NANNIES, MIGRATION AND EARLY CHILDHOOD EDUCATION AND CARE

An international comparison of in-home childcare policy and practice

Elizabeth Adamson

First published in Great Britain in 2017 by

Policy Press
University of Bristol
1-9 Old Park Hill
Bristol
BS2 8BB
UK
t: +44 (0)117 954 5940
pp-info@bristol.ac.uk
www.policypress.co.uk

North America office:
Policy Press
c/o The University of Chicago Press
1427 East 60th Street
Chicago, IL 60637, USA
t: +1 773 702 7700
f: +1 773-702-9756
sales@press.uchicago.edu
www.press.uchicago.edu

British Library Cataloguing in Publication Data
A catalogue record for this book is available from the British Library

Library of Congress Cataloging-in-Publication Data
A catalog record for this book has been requested

ISBN 978-1-4473-3014-1 hardcover
ISBN 978-1-4473-3380-7 ePub
ISBN 978-1-4473-3381-4 Mobi
ISBN 978-1-4473-3015-8 ePdf

Cover design by Policy Press
Front cover image: istock
Printed and bound in Great Britain by CPI Group (UK) Ltd, Croydon, CR0 4YY
Policy Press uses environmentally responsible print partners

MIX
Paper from
responsible sources
FSC® C013604

Contents

List of tables

Acknowledgements

I would like to acknowledge the various individuals that made this book possible. First, thank you to Deb Brennan and Fiona Williams for instilling the idea, and for your mentorship and inspiration in helping me to achieve my goals. To my friends and colleagues at the Social Policy Research Centre, thank you for your support and encouragement to keep writing.

To Mom, Dad, Heather and Geoff, thank you for your constant love and friendship. Whether in person or over the phone, you are always there to help celebrate the good times and work through the challenges. To Pete, I cannot thank you enough for always being by my side – even from the other side of the country. You continue to challenge and support me to reach my goals, and provide endless love and laughter along the way.

To all the research participants, thank you for sharing your time and knowledge with me. The rich information you provided has contributed to an understanding of the dynamics and complexities of childcare, nannies and early education that extends far beyond the scope of this book.

Last but not least, I would like to acknowledge the support of the Australian Research Council and the Faculty of Arts and Social Sciences and Graduate Research School at the University of New South Wales for making earlier stages of this research possible.

Elizabeth Adamson, May 2016

Introduction

In-home childcare, commonly referred to as care by nannies and au pairs, is not new. These forms of childcare[1] and domestic care work have existed for centuries in some countries. What is worthy of attention is the fact that these forms of childcare until recently remained firmly in the informal and private care domains. The restructuring of welfare state services – primarily through marketisation – has changed the nature of such forms of childcare. Through childcare funding and regulation, forms of in-home childcare that previously were situated in the private and informal sphere are being repositioned across the public and formal sphere. At the same time, in some countries, migration policy facilitates in-home childcare. Just as other forms of childcare and early education (such as kindergarten, preschool, centre-based services and family day care) have developed in distinct ways across countries, so too have forms of in-home childcare.

The childcare and early education field has gained visibility and momentum on the policy agenda as scholars and international organisations have demonstrated the various benefits of quality early learning and childcare for young children and their families. Governments and international organisations have, albeit to different extents, embraced the term 'early childhood education and care' (ECEC) to promote the dual focus of children's education and care on policy agendas. Increased public and private investment has been driven by demographic changes, such as increases in women's workforce participation, and also by evidence that demonstrate the benefits of high-quality ECEC for children's development and wellbeing. ECEC does not, however, always address the needs of mothers and children at the same time. Some ECEC programmes are designed specifically to meet the needs of children through high-quality early learning programmes, notably part-day preschool or kindergarten for children in the year before school. Others, such as full-day care in centre- and home-based settings are typically designed to also facilitate parents' employment. Children's participation in these types of regulated, centre-based ECEC has increased in most developed (and developing countries) since the 1960s, including in the three liberal English-speaking countries that are the focus of this book: Australia, the United Kingdom[2] (UK) and Canada.[3]

Despite the trend towards regulated and centre-based ECEC, many parents still rely on more informal home-based care by grandparents, other relatives and friends. In addition to reliance on these informal care arrangements, some families are increasingly seeking flexible, in-home childcare provided by non-relatives – such as nannies – as their primary or supplementary choice of care. The need for flexible in-home forms of ECEC is associated with longer work hours and non-standard forms of employment. Some governments across the developed world are redesigning ECEC funding and regulatory mechanisms to support these forms of care (DfES, 2002; Morel, 2007; Sipilä et al, 2010; Fagnani and Math, 2011; Australian Government, 2015). Such support can appear perplexing, given the strong government rhetoric in some countries about the need for increased 'social investment' through expenditure on high-quality, universal ECEC services, generally assumed to be centre-based services (OECD, 2006, 2012).

ECEC has moved from a peripheral to a central place on governments' agendas and, at the same time, there have been changes in the way governments fund and deliver services. There have been shifts in emphasis from care to education, from community-based to market-provided services and from supply-side to demand-side funding. Therefore, while many governments can be applauded for increasing spending on ECEC and children more broadly, attention should be given to the design of childcare and how welfare state restructuring is shaping the purpose and outcomes of ECEC services. There are active debates about the optimal approach to ECEC provision within international organisations, across regimes, and within countries and regions. While many countries across the globe have adopted the term 'early childhood education and care' to denote a unified approach to care and education for young children, the extent of governments' involvement and responsibility for funding, delivering and regulating services remains varied (OECD, 2006). And, in many cases traditional spheres of 'care' and 'education' remain divided along political, ideological and cultural lines (Jenson and Sineau, 2001; Kremer, 2007).

Debates about provision and funding of ECEC are therefore not simply about how much government should spend; just as important are the mechanisms through which subsidies are transferred to services and families. A key distinction is whether governments favour supply-side funding, where subsidies are delivered directly to service providers, or demand-side measures such as tax credits and vouchers, which put cash or its equivalent in the hands of 'consumers' to enable them to purchase services. Supply-side funding can be directed towards public or private (for-profit or not-for-profit) services, while demand-side funding follows the child, encouraging reliance on the market to meet demand.

Childcare has been professionalised through the expansion of regulated, centre-based services provided by qualified staff (increasingly referred to as teachers and 'educators'); but, at the same time, there have been moves in some countries to formalise (or modernise) informal care through the introduction of registration processes, tax credits and demand-side vouchers that can facilitate and subsidise non-parental care provided in the child's home. Such forms of childcare are not necessarily provided by workers trained in early education or childcare. Thus, while governments' expenditure on ECEC has increased across most Western countries in the past four decades, the funding and regulatory structures have shifted in significant, and sometimes divergent, ways. Some of these changes support the provision of in-home childcare by making this type of childcare arrangement more affordable to families through subsidies and registration mechanisms.

ECEC funding and regulation does not, however, reveal the whole story of in-home childcare; in many countries, migration policy also shapes its prevalence and position. The capacity for employers, including private families, to recruit and employ care workers relies not only on the structure of funding and regulations of childcare and related employment regulations, but also on migration policies. This is because migration policies and visa categories can offer a main pathway to recruit a low-paid and commoditised care workforce. The intersection of care/domestic work and migration policy is a pressing issue for many governments as they respond to a 'care crisis' (Estévez-Abe and Hobson, 2015), and governments are increasingly looking to other countries to recruit low-paid care workers (Lutz, 2008; Ruhs and Anderson, 2010). These workers may be recruited to the formal care sector (in centre- or home-based settings), but they may also work in more informal home-based settings. In the latter case, care provision is often regarded as a private responsibility and, for the most part, is at the periphery of sector regulation with minimal oversight (Busch, 2014).

Liberal countries, which are the empirical focus of this book, have traditionally viewed the care of young children as a private matter for families. These countries have always had – and still do have – a strong reliance on private approaches to childcare and ECEC, provided either by family or the market (O'Connor et al, 1999; Baker, 2006). Australia, the UK and Canada are selected for their similar approach to market-led ECEC, as well as for their distinct differences with respect to the policy treatment of in-home childcare in the ECEC and migration domain. In terms of migration policy, these three countries are all destination countries for global migration, although the policies and programmes to recruit and regulate care workers differ. Australia, the UK and Canada are regularly grouped together as liberal countries, a group that also includes the US and sometimes New Zealand and Ireland. The key tenet of liberal theory that is common across the three study countries (as well as other countries in the liberal group) is the reliance on the market for the delivery of services, which leaves the responsibility for ECEC in the private domain. This reliance on the market for service delivery encourages policy mechanisms that are designed to promote individual choice (O'Connor et al, 1999; Wincott, 2006; Mahon, 2008; O'Connor and Robinson, 2008; Mahon et al, 2012).

With the restructuring of government subsidies and regulatory frameworks, in-home childcare is increasingly situated at the intersection of informal/formal and public/private care. In-home childcare therefore offers a new lens through which to analyse the continuum of formal and informal, public and private, and sometimes familial and non-familial care. How does in-home childcare differ across these countries? How and why has in-home childcare been transformed as a result of welfare state restructuring? What are the potential implications for children, families and care workers? And what are the implications for policy design? These are the questions addressed in this book.

Definition and scope

The book focuses on 'in-home childcare' as a form of ECEC provision. It considers how different forms of in-home childcare, for example nannies and au pairs, are situated across formal/informal, regulated/unregulated and public/private domains. According to some commentators and scholars, nannies are 'qualified childcare professionals' akin to formal carers, and 'are responsible for providing a caring and stimulating environment for their charges' (Cox, 2006b, p 72). However, it is also common for trained and 'professional' nannies to remain in the private, informal sector (Busch, 2012). Referring to nannies in the UK, Rutter and Evans suggest that they 'largely work unsupervised and are employed by a family or group of families on a live-in or live-out basis' (2011, p 13). Untrained 'nannies', such as au pairs and other domestic workers, are regarded as informal carers, yet sometimes receive public funding despite the absence of any qualifications or regulation.

The complexities of defining in-home childcare exist in part because there is no internationally consistent definition for informal and formal childcare, let alone in-home childcare. Rutter and Evans define informal childcare as being 'largely unregistered by the state for quality control, child protection and/or taxation purposes' (2011, p 5). Domains of care are also distinguished by the location of care, relationship to the carer, and the form of reward (Land, 2002, p 18). Some scholars simplify the distinction by defining informal arrangements as those that are 'not formalised with contracts or employment rights' (Holloway and Tamplin, 2001, p 2). Overall, there is little consistency in the way informal and formal care is defined and these inconsistencies are often evident in national administrative and policy definitions (Doherty et al, 2003, Cassells et al, 2007; Bryson et al, 2012). In-home childcare therefore straddles an already blurred line between informal and formal care: it is provided in the home of the child, it is usually (but not always) paid and sometimes publicly funded by subsidies or tax measures, and care workers are sometimes required to hold ECEC qualifications (albeit at a relatively low level) and meet other sector standards.

The focus of this book is in-home childcare defined as paid care provided by non-relatives in the child's home. When applied conceptually, the different characteristics and position of in-home childcare in Australia, the UK and Canada begin to emerge. For example, in Australia, a distinction is made between formal in-home care educators (employed through the regulated In Home Care programme) and 'nannies' (often including au pairs) who are privately employed by families.[4] In the UK, the 'professional nanny', noted by Cox above, may be less common than two decades ago (Gregson and Lowe, 1994); however the term 'nanny' increasingly refers to other forms of in-home childcare, namely au pairs, but also babysitters, mothers' help and domestic workers with childcare responsibilities (Leach, 2009; Social Issues Research Centre, 2009; Bryson et al, 2012; Cox and Busch, 2014a). In Canada, the term 'nanny' or 'live-in' most often refers to migrant caregivers recruited through the former Live-In Caregiver Program,[5] distinct from 'local' or 'trained' nannies.

It is important to consider the scope of these groups of childcare workers in each of these countries. Anecdotal evidence suggests that despite the rise in attendance of children in centre-based services there is still sustained demand for nannies and au pairs (Australian Nanny Association, 2014; CAPAA, 2014; Cox and Busch, 2014a). However, the exact numbers and trends cannot be confirmed because of the changing nature of government support for different forms of ECEC, and because of challenges with measuring au pairs through different migration visa pathways (Cox and Busch, 2014b; Berg, 2015). One characteristic we can look at is the number of in-home childcare service providers and caregivers that are part of the formal ECEC sector (in

Australia and the UK) and part of a formal immigration programme (in the case of Canada).

In Australia, there are approximately 70 services providing formal (approved) care under the In Home Care scheme, where the families are eligible for receipt of public subsidies. These services represent approximately 1,000 educators, who provide care and education to approximately 5,600 families. It should be noted that approximately 65 per cent of these workers hold an ECEC-relevant qualification, mostly a two-year diploma or a certificate III or IV (Social Research Centre, 2014). Outside this formal In Home Care programme, there are an estimated 30,000 nannies and au pairs in Australia (Productivity Commission, 2014a); however, there is no way of knowing the types and levels of qualification held by workers in these groups. Similarly, there is no reliable way of measuring the numbers of in-home childcare workers in England, or the UK more broadly. In-home childcare workers in the UK are generally distinguished between nannies and au pairs. While there is no official distinction between nannies and au pairs in the UK (Rutter and Evans, 2012a), nannies are more likely to hold qualifications and to be registered with Ofsted, the regulatory body for early years services. There were approximately 11,000 nannies registered with Ofsted in 2014 (Ofsted, 2015), but there are an estimated 100,000 nannies and au pairs in England (Simon et al, 2015) – meaning that only about 10 per cent of in-home childcare workers in England are registered. This figure is contestable, as it includes au pairs who may only be looking after older children and may have considerable domestic duties. However, it is difficult to measure the distribution between groups of in-home childcare workers (nannies and au pairs) because there is no clear definition of either group. Another recent study on the nanny workforce in England used the General Household Survey and estimated that there were 63,000 nannies and mothers' help (Social Issues Research Centre, 2009). To put this in context, the 2006 Childcare and Early Years Provider survey reported a total of 347,300 staff working in the formal childcare and early years sector[6] (Brind et al, 2011), which would indicate that up to 15 per cent of workers caring for and educating young children in England are working in the child's home – in both formal and informal capacities. In this study, nannies are distinguished (from au pairs and mothers' help) by two particular features: they are qualified and/or experienced, and are in sole charge of the children. According to this definition, it was estimated that, in 2009, there were 30,000 nannies in England. Eighty-two per cent of nannies who completed the survey reported having a childcare-related qualification (Social Issues Research Centre, 2009, p 26).

Canada differs from the other two countries in that in-home childcarers are not registered with any ECEC government agency or regulatory body. The 2011 National Household Survey indicates there were over 60,000 workers classified as 'home childcare providers' under the occupations category 4411. This compares with approximately 187,000 workers in the occupation classification, 'early childhood educators and assistants' category (Statistics Canada, 2011). These figures suggest that in-home childcare workers may represent close to 30 per cent of the total childcare workforce in Canada. Immigration policy facilitates the use of in-home childcare through the (former) Live-In Caregiver Program, which, until it ended in November 2014, brought in approximately 14,000 caregivers per year. The qualification levels of caregivers entering under the Live-In Caregiver Program increased significantly since the 2000s, with 2009 figures indicating that over 60 per cent held bachelor degrees. However, these qualifications are not necessarily related to ECEC (Kelly et al, 2011). Some of these characteristics and nuances in relation to their position within the ECEC regulatory framework are outlined later in this chapter.

Given the nuances of in-home childcare, why should we, as members of the research and policy communities (and society more broadly) care about how in-home childcare is classified? Does it matter how government supports in-home childcare? There are many reasons why we should care, and these include the implications for the equality and equity of care users (mothers/families), the quality for care receivers (children), and the quality and working conditions for the care worker, or nanny, providing the care.

Why is in-home childcare important?

In-home childcare straddles different policy domains, namely ECEC and migration. But, as a form of ECEC, it has not received adequate attention in either domain. In-home childcare is worthy of policy attention; there has been an 'internationalisation' of ECEC policy, which has been driven by new ideas about the importance of investment in early education, the knowledge economy, and maternal workforce participation (Mahon, 2010b; White, 2011). There has also been an internationalisation of in-home childcare and domestic care work as care workers themselves are recruited from developing to wealthier countries in response to the 'care crisis'. That is, in some cases, migrant care workers move across borders to fill the gap in supply of local workers willing to work in lower-paid jobs. This gap in care labour supply can be attributed to an emphasis on increased participation in paid labour (outside the home), and the rise of the '24-hour economy'. In particular, the shift to casualisation and non-standard work is seen to enhance productivity and countries' tax income. These changes in employment patterns generate demands for more flexible, individualised, consumer-led childcare services, such as care by nannies, au pairs and other forms of domestic care. Individuals, employers, agencies and governments alike have looked outside the local market to fill this gap. This movement of migrant workers is not limited to in-home childcare; the trend is also apparent in formal, centre-based care work, such as nursing and aged care, and also in childcare centres. However, care provided in the home – for children, for frail and elderly people, and to perform other cleaning and household tasks – is viewed as more flexible and affordable than formal, centre-based options (Morel, 2015).

Many of the trends described above are linked to a shift towards a 'social investment' approach to social policy, which is prominent among liberal countries and other regimes types, but also Western countries more broadly (Morel et al, 2012). A liberal social investment approach to social policy emphasises human capital, in relation to children and women alike. It is viewed that investment in children, for example through the provision of high-quality ECEC, has positive outcomes for the child in the future. At the same time, government investment in flexible childcare (and other forms of domestic work) can enhance women's productivity in two ways. First, the hiring of in-home care helps to reconcile work and care responsibilities for skilled workers (mothers), who are then able to increase their economic contribution in the knowledge economy. In-home childcare is especially appealing for 'modern' women working outside the home. In families with multiple school-aged and younger children, in-home provision offers convenience by removing the added pressure of meeting school and external childcare drop-off and pick-up times to fit with work schedules and routines. Second, the provision of childcare and domestic work in the home through formal policy measures creates legitimate jobs for (generally) lower-skilled female workers (Morel, 2012, 2015). Under this latter approach more vulnerable workers increase their earnings, overall employment rates increase and, in theory, public expenditure on welfare benefits is reduced.

Government involvement in in-home childcare is therefore relevant to a number of policy areas and debates. First, it is relevant to increased international attention on the provision of high-quality ECEC as a form of investment in children to improve their short-term wellbeing and long-term outcomes. Second, governments are interested in ways to boost employment, particularly among women and mothers, which requires flexible and affordable care (ECEC and elderly care) options to help reconcile work and care responsibilities. And, third, employment in the domestic sector opens up opportunities for lower-skilled workers, local and migrant, who might otherwise be unemployed or working in the informal economy. The focus of this book developed out of an interest in comparative ECEC policy; however, an examination of in-home childcare policy must include all three dimensions.

To date, there has been little examination in comparative ECEC policy (and social policy more generally) of the rationales behind governments' support for in-home childcare. Indeed, such support can appear perplexing, given the strong government rhetoric in some countries about the need for increased 'social investment' through expenditure on high-quality, universal ECEC services, generally assumed to be centre-based services.

ECEC has gained a central position on liberal governments' policy agendas based on evidence of the benefits of increased public expenditure on high-quality care. Much of the research evidence on ECEC policy is based on formal, centre-based care and, as a result, in-home childcare has been at the periphery of provision and analysis. By extending the analysis beyond centre-based, mainstream ECEC, this book addresses an important gap in childcare policy research. In an innovative way, this research also extends analysis to include migration as an integral part of policy that intersects with governments' funding and regulation of ECEC.

Although not typically discussed in analyses of childcare policy, immigration policy that facilitates the recruitment of migrant domestic care workers can increase the supply of more affordable care labour. However, there are concerns that within an unregulated market for care, there may be implications for the quality of the care provided for children and the working conditions for care workers. Government involvement in in-home childcare therefore has implications for quality and affordability for care users, and can also reinforce gender and income inequalities (Williams, 2004, 2012b; Baker, 2006; Lewis 2008). The consequences of government involvement (or lack of involvement) in ECEC have been well documented in relation to gender equality issues for the family (mother), and issues of access and quality for children (Michel and Mahon, 2002; Penn, 2011b). Government involvement in in-home childcare also extends to care workers. That is, markets that facilitate the employment of in-home care workers stimulate demand for low-wage migrant workers (Williams and Gavanas, 2008; Williams, 2010b). The implications are relevant to governments as funders and regulators of in-home childcare, and also to service providers, users (families) and care workers.

Demand can be stimulated through government initiatives, such as childcare policy (for example, vouchers and tax measures) as well as formal migration schemes to recruit care workers. Demand for affordable in-home childcare is also driven by the absence of adequate systems for regulated ECEC. This book delves into some of these intersections and complexities in relation to in-home childcare. While the analysis and comparison focuses on three liberal English-speaking countries – Australia, the UK and Canada – the overarching trends and conceptual analysis are relevant to an international audience. Next, a snapshot of demographic trends, including maternal employment and ECEC enrolment rates, is outlined to better identify the users of in-home childcare and ECEC more broadly.

Trends in maternal employment and ECEC usage

There has undoubtedly been a broad cultural shift in recent decades that has witnessed the increase in women's and mothers' workforce participation. At the same time, research about children's development and future productivity has driven the uptake of early education (opposed to only 'care') services (for example, see Esping-Andersen, 2002). Corresponding to these trends, the number of children attending non-parental childcare (formal and informal), and the amount of care they use, is increasing as more women enter or return to the paid labour force, with many working longer and/or more non-standard hours than previously (Australian Bureau of Statistics, 2008; Cleveland et al, 2008; Smith et al, 2010). Across the OECD countries, the average maternal employment rate was 52.9 per cent and 66.3 per cent for mothers with a youngest child 0 to two years, and three to five years, respectively (OECD, 2015). As outlined in Table 0.1, maternal employment for families with young children (0 to three years) has increased by approximately 20 to 25 per cent in the three study countries over the past three decades: in Australia, from 30 to 56 per cent for mothers with children 0 to four years; in the UK from 38 to 56 per cent for mothers with children 0 to two years; and in Canada from 40 to 65 per cent for mothers with children 0 to two years.

While take-up of formal ECEC services has also increased over the past few decades, participation has not kept pace with maternal employment trends. Data suggests that a large number of families,

Table 0.1: Increase in maternal workforce participation

	1981 (or earliest year[1])	2011
Australia[2] (0-4 years)	30	56
United Kingdom[3] (0-2 years)	38.3	56
Canada[4] (0-2 years)	39.6	64.5
OECD average (2013)		
(0-2 years)		53.6
(3-5 years)		66.8

[1] UK figure is 1995.

[2] For Australia, see Baxter (2013, p 6).

[3] For the UK, see Thompson and Ben-Galim (2014).

[4] For Canada, see OECD (2005, p 70, 2015).

particularly with children 0 to three years, use informal, unregulated options. As Table 0.2 shows, across the OECD, while approximately 54 per cent of mothers with children 0 to two years were employed, less than one third were enrolled in formal ECEC services. However, the opposite pattern exists for children aged three to five, which likely reflects the high proportion of children aged four and five attending publicly provided preschool and the fact that, in most countries, children start school by age five. These figures do not reflect the fact that children often attend preschool and kindergarten part-time, which does not fit with most parents' working patterns. In Australia, almost half of mothers with young children aged 0 to three years work, but only one third are enrolled in formal ECEC services; and in the UK, approximately 57 per cent are employed and 42 per cent enrolled in formal ECEC schemes (OECD, 2015, LMF1.2, PF3.2). In the province of Ontario in Canada, 2011 figures suggest that over 70 per cent of mothers with children aged 0 to five years are employed, yet there are only regulated spaces for approximately 22 per cent of children in this age group (Friendly et al, 2013, Table 9).

So, who is caring for these children while parents are employed? And (how) are governments assisting families with these arrangements? We know that grandparents, other family members and parents working from home care for many children. These informal care arrangements can be a positive choice for families; however, in other circumstances, there may be few alternatives. This is especially pertinent where one or both parents are participating in casual, non-standard or precarious employment.

Table 0.2: Workforce participation of mothers by age of youngest child (2011) and enrolment rates in formal childcare and preschool (per cent), by age (2010 or latest year)

	0 to 2 years		3 to 5 years	
	Workforce participation	Enrolment in formal ECEC	Workforce participation	Enrolment in formal ECEC
Australia	48.7	33.2	61.6[2]	80.1
United Kingdom	56.9	42	61.2	93.3
Canada (Ontario)	64.5 70.6[1]	22.5[1] (a)(b)	70.4 75.3[1]	47.3
OECD average	52.9	32.9	66.8	81.0[3]

(a) 0 to 5 years.
(b) This refers to the proportion of children for whom there is a regulated space (for Australia and the UK, this is the proportion of children enrolled in formal ECEC).

[1] Friendly et al (2013, Table 9).

[2] Baxter (2014).

[3] Author's calculations from OECD (2015, PF3.2).
Other sources: OECD (2015, LMF1.2, PF3.2).

It is difficult to compare participation in specific types of childcare because of the different terminology used, and also because of inconsistent approaches to data collection and school starting age[7] (OECD, 2015, PF3.2). To compare the prevalence of in-home childcare across the three countries, we can use national datasets surveying parents' use of childcare arrangements, but the different categories and methods for collecting the information means they are not directly comparable. They do, however, offer some idea of how patterns of in-home childcare use differ, as well as identify challenges for comparison.

Australian census data from 2014 suggests that approximately 4 per cent of children from 0 to four years are cared for informally by a non-relative (Australian Bureau of Statistics, 2015). In England, the 2012–13 annual survey of parents found that 3 per cent of 0- to four-year-olds were cared for by a nanny, au pair or other non-relative carer (in formal or informal arrangements) (DfE, 2014). However, the Office for National Statistics found that in 2004, the proportion of children cared for by nannies or au pairs was much higher, at 10 per cent for children aged 0 to three years, and 14 per cent from children aged three to six years (OECD, 2005, Table 4.3). Research has also suggested that a decline in registered childminders may reflect a corresponding increase in unregistered in-home childcare (Simon et al, 2015). In Ontario, in Canada, in 2002-03, it was estimated that almost 9 per cent of children from six months to five years were cared for in their own home by a non-relative (Bushnik, 2006). More recent figures from 2011 indicate that almost one third of children under four years received centre-based care, almost one third received home day care (in the home of the care provider) and 28 per cent were in private arrangements. Private arrangements include grandparents, other relatives and nannies (Sinha, 2014). In sum, current data sources make it difficult to determine the prevalence of in-home childcare in each of these countries. The data available is inconsistent in measuring in-home childcare as informal or formal care.

The decisions families make about formal and informal childcare are reflective of individual preferences and constraints as well as policy settings that determine the availability and affordability of different care options, and these individual preferences and institutional settings are both reflective of broader institutional norms and cultural attitudes (Pfau-Effinger, 2005a; Kremer, 2007). The next section outlines the main features of each ECEC policy system, with a focus on in-home childcare.

Policy snapshot

It is inevitably difficult to measure and compare the generosity and eligibility of ECEC in different countries. Across the OECD, investment in ECEC as a proportion of gross domestic product (GDP) has increased over the past two decade, from an average of 0.5 per cent in 1998 to 0.8 per cent in 2011. The Nordic countries, in particular, stand out for their high level of investment – increasing from 1.4 to 2.0 per cent of GDP in Denmark in this period. Australia doubled investment from 0.3 to 0.6 per cent of GDP[8], and the UK almost doubled its investment, from 0.6 to 1.1 per cent. However, Canada's investment as a proportion of GDP did not increase and remains the lowest at 0.2 per cent (OECD, 2015). There are, of course, limitations to cross-national comparisons of GDP expenditure, as there are complex considerations about what types of care and education are included. For example, expenditure on kindergarten is not included in the case of Canada, while expenditure on reception classes for four-year-olds is likely included for the UK (Penn and Lloyd, 2013, p 19).

In addition to different ways of measuring expenditure, just as important (if not more so) are the details and structure of spending (Jenson and Sineau, 2001; Baker, 2006). The policy landscapes shaping in-home childcare in Australia, the UK and Canada are rapidly changing (and will likely have changed between the time of writing in January 2016 and publication). In Australia, ECEC services are legislated by a national framework, the National Quality Framework (NQF) for Early Childhood Education and Care, which was fully implemented in 2013. The national regulation covers most approved services, which are long day care, family day care, preschool and outside school hours care. The major Commonwealth subsidies, Child Care Benefit (CCB) and Child Care Rebate (CCR),[9] are administered by the Department of Education,[10] and available to families using 'approved' ECEC. What is important to note here is that while all services legislated under the NQF are approved to receive Commonwealth subsidies (with the exception of preschool services funded by states), there are some 'out-of-scope' services approved to receive subsidies that are not legislated and regulated by the NQF. The approved In Home Care programme is one of these services. The Coalition government recently implemented the Nanny Pilot programme, which extends subsidies for families hiring nannies as part of a two-year trial from 2016-18.[11] This is a shift from the current system, which provides targeted funding under the In Home Care programme for families meeting specific eligibility criteria that prevent them from accessing mainstream services, such as long day care or family day care. In the migration domain, the Department of Immigration and Border Protection has responded to calls by families and nanny agencies to extend the current limitation on the Working Holiday Visa, to allow temporary migrants on this visa (mostly backpackers) to work with the same employer for 12 months, rather than the current six-month limit with one employer. This change took place in July 2015.

In the United Kingdom, the responsibilities for regulation are administered at the national level. In England, the Office for Standards in Education, Children's Services and Skills (Ofsted) is responsible for regulating and inspecting ECEC services. It is mandatory for centre-based nurseries, preschools and childminders to register with Ofsted, while home childcare (including nannies and au pairs) and playgroups (among others) are part of the voluntary register. As mentioned, estimates of the total number of nannies and au pairs (Simon et al, 2015) indicate that a relatively small proportion of nannies and au pairs are registered with Ofsted (approximately 10-12 per cent). This is arguably because the register is voluntary and most nannies only register at the request of their employer, for subsidy purposes (Nannytax, 2015). In Scotland, by contrast, nannies are registered with the Care Inspectorate as part of a childcare agency (rather than as individuals).

Across the UK, the childcare element of the Working Tax Credit (WTC) and employer-sponsored childcare vouchers are available to families using registered care (with Ofsted in England and with the Care Inspectorate in Scotland), and who are eligible under the work and income tests. WTCs are eligible to working families under a certain income threshold, while childcare vouchers are accessible mostly by middle-income families whose employer is signed up with a childcare voucher scheme. These are the same funding mechanisms that are available for centre-based (day nurseries) and home-based care (childminders). However, the majority of funding for ECEC in England is directed to the early years entitlement, which offers 15 hours per week of free ECEC for three- and four-year olds (and some two-year-olds) in nurseries and preschools and with some childminders. In-home childcare – even nannies registered with Ofsted – is not included under the early years entitlement. In-home childcare is affordable for many families as a result of the expansion of the European Union in 2004, which increased the number of young women from Eastern Europe moving to the UK to work as au pairs. A separate Youth Mobility Scheme also allows young people from non-member nations to work as au pairs in private homes.

In Canada, there is no national legislation or regulation for ECEC. Instead provinces and territories regulate ECEC. In the province of Ontario, the focus of this research, the Child Care and Early Years Act 2014 regulates licensed home-based care (in the home of the caregiver), although unregulated home-based care is permitted. Provincial means-tested subsidies are available for families using Licenced Centre-based Child Care and Licensed Home-based Child Care. Kindergarten is delivered at the provincial level and in Ontario full-day kindergarten is available for four- and five-year-olds. At the federal level, the Child Care Expense Deduction (CCED) and Universal Child Care Benefit (UCCB) provide minimal financial assistance for families using any type of formal/informal or regulated/unregulated care. There is no subsidy specific for in-home childcare. The current UCCB gives families $160/month for each child under seven years old. Families can also claim the CCED for childcare expenses regardless of the type of care used. In addition to these cash benefits and deductions that can subsidise informal in-home childcare, the Caring for Children Pathway under the Temporary Foreign Worker Program (and former Live-In Caregiver Program) offers a formal route for recruiting migrant care workers to live in the family home to care for children, the elderly and people with a disability. Some provinces, including Ontario, have discretion to provide additional subsidies for families on welfare assistance using informal childcare to facilitate employment.

The high cost of formal ECEC is a significant factor contributing to the demand for informal arrangements, including in-home childcare, in the three study countries. The average cost of childcare across OECD countries is estimated at 27.6 per cent of the average wage. Canada, Australia and the UK are placed at the higher end of this spectrum, at 39 per cent, 49.2 per cent, and 53 per cent, respectively. These figures are based on the gross cost of services; however (as detailed in Chapter Three), even after subsidies are taken into account, the cost in all three countries is above the OECD average (OECD, 2015).

Government involvement in funding and regulating ECEC is designed to address issues of quality, affordability and accessibility of ECEC services. Funding and regulation for ECEC can be designed to exclude certain types of care from the formal sector; however, the introduction of new policy mechanisms can also be designed to integrate previously informal or 'grey market' services into the formal mixed market of care (Morgan, 2005; Lister et al, 2007; Warner and Gradus, 2009; Williams, 2010a). The introduction of subsidies for new forms of ECEC – previously in the private and informal domains – can be effective in reducing the out-of-pocket costs for families. The availability of public subsidies for in-home childcare may enhance the affordability of this option for more families. However, without adequate regulation, the availability of subsidies to forms of informal and unregulated childcare can affect the distribution of subsidies and, as a result, lead to inequitable outcomes in ECEC systems. This may mean that families that would benefit the most cannot afford the care they need and, at the same time, publicly subsidised services may not be good quality. The presence of a formal avenue for families to recruit migrant care workers also affects the availability, affordability and quality of in-home childcare.

However, it must be emphasised that informal care can be a 'positive choice' for parents (Land, 2002; Skinner and Finch, 2006; Vincent and Ball, 2006; Land and Himmelweit, 2010; Rutter and Evans, 2011; Bryson et al, 2012); however 'rewarding, regulating and sustaining providers of informal care raise complex and controversial issues' (Land, 2002, p 13), which provides the motivation for writing this book.

Overall, the funding and regulation of in-home childcare is receiving increasing attention in policy and public debates, although limited attention has been given to the implications for different policy settings. ECEC policy settings as well as migration policies shape the position of in-home childcare within a country's ECEC system. In the three liberal countries chosen for this study, policy mechanisms have been introduced in the past two decades (and earlier in Canada) to support and facilitate the use of different forms of in-home childcare. The ECEC usage and attendance rates outlined above are partially reflective of each country's ECEC policy systems and mechanisms to support different forms of care. But, as will be explored in later chapters, the policy structures are not the only explanation – embedded cultural norms and attitudes are also used to explain developments and divergences.

Empirical approach

In order to gain a richer understanding of the embedded norms and attitudes shaping policy developments and rationales for policy reform, primary data for this book was collected through interviews with key stakeholders, carried out in each of the three study countries. A total of 60 interviews (20 in each country) were conducted between May 2012 and March 2013 in Canada, the UK and Australia. Key stakeholders were recruited as individuals and as representatives of organisations from the ECEC, in-home childcare and nanny sectors. Pilot interviews were conducted with key stakeholders from three different stakeholder groups (provider organisation, peak organisation, nanny agency) in Sydney, Australia in May and June 2012. These interviews were used to modify the interview schedule. Interviews were conducted in the province of Ontario (in Canada) in July and August 2012. Most were in the Greater Toronto area, with four participants from other local areas. The interviews in the UK were conducted in September and October 2012; 16 were in England and four in Scotland. The remaining 17 interviews in Australia were conducted between October 2012 and March 2013. Most were in the greater Sydney area in New South Wales, and three were conducted in South Australia. A minority of interviews were conducted in different jurisdictions[12] in order to identity how local policy and cultural contexts shaped views about the role and position of in-home childcare. In Canada, there is no national responsibility for ECEC, and therefore it was decided to choose Ontario for the empirical research. It is the most populated province, it has a long history of childcare advocacy, and it has the most of number of migrant workers under the Live-In Caregiver Program, compared with other provinces.

The recruitment strategy aimed to generate a mix of representatives from each country, including government, peak organisations, provider organisations, and nanny agencies and associations. A fifth group, key informants, was added where participants did not fall in the other groups. Key stakeholders were selected because of their potential to identify new themes and issues related to the emergence of government support for in-home childcare and the way it is situated within the broader ECEC sector.

The interviews conducted were semi-structured and varied in length from 25 minutes to almost two hours. Most were between 45 and 55 minutes. The research activities were approved by the University of New South Wales' Human Research Ethics Panel. Participants were recruited through email and phone contact. They were first introduced to the project and asked whether they or anyone else they knew in a similar position were interested in participating. An information and consent form was sent, which included further detail about the types of questions that would be asked and the approximate duration of the interview. Information about ethics approval and complaints, and a consent and withdrawal form were attached. All participants signed the consent form, which gave their consent to use the information they provided, but did not give approval to use their names or organisational affiliation. Table 0.3, below, outlines the distribution of key stakeholders across countries and sector groups.

Table 0.3: Key stakeholder interviews, by country and affiliation

	Australia	United Kingdom	Canada
Government representative or national authority[1]	4	4	3
Provider organisation[2]	4	4	4
Peak organisation[3]	7	5	4
Nanny agency/association[4]	5	5	5
Researcher and/or other key informant	0*	2	4
Total	20	20	20

* While there were no Australian interviewees identified as 'researcher and/or other key informant', two of the representatives in the 'peak organisation' group could be included in either group.

[1] Government representatives included public servants, ministries at the local and national level, and government agencies and authorities responsible for regulation and monitoring.

[2] All provider organisations included in the study provided multiple services, including home-based care (not necessarily in-home childcare). They were selected because of their reputation at national/ provincial levels in providing ECEC services across multiple settings. Many of them were also involved with training ECEC workers.

[3] Peak organisation refers to non-government organisations that represent service provider organisations and/or ECEC/care workers in a specific sector. It is defined as 'an advocacy group, an associated of industries or groups with allied interests'. Peak organisations are generally established for the purposes of developing standards and processes and to act on behalf of members (Fitzgerald, 2006). For this study, membership and professional organisations were also included in this group (including unions).

[4] Nanny agencies and associations were grouped together for the purpose of identifying stakeholders in this study. In some circumstances, 'nanny associations' also could be classified as 'peak organisations', representing nannies and in-home childcare workers.

The interviews covered four key topics designed to elucidate the interviewee's understanding of the role and functions of the department/organisation within the ECEC sector, and how they viewed their role in advocacy and policymaking, and the role of the government in supporting different types of childcare and ECEC:

- role and function of department or organisation;
- ECEC policy and advocacy;
- attitudes towards in-home childcare;
- role of government in ECEC and in-home childcare.

As expected, some issues were more salient among some groups and countries. Thus, while the topics outlined do not explicitly ask about the role of migration in in-home childcare, the issue was raised by the participant in many circumstances and, where it was not, participants were probed for their views as part of broader questions about governments' role in funding and regulating in-home childcare. As will be discussed in later chapters, the issue was very salient among some stakeholders, but held at arm's length by others. This, in itself, was a finding that distinguished the country and affiliation of the stakeholder.

The transcripts from the interviews were uploaded and analysed using NVivo software. The query function in NVivo was used to explore and compare the frequency of different themes across countries and by stakeholder group. The findings from the interview data were analysed in relation to findings from secondary policy and documentary analysis, and are used primarily in the discussion in Part Two of the book. The interviews confirmed many of the findings from the policy and documentary analysis and provided insight into specific aspects of policy detail and debate.

Book structure and chapter outline

The book is organised into two parts, each with three chapters. Part One (Chapters One to Three) introduces the topic: it outlines the key terms, trends and concepts, and describes the policy structures and mechanisms that support in-home childcare in the three study countries. It focuses on broader trends in welfare state restructuring, particularly in relation to the care domain. Chapters One to Three primarily use secondary sources, including existing literature and policy information describing the past and current policy settings under investigation. Chapter One presents key terms and concepts used to analyse the restructuring of care and illustrates how key care and migration trends are contributing to the restructuring of care. Using these key trends and themes, it explains what restructuring means for in-home childcare, and ECEC more broadly. Chapter Two outlines significant historical developments in the three countries that are the focus of this book: Australia, the UK and Canada. In doing so, it illustrates how these policy changes correspond to the key processes of welfare state restructuring introduced in Chapter One. In particular, developments in policies shaping in-home childcare are situated within the context of ECEC and migration policy in each country. Chapter Three details the contemporary policy structures of in-home childcare in Australia, the UK and Canada, focusing on the intersection between funding, ECEC regulation and migration. Similar to Chapter Two, this chapter compares in-home childcare across the three study countries, and also with other ECEC types within each respective country.

Part Two (Chapters Four to Six) delves into the key empirical research findings, which focus on two key themes: first, the implications of these policy differences for families and care workers and, second, the historical, discursive and cultural reasons why the three study countries support in-home childcare differently. Chapters Four to Six, in particular, draw on a mix of analysis of primary and secondary documents and sources, as well as the data collected through 60 interviews with stakeholders, as described earlier. Chapter Four builds on Chapter Three by examining why policies differ. In particular, it focuses on the different rationales for supporting in-home childcare, examined through a 'social investment' framework, introduced in Chapter One. Chapter Five explores the implications of policy intersections for families and care workers in relation to the intersecting inequalities of gender, class/income and race/migration. Chapter Six returns to the concept of care culture to present an explanation for why the three study countries have developed different reasons and policies to promote in-home childcare. The Conclusion summarises what has changed, why these changes took place, and why it matters for social policy.

Notes

[1] 'Childcare' is used throughout the book to refer to the provision of all forms of non-parental care for young children. This includes informal and formal, regulated and unregulated arrangements. Where applicable, 'childcare' is used to maintain consistency with the original source. 'Early childhood education and care' (or 'ECEC') is used interchangeably with 'childcare', which reflects contemporary and policy-specific uses of the term.

[2] For the purpose of this book, in the UK data and analysis tends to focus on England, but comparisons with Scotland are incorporated.

3   For Canada, analysis focuses on the province of Ontario, as it is the most populated province, has an active childcare movement, and a high proportion of in-home childcare due to the lack of available and affordable regulated childcare spaces.

4   In addition, in 2015 the Australian government announced the introduction of the Nanny Pilot programme, a two-year trial running from 2016 to 2018. The programme offers subsidies for a capped number of families using nannies employed through an approved service provider.

5   The Live-In Caregiver Program was amended in November 2014. Migrants who entered under the Program prior to this date remain in the Program. The Program has been replaced by the Caring for Children Pathway, under the Temporary Foreign Worker Program. The former name, 'Live-In Caregiver Program', is retained throughout the book as it was the name of the Program during the time of data collection and analysis.

6   Includes full-day childcare, sessional childcare, after school childcare, children's centres, childminders, nursery and reception classes, nursery schools.

7   For example, in Ontario, a kindergarten programme (full-day since 2014) is free through the school system from the age of four years. In contrast, in most states in Australia children do not start kindergarten until age five or six.

8   Latest available figure for Canada is 2009.

9   In July 2018, the CCB and CCR will be replaced by a single Child Care Subsidy.

10   The subsidies were administered by the Department of Social Services between September 2013 and November 2015.

11   In May 2016, it was announced that the trial would be extended for a further six months.

12   South Australia (Australia), Scotland (UK) and four municipalities outside Toronto (Ontario).

Part One
Conceptual and historical analysis of in-home childcare

ONE

Restructuring care: concepts and classifications

Welfare state restructuring since the 1970s has reshaped the role and responsibilities of government in delivering a range of social services and benefits. Early childhood education and care (ECEC), as well as the care domain more broadly, is no exception to debates about how best to fund, regulate and deliver services. Governments may assume a variety of roles in the provision of social care services, including direct provider, contractor, funder and regulator. In recent decades, there has been a shift away from government as direct provider of services, which means that governments are increasingly contracting services to private providers. This is often achieved through a shift from supply-side to demand-side funding by putting public money in the hands of consumers through the use of vouchers and tax credits (Salamon and Elliott, 2002; Bonoli, 2005; Clasen and Siegel, 2007). These changes reflect the process of marketisation, whereby services are purchased by service users, constituted as consumers, through a mixed market of public and private providers. That is, rather than *provide* services, governments increasingly *subsidise* services through tax rebates or cash benefits to assist with the costs of care services, including childcare. The action of putting public funds in the hands of consumers to purchase services is often called 'cash for care' (Sipilä et al, 2010). Cash-for-care schemes represent one of many ways that governments have shifted responsibility for care provision to private providers and users themselves.

Care services, including childcare, have been affected by broad shifts in welfare state design, but changes to childcare policy are also a result of demographic and labour market changes that contribute to increased demand for paid, non-familial care provided in the public sphere, opposed to familial care in the private home. Demographic changes in the past few decades include an increase in the number of women in the labour market – especially mothers with young children. This means that childcare is increasingly provided by other family members (particularly grandparents), and by non-relative carers in both formal settings (mostly regulated and centre-based) and informal settings, such as by neighbours and by professional care workers in the private home.

At the same time that women and mothers' workforce participation has increased, there have also been shifts in the composition of the labour market, as full-time permanent work is being replaced with a rise in part-time, casualised and non-standard positions.

In many countries, including Australia, the UK and Canada, parents are increasingly likely to have non-standard, short-term, insecure, or unpredictable work hours. Participation in such work arrangements requires families to seek flexible childcare that is not always available in 'typical' formal services, namely centre-based childcare or childcare provided in the caregiver's home. Many families therefore rely on informal services. As introduced in the previous chapter, these informal arrangements can be paid or unpaid, provided by relatives or non-relatives, and provided in or outside the child's home. Thus, while the number and proportion of children attending formal ECEC settings – such as preschool and other centre-based childcare – has increased, there are still pressures from families to secure affordable and flexible childcare to accommodate non-standard and unpredictable hours (Rutter and Evans, 2012b; Brady and Perales, 2014). These demands call for a restructuring of care that better addresses parents' long and non-standard work hours. This is especially true in liberal market-orientated countries where there is an emphasis on women's workforce participation and productivity, yet a lack of available and affordable childcare.

Changes in the labour market are shaped by demographic shifts such as the rise in women's workforce participation, by increases in non-standard employment patterns, noted above, and also by global changes. Changes in the global labour market mean that workers increasingly move across national borders in search of employment opportunities. Migrant workers are part of the rise in non-standard and precarious work, including in the care sector. They fill the gaps in care needs for families working long hours and, in doing so, also work long and sometimes unpredictable hours themselves. The movement of migrant care workers, mostly from poor to rich countries, also contributes to the gap in care for their own children, who are often left behind to be cared for by other family members. This trend, termed the 'global care chain' (Parreñas, 2001; Yeates, 2005), represents an important global trend contributing to the restructuring of care responsibilities. This chapter discusses the interrelated shifts that have contributed to the restructuring of care responsibilities that affect the supply and demand of in-home childcare: the rise in non-standard work, the reconceptualisation of care, markets and migration, the rhetoric and rationales behind care restructuring, and shifting ideals of care.

Rise in non-standard employment

In addition to increases in female and maternal employment, there have been shifts away from standard employment, where employees generally work Monday to Friday, from between the hours of 8am and 6pm. Increases in non-standard work patterns can be linked to welfare state restructuring and the decline of the full-time permanent worker model. This trend is associated with the rise of the '24-hour economy', particularly among female-dominated service industries (Presser et al, 2008). In Australia, in 2007, nearly 60 per cent of all couple families had one or both parents usually working between 7pm and 7am. In 41 per cent of families, one or both parents worked shift work, and in 15 per cent of families one or both parents worked weekends (Australian Bureau of Statistics, 2009). In the UK, a survey found that only 35 per cent of employees worked a standard week, defined as Monday to Friday between 8am and 6pm (Statham and Mooney, 2003). Another study found that 80 per cent of working fathers worked atypical times, and half of working mothers (lone and couple) worked atypical times (Barnes et al, 2006, p 34). In Canada, in the late 1990s, one third of workers were in non-standard jobs, an increase from 28 per cent less than a decade earlier (Strazdins et al, 2004; Rapoport and Le Bourdais, 2008).

Non-standard employment among families with young children may reflect a positive choice by parents to work more flexible hours in order to maximise parental care. The absence of affordable formal or stable informal childcare may also prevent families from taking up standard employment (Le Bihan and Martin, 2004; Rutter and Evans, 2012b). In these circumstances, non-standard work can contribute to demand for more flexible ECEC options, including in-home childcare (Rutter and Evans, 2012b). As discussed in the previous chapter, in-home childcare traverses the informal/formal and public/private domains, which is often complicated by shifts in welfare state policies and the reclassification of care types.

Conceptualising care, redistributing responsibilities

The way governments fund and provide ECEC, and other human services, contributes to the development of care classifications and care regimes, which have been compared and critiqued in relation to broader welfare regimes typologies (O'Connor et al, 1999; Jenson and Sineau, 2001; Michel and Mahon, 2002; Lewis, 2006; Brennan et al, 2012; Anderson and Shutes, 2014). Comparative welfare regime scholars, particularly those interested in gender and care, have mapped out the ways that welfare state changes contribute to changes in care provision in the paid/unpaid, familial/non-familial and public/private spheres (Lewis, 1992; Jenson, 1997; Leira and Saraceno, 2002; Pfau-Effinger, 2005c; Kremer, 2007).

Welfare state changes are explained through processes of marketisation, commodification, privatisation, re-familisation and commercialisation, among others. These processes shift the distribution of responsibilities for care across the different domains – particularly between unpaid and paid work, and between the private (family or market) domain and the public domain. The dynamic between the public and private domains is, however, very complex. As Jane Jenson argued, typologies must move beyond the division of unpaid and paid work. We must ask *who* cares, *who* pays, and *how* the care is provided (Jenson, 1997, p 182–87). By asking these questions, distinctions within the private sector are made and the complex dynamic between public funding of private delivery is revealed. In particular, 'the mere absence of public provision of care does not tell us which private source – markets, voluntary organisation or families – will provide care' (O'Connor et al, 1999, p 30).

The liberal type – where Australia, the UK and Canada are regulatory grouped together in welfare regime classifications – is characterised by its 'distrust of public policies and the role of the state' (O'Connor et al, 1999, p 45). In these countries, the provision of care usually falls to the private family or private market. Increasingly, public funding through cash-for-care schemes and tax measures supports private care, including in-home childcare. In-home childcare is not, however, unique to the liberal welfare states. Cash for care and other funding models to encourage in-home childcare are common across Europe (Sipilä et al, 2010; Fagnani, 2012; Morel, 2012).

Governments are continually reforming policy structures and mechanisms for delivering social and care services, and childcare is no exception. When governments introduce new policy structures for providing childcare and early education, for example, the responsibility for funding, regulating and delivering services usually shifts between the family, market and public sector. As mentioned earlier, countries across the developed and developing world have witnessed a shift toward market-led provision of ECEC and other care services. Market-led approaches to delivering care services tend to shift responsibility for *paying* for services to the user (family), and *delivering* services to private organisations or individuals. Private organisations can be non-profit or for-profit, and for-profit services are sometimes commercialised or, where shareholders are involved, corporatised (Press and Woodrow, 2005; Brennan, 2007). Market-led approaches also tend to put government funds (public money) in the hands of families, allowing service users to purchase care from organisations and, sometimes, individuals. Market-led childcare can be part of the formal and, sometimes, informal domains. Whether provided by private companies or private individuals, the marketisation of care services promotes the commodification of care work as it moves from the unpaid and familial setting to the paid and non-familial domain. When provided by private companies, marketisation tends to formalise services; when marketisation allows for care by private individuals, it may also lead to informalisation.

The complexities of defamilisation, marketisation and privatisation have been conceptualised by scholars in various ways. Defamilisation, for example, has been defined as a 'process of unburdening the family' from care responsibilities (Clasen and Siegel, 2007, p 11). Sweden is often cited for its childcare policies, which, to some extent, defamilised childcare provision in the 1970s through the expansion of publicly funded ECEC services that allowed mothers to give up (some of) their unpaid caring responsibilities to work in the paid labour market. Here, the process of defamilisation occurred side by side with the formalisation of care for children. Commodification, on the other hand, refers to the inclusion in the market *without* formalisation, and delineates the process of moving care from the unpaid to paid labour market, but it does not always require defamilisation (Pfau-Effinger, 2006; Lewis et al, 2008). Leira's (2002) framework illustrates how commodification can reflect both familisation through cash benefits supporting parental childcare, or defamilisation through state-subsidised childcare services or benefits for non-parental childcare (presented in Lister et al, 2007).

The processes of defamilisation and commodification, noted above, are intertwined with the processes of formalisation and informalisation. In-home childcare sits at the nexus of informalisation and formalisation, where care shifts to the paid labour market (the process of commodification) and *sometimes* also shifts from the informal to the formal sector through the introduction of government funding and regulation. Birgit Pfau-Effinger highlights the blurred boundary between informal and formal care. She conceptualises how informal care can shift to paid care through processes of formalisation and commodification. In particular, care can be in the form of undeclared work in private households, that is commodification without formalisation; it can be a semi-formal, welfare state-supported form of 'care' in private households; and it can be formal paid work (Pfau-Effinger, 2006, p 139). In-home childcare may fall into any of these three categories: the 'traditional' nanny in the private home, paid for by private money resembles Pfau-Effinger's first pathway; partially subsidised and registered or regulated nanny care is increasingly common in a market environment, which resembles semi-formal care in private households; and, lastly; in-home childcare may also exist as subsidised and regulated paid care in the child's home, akin to formal services (regulated centre-based care or family day care). The introduction and removal of different policy elements, such as funding and regulation, can easily blur these lines for in-home childcare. In countries where migration policy and patterns also facilitate the recruitment of private in-home childcare, the processes of formalisation and informalisation are even more complex.

Migration, and migration policy, is another factor in welfare state change. Global migration trends and national immigration policy contribute to new care arrangements and classifications beyond the paid/unpaid, familial/non-familial, informal/formal and public/private dichotomies (Morel, 2007, 2012; Williams and Gavanas, 2008; Cox, 2012; Williams, 2012b). For example, in both Southern Europe (Bettio and Plantenga, 2004; Simonazzi, 2009) and Asia and North America (Michel and Peng, 2012), market mechanisms in combination with migration have led to a shift from familialist care regimes to 'migrant-in-the-family' care regimes.

Childcare and early education is increasingly 'going public' as care provision moves from the home to outside the home, from the unpaid to the paid sector, and from familial to non-familial care. The alleviation of childcare responsibilities can occur either through the provision of public services or, as presented above, through *public financing of private services*. Childcare is therefore also going public as new forms of, formerly private, childcare are attracting public subsidies. Overall, it is evident that care domains are at best a set of fuzzy categories to describe different forms of care provision, and different processes for redistributing care responsibilities. Despite the blurred categories for classifying care, the concepts themselves – that is, privatisation and formalisation – offer frameworks for understanding differences between care regimes and changes over time within specific countries and local contexts.

Markets, regulation and migration

As described above, the line between informal and formal is blurred, and the classification of care is shaped by government subsidies and regulation. Overall, public subsidies for private care arrangements represent a shift from care provided in the informal toward the formal domain. The introduction of public subsidies for unregulated care is attractive not only to families who receive the subsidy, but also to governments paying for the subsidies. This is because the formalisation of care work performed by workers previously in the informal and private domain is likely to increase revenue from income tax, by making previously undeclared work more visible. Moving care work from being undeclared to declared for tax purposes improves official employment figures and increases tax revenue. Jenson and Sineau point out how tax credits 'fit well with neo-liberalism's enthusiasm for seemingly lower "state expenditures" as well as greater "choice"' (Jenson and Sineau, 2001, p 255). There are therefore incentives for governments to introduce market mechanisms, such as voucher schemes, as a way to discourage a black market for care workers.

However, the formalisation of services is shaped not only by public subsidies, but also by the introduction of sector regulation, industry standards and other employment policies. The intersection of care and employment policy also has implications for the division of care responsibilities (Morgan, 2005; Simonazzi, 2009). Sector regulation can impose sets of standards that provider organisations must meet in order to be eligible for receipt of public subsidies. This may include specific procedures, practice guidelines, or the requirement that all (or a specific proportion of) staff hold relevant qualifications or skills. Market mechanisms (such as cash vouchers and tax deductions) that promote commodification in the absence of regulation tend to open up pathways for a low-paid workforce, where workers may not be required to hold specific qualifications or demonstrate a particular skill set. For example, Morgan (2005) shows how the more regulated labour markets in Western Europe limit the growth of a private childcare market, while in the US the low-wage labour force (and lack of formalised childcare) drive a market for private childcare. However, even in Europe, cash benefits and tax measures have expanded the market for commodified care – for childcare, elderly care, and other low-skilled domestic work (Morel, 2015).

Global migration, national immigration policies and the shift to funding commodified forms of care result in migration and care being intrinsically linked in the way governments support different types of care and domestic work.[1] The process of commodification through marketisation has led to a global restructuring of care work as workers from developing countries move to developed countries to provide low-paid care work (Lutz and Palenga-Möllenbeck, 2011; Anderson and Shutes, 2014). Where migration pathways exist in combination with cash benefits and other subsidies for childcare there are further opportunities for families to recruit low-paid, in-home childcare workers.

The recruitment of migrant care workers may appeal to governments, employers in the care services sector and families for different reasons. For government, migrant workers offer a new source of human capital, which can in turn boost productivity. Governments use migration programmes as a means to fill gaps in the care workforce, whether in institutional or home settings. Governments may also promote care worker migration schemes because they provide affordable care labour so that parents (almost always mothers) can enter or return to the labour market in positions that contribute to the economy. Some employers in the care sector view migrant care workers as a more affordable form of labour, which can reduce the costs of running a service. Families, too, may perceive migrant workers as offering more flexible and affordable childcare. For families with young children, a care worker living as part of the family can allow the second earner in the family to work longer or non-standard hours. Of course, locally born workers can also live in the home, but it is more common for migrant care workers to do so, through au pair schemes or similar room-and-board arrangements. The hiring of migrant workers thus supports government and employer objectives to enhance productivity, achieved partly through lower wages. At the same time, migrant workers support the demands and pressures of modern families seeking greater flexibility to work longer, non-standard and unpredictable hours.

The movement of workers across national borders is a significant global phenomenon (Ehrenreich and Hochschild, 2003; Lutz and Palenga-Möllenbeck, 2012). The movement and recruitment of migrant workers is not restricted to the care sector; however, the high demand for care and domestic workers in institutional and private (home) settings has driven the recruitment of migrant workers, mostly women, from less developed countries (see Anderson and Shutes, 2014). They often leave behind their own children who are then cared for by other family members, resulting in the 'global care chain' (Parreñas 2001; Ehrenreich and Hochschild, 2003; Yeates, 2012). These migrant care workers leave their home countries in the hope of earning money to send back to their own families and children. In turn, they provide care for other children (and also elderly and disabled people) so that their employers (host family) can work longer and earn more money for themselves.

The migration of care workers and the marketisation of care work are intrinsically linked by a shared discourse between families, government, employers hiring care workers and, sometimes, care workers themselves; there is an emphasis on employment, productivity and the economic contributions of all members of society. Governments benefit from higher taxes paid by families earning higher wages and, when care work is formalised through government regulation, the care worker declares their income, which supports an increased employment rate. This focus on employment, human capital and productivity is central to neoliberalism and a social investment approach to social policy. This framing of investment in human capital also dominates debate about early childhood education and care policy in many Western countries (Jenson, 2008; Mahon 2008, 2013; Adamson and Brennan, 2014).

Rationales for restructuring: the shift to 'social investment'

The restructuring of care is not only about reforms that alter the way governments spend and support unpaid and paid care; it is also about the ideas and rationales that underpin government and societal attitudes about the provision of care. The restructuring of care responsibilities – through both marketisation and migration – is consistent with global neoliberal trends about the role and responsibility of government in the provision of care services, and welfare state spending more broadly. Scholars and policy thinkers have coined the term 'social investment' to describe this type of restructuring of spending on care and social services. Social investment represents a shift from policies aimed to protect individuals from the market through social protection towards 'productive welfare', reflected in active welfare measures, and a focus on skills, labour force participation and early education (see Giddens, 1998; Esping-Andersen, 2002; Morel et al, 2009). Early childhood education and care is part of this trend, which emphasises investment in human capital. In particular, investment in children's early learning and development benefits the outcomes and productivity of future citizens. In the past two decades, the flurry of policy activity in ECEC at the national and international levels has been driven by a social investment agenda – particularly the revenue from mothers' current workforce participation and the savings in spending on children in the future. These shifts are evident through increased public (and private) expenditure on early education and intervention services for young children and also on activation measures to support mothers' workforce participation (OECD, 2015). The emphasis on mothers' workforce participation has been the focal point of policies and programmes to support families' use of in-home childcare.

The future-oriented approach to social investment gained momentum through Gosta Esping-Andersen's book, *Why we need a new welfare state* (2002). Here, he argued that a human capital approach to investing in children is needed to address shifting labour force trends and demographic changes. As he explains, spending on children in the present produces benefits to them and society in the future:

> If we aim for a productive and socially integrated future society, our policy priorities should centre on today's children and youths. Solid investments in children now will diminish welfare problems among future adults. (2002, p 51)

Similarly, Ruth Lister (2004) conceptualises social investment in three ways: as a 'pragmatic response' to the 'perceived economic and social challenges facing mature welfare states'; as an 'analytical tool' to explain contemporary developments in liberal welfare states; and as a 'normative ideal' where children stand as 'emblems of a future, prosperous, cohesive, and inclusive society' (Lister, 2004, p 157).

Frames for thinking about ECEC are shaped by various bodies of research, not to mention the significant role of ideology (Penn, 2011a). These include scientific research about the costs and benefits of investing in children's development (McCain and Mustard, 1999; Heckman, 2006); popular science about children's learning and development (Smyth, 2014); social movements (for example, feminism and children's rights); demographic pressures (such as low female employment rates and low fertility rates) and cost–benefit analysis (for example, reduction in poverty and crime rates). Economists and social scientists have lauded ECEC as a worthwhile investment based on both economic and social rationales showing that benefits outweigh costs in the short and long term (Cleveland and Krashinsky, 1998, 2003). This body of research is critical in shaping debates about alternative models and best practices in ECEC.

Rationales reflect the way 'problems' are articulated, and influence the policy structure and programme design promoted by government. For example, Jane Jenson proposes that when ECEC rests only on a labour force participation rationale, 'babysitting and unregulated care may be considered sufficient' (2008, p 366), whereas when focused on child development and early learning, centre-based, regulated care is promoted. Rianne Mahon summarises as follows:

> If [the problem] is framed in terms of the 'development needs of the child' the appropriate response would be universal part-day education (or high quality care) for children from two and a half to school age, with strict regulations concerning personnel training, staff–child ratios, physical facilities, and parent involvement. If framed in terms of 'equal life chances,' it would take the form of a mix of educational (part day) care supplemented by social services, targeting the children of working and single parents, immigrants, and those from deprived homes. If framed as a service for working mothers, expanding the number of full day, full year places would be a priority. (Mahon, 2010b, p 203)

Early childhood advocates and policy actors increasingly promote investment through a human capital approach to social policy – where ECEC is framed around children's 'early learning and development' and concerns about child poverty, which often extends to include parents' workforce participation (Dobrowolsky, 2002; DfE, 2003; Australian Government, 2009; Council of Australian Governments, 2009; HM Government, 2009; Mahon, 2009). The child-centred approach to social investment is critiqued by gender and care scholars, among others, for its limitations in addressing gender equality for women. It is also critiqued for its focus on the future benefits of children, to the neglect of their current wellbeing (Jenson and Saint-Martin, 2003; Dobrowolsky and Jenson, 2004; Williams, 2004; Lister, 2006; Lister et al, 2007; Lewis and Campbell, 2008; Lloyd, 2008; Jenson, 2009; White, 2011). This 'narrow' human capital approach to social investment ignores the potential for a more holistic approach to investment in ECEC – that is, investment in universal, high-quality care to address children's rights and wellbeing and the quality of employment for the care workers.

In ECEC, a neoliberal discourse translates support for public funding to subsidise private care arrangements. There are two interrelated discourses at play: first, a discourse of economic benefits and productivity, noted earlier, that advocates childcare as a means to facilitate mothers' workforce participation; and, second, a discourse of *choice* and individualism that promotes the use of cash subsidies and demand-side market mechanisms because, in rhetoric, they offer families' choice in childcare arrangements. That is, publicly funded subsidies, vouchers and tax measures are promoted by policymakers, employers and families themselves as the best model to support parental choice to use formal/informal, regulated/unregulated and centre- or home-based childcare. In Canada, the discourse of choice underpinned the Conservative government's introduction of the Universal Child Care Benefit in 2006 (Richardson et al, 2013). And, in the UK, Williams and Gavanas (2008) illustrate how discourse around consumerism and choice act to legitimise acceptance for in-home and migrant care workers, thereby justifying public funding for private, informal and commodified care arrangements. Similarly, in Australia, the recent introduction of the Nanny Pilot programme in 2016 was promoted through both an emphasis on parental workforce participation and calls by some advocacy groups for equal access to subsidies if they choose to use nannies (Productivity Commission, 2014a).

While the restructuring of care policies through marketisation and privatisation can support the rights of parents to use informal care provision *as consumers*, there are implications for equity of access by parents, for the rights of children to access high-quality childcare, and the social rights of care workers, particularly caregivers working in the informal sector who may be undocumented as workers or citizens. Scholars critique the narrow human capital approach in liberal countries, which encourages mothers' workforce participation, within the context of inadequate provision of ECEC services driven primarily by market principles. That is, subsidies and tax measures are promoted to provide consumer choice and to reconcile some of the costs of non-parental care, but the availability and quality of formal ECEC is not prioritised.

Ideals of care

As discussed above, countries' care arrangements can be explained through differences in the structural mechanisms that support childcare settings, and by different rhetoric and rationales for childcare. Both structures and discourses are reflective of embedded cultural norms and attitudes. Cultural norms and values about ECEC are grounded in historical structures and norms, but can also be shaped by new discourses about the place of women and children in society and, ultimately, the purpose of ECEC. Cultural norms about ECEC and care more broadly thus shape, and are shaped by, policy structures and discourses. Cultural norms can be embedded in historical structures, but may also change to reflect new ideas about the purpose and responsibility of ECEC.

Monique Kremer conceptualises divergences and changes in countries' care responsibilities as 'ideals of care'. Kremer's (2002, 2006, 2007) framework identifies four ideal type care arrangements that denote different ideas about the division of care responsibilities and the appropriate care of young children. The 'starting point' is full-time mother care, or the male breadwinner model, and there are four alternative models that reflect interactions between embedded policy structures and care cultures: surrogate mother care, intergenerational care, parental sharing and professional care. Williams and Gavanas define 'care culture' as 'dominant national and local cultural discourse on what constitutes appropriate childcare, such as surrogate mothers, mothers working and caring part-time; international help; shared parental care, or professional care' (2008, p 16).

In-home childcare is a type of care that does not fit neatly in any one of Kremer's or Williams and Gavanas' 'ideals of care' **or** 'care cultures', but could cross over many of these ideal types: nannies, for example, are often considered to represent surrogate mother care, but can also be professional carers. The extent to which in-home childcare reflects either, both – or none – of the ideals is shaped by the ways governments support this form of care in policy *and* rhetoric. As noted earlier, in-home childcare can be formal or informal, regulated or unregulated, and funded through public or private money – or a mix of these.

Scholars in Europe have given greater attention to the normative values that shape these different care ideals, and the government and public acceptance of new policy ideas (for example, Sipilä et al, 2010). The relationship between informal and formal care has been conceptualised in a European context to illustrate how both historical structures and cultural values affect individuals' attitudes and choices of care arrangements (Pfau-Effinger, 2005c; Kremer, 2006; Kremer, 2007; Morel, 2007; Van Oorschot et al, 2008; Williams, 2008, 2012b; Williams and Gavanas, 2008; Padamsee, 2009). Limited work has traced or conceptualised the relationship between different forms of childcare in liberal English-speaking countries, addressed in the remaining chapters of this book. To begin with, the next chapter outlines key historical developments that have shaped ECEC and in-home childcare policy in Australia, the UK and Canada.

Note

[1] For recent European accounts discussing the intersection between shifts in government policy and the recruitment of migrant workers to perform care and

domestic work, see Arat-Koç (1999), Cox (2006b, 2012), Williams (2010b, 2012b), Morel (2012), Nordberg (2012), Shutes and Chiatti (2012) and Busch (2013).

TWO

Restructuring care: comparative policy developments

The developments of early childhood education and care (ECEC) policy trajectories are shaped by various cultural, social and political contexts. Australia, the UK and Canada's respective approaches to supporting different forms of ECEC, and children and families more generally, were established at different times, and shaped by different groups of policy and public stakeholders. The feminist movement played a pivotal role in advocating for women's right to work and the expansion of childcare in all three countries; however, the way these movements played out, the actors involved, and their various goals and achievements diverged in critical ways.[1] For example, trade unions, femocrats, and lobby groups played a significant role in Australia (Brennan, 2002); trade unions and local employers influenced the trajectory of childcare in the UK (Randall 1995, 1996); and federal-provincial negotiations are identified as a key factor in progress and retreat of childcare in Canada (Mahon and Phillips, 2002). The directions and goals of movements were largely shaped by collective beliefs, political and advocacy mobilisation and negotiations about what is best for mothers and children (Michel and Mahon, 2002). The development of policies and programmes also reflects different regional and local norms.

Despite the distinct histories and care trajectories, there are clear patterns of convergence in the use of market mechanisms to fund and deliver ECEC and other care services (Brennan et al, 2012; Mahon et al, 2012). However, the marketisation of care services can reflect distinct processes of care restructuring. In liberal countries, including Australia, the UK and Canada, marketisation has fostered a different form of privatisation of care arrangements, compared with Nordic and southern European countries – from the private family to private services and commercial providers. Private providers include large corporations as well as individuals working largely in the informal sector. Australia, the UK and Canada have never had universal childcare, and therefore the restructuring of services in these countries cannot be explained as a shift away from universalism as in many Nordic and European countries (Brennan et al, 2012). In liberal countries, restructuring involved shifting priorities (between women and children), the redesign of funding and regulation to include and exclude different forms of subsidised childcare, and the introduction of policies and programmes targeting different groups of children and families.

The historical overviews that follow illustrate the differences in these liberal countries' childcare trajectories, with particular attention given to debates about how childcare policies and funding have positioned home-based care arrangements – in both the caregiver's and the child's home – across the public, private, informal and formal domains.

Australia

Australia's Child Care Act, introduced in 1972, established the Commonwealth government's responsibility to regulate and fund centre-based care (now called long day care). While in-home childcare, such as care provided by nannies, was not promoted in the Child Care Act 1972, parental care was the preference and 'family-like' care was the next best alternative. Thus, centre-based services were not the preferred form of childcare, unless they were used for educational purposes or as a welfare measure. In parliamentary debates, Senator Margaret Guilfoyle stated she hoped that centre-based care would not be used for children under the age of three or four, unless parents were single or ill (Brennan and O'Donnell, 1986, p 24). This preference for family-like care dominated debates about the distribution and funding of children's services through the 1970s and 1980s.

Family day care – group care provided in the caregiver's home – originated as a pilot scheme by the Brotherhood of St Laurence in Melbourne in the early 1970s. Evaluations of the programme recommended it be considered as an alternative and complement to centre-based care, rather than a solution to meeting the childcare needs of working mothers (Brennan, 1998, pp 132-3). At the time that the Child Care Act was introduced, family day care did not come under the Commonwealth's childcare programme. The 'mother-substitute' ideal shaped the informality and flexibility that family day care offered. But shortly after, in 1975, the Commonwealth government formally incorporated family day care into its childcare programme (Jones, 1987, p 90).

Tensions existed around the place of family day care because it was perceived as informal and based on a preference for the 'mother ideal' nature of care, rather than a service provided by qualified staff. Family day care was promoted because it was believed that home-based care provided a family-like environment for children; it also aligned with ideas about the division of labour and the role of women as unpaid caregivers, rather than paid workers. In 1973, the role of family day care was contested in a report, by the Social Welfare Commission, called *Project Care*, by Joan Fry (cited in Brennan, 1998, p 134). The report discussed two alternative approaches to family day care: the first rested on the mother ideal that 'incorporates an extra child or children into her household', and the second viewed caregiving as an occupation, whereby remuneration should be 'commensurate with out-of-home employment'. The Social Welfare Commission advocated that the former approach 'would be more in keeping with the spirit of family day care for the caregivers to be regarded as housewives carrying additional duties, rather than as workers' (Brennan, 1998, p 134).

Similar to the UK and Canada, discussed later, family day care was used mostly by families where work was a necessity for the second, or sole, earner, and children required a safe environment while their mother worked. Non-working parents looking for an educational programme for their children more often used centre-based care, such as preschool. Families used family day care for non-standard hours, including evenings, weekends and overnight. Studies in the mid-1980s, arguably at the height of family day care, found that such care was used predominantly for children whose parents were both in the workforce, whereas for children in centre-based care, only half of their parents were in workforce. Family day care was also more likely to be used for children with special needs, for infants, and for the provision of care in remote and sparsely populated areas (Kingdon, 1984, cited in Jones, 1987, p 94). The groups of children identified as being more likely to use family day care in the 1980s are the same groups of children and families for whom the In Home Care programme was developed 15 years later.

Pressures from the government, providers and families all shaped the formalisation of the family day care sector. The Commonwealth government needed to hold publicly funded services accountable; care workers realised that in order to improve their occupational status they needed to conform to prescribed standards to improve the public perception that family day care schemes were of high quality; and families' expectations and decisions took account of the quality, reliability and accountability of providers. These pressures prompted some 'family day care mothers' to change their description of themselves to 'home-based childcare workers'. This name change was the first step towards attaining award wages[2] and working conditions (Jones, 1987, p 98). As Jones writes in 1987, 'the original model of informal, motherlike care is gradually ceding ground to the idea that family day care should be a formal, quality service akin to that provided in childcare centres' (Jones 1987, p 96).

Under the Hawke and Keating Labour governments (1983–96), childcare moved to a central position on the government agenda, through shared interests by the union movement and women's groups for work-related childcare (Brennan, 2002, p 100). Throughout the late 1980s, funding for centre-based services shifted toward family day care services, viewed by critics as a 'cost-cutting exercise' (Brennan 1998, p 189). The Victorian Home Based Caregivers Association criticised the government's decision to support family day care for economic reasons, rather than in recognition of the value of family day care. However, some voices within government, including Finance Minister Peter Walsh, fiercely stated that the expansion of childcare services in the previous decade could not be sustained, and that responsibility should occur within the private sector (Brennan, 1998, p 189). Walsh's announcement brought some positive attention to the childcare fight. A report from the Centre for Economic Policy Research at the Australian National University noted the economic benefits to investment in childcare and provided a counter-argument to Walsh's comments. This report arguably brought benefits and negative consequences to the community childcare lobbyists.

The 1988 Childcare Strategy latched on to findings from the Centre for Economic Policy Research, and opened doors for new funding approaches and private sector actors to enter the stage (Brennan 1998, 190–197). The strategy proposed to meet all demand for work-related childcare by 1990. It created space for commercial providers and also maintained the economic rationale for supporting family day care because it was more cost-effective. However, the capacity of services (centre- and home-based) to deliver affordable, flexible care diminished under financial constraints spurred by per capita funding (in place of capital funding) and increasing expectations for standards and accountability (Jones, 1987). Family day care providers' autonomy was restricted in the sense that they were required to report on children's attendance and service standards. These are acknowledged as positive criteria for any person receiving public funds to look after children; however, with a lack of proper funding, these changes also constrained caregivers' autonomy and capacity to deliver services to meet the needs of families in their community.

By the late 1980s, there were also women's groups advocating for tax deductibility for childcare expenses, driven by professional women's organisations that argued childcare was a legitimate expense for working parents (Brennan 1998, p 179). Similar groups of women's organisations have, over the past decade, supported the subsidisation of in-home childcare (Australian Women Chamber of Commerce and Industry, 2013), discussed further in Chapter Four. Achievements in the 1970s towards a progressive, community-based programme encouraged by alliances between feminists, trade union leaders and Labour governments were, by the end of the 1980s, overshadowed by an emphasis on private provision (Brennan, 1998, p 109).

Reforms in the 1990s drastically shifted government's responsibility in planning and regulating childcare services: the 1991 expansion of fee subsidies (renamed Childcare Assistance) to private providers reflected a shift towards private responsibility for ECEC. By removing the government's role in planning the provision of not-for-profit services, private providers were able to establish services at their will, and there was little accountability for the quality of services attracting public subsidies. The removal of operational subsidies to not-for-profit services in 1996 also shifted responsibility further towards the private sector. Together, these reforms signalled clear preference for a market-based system that rested on demand-side funding mechanisms (Brennan, 2007).

The Childcare Cash Rebate introduced in 1994 (following means-tested Childcare Assistance from 1991) subsidised up to 30 per cent of work-related childcare for families, which included informal (but registered) care by relatives and non-relatives alike, but this measure was removed for informal care by the end of the 1990s. In 2000, the Child Care Benefit replaced Child Care Assistance and the Childcare Cash Rebate – at the same time that the In Home Care scheme was established (McIntosh and Phillips, 2002). In the mid-2000s, the Child Care Rebate was introduced (in 2004) and increased (in 2007), to subsidise the out-of-pocket costs of approved childcare. This includes the formal In Home Care programme.

The history of ECEC in Australia reveals no 'natural moments' that legitimised informal in-home childcare. Australia stands out among the three countries examined here for its limited financial support for families that use informal home-based childcare (in either the caregiver's or child's home). The restructuring of the children's services sector in 1980s and 1990s shifted the place of family day care and created a gap in the market for more flexible childcare provision. Writing in 1987, Jones indicates how family day care providers started advocating for greater remuneration to recognise their work in line with that of other women working outside the home. At the same time, the government imposed new monitoring and reporting requirements that affected the number and patterns of hours of care provided by individual family day care providers. These changes reshaped understandings about the importance of caregiver training and quality care and, in turn, affected parents' demands for more regulated services. The restructuring of family day care thereby created a gap in flexible, affordable care for families. Arguably in response to mounting pressures for more flexible care throughout the 1990s, the In Home Care programme was introduced to meet this 'gap' in the family day care sector. It started as the Sick Care Pilot, to fill a gap in the need for home-based special needs care that had faded away through a series of reforms that 'formalised' the family day care sector. By the end of the 1990s, pressures for flexible provision to address special needs and non-standard work patterns strengthened and continue today under increasing demand for affordable and flexible options to meet the needs of working families.

The pressures for flexible and non-standard childcare are at the centre of current policy developments in Australia. However, the pressures driving demand for flexible and affordable childcare are in stark contrast to those of the 1970s when subsidisation of family day care was supported under the rationale that some mothers needed to work and appropriate care should be provided to their children. Today, in-home childcare receives attention as a way to encourage women's workforce participation. In 2016, the Coalition government introduced a two-year Nanny Pilot programme, which establishes subsidies for a capped number of families to access care by nannies. The Nanny Pilot is contentious among the ECEC sector because of the lack of regulations and oversight, which goes against the improvements to quality standards across most other ECEC services.

At the same time, recent changes to migration policy are entangling debates about the work of in-home childcare. The Working Holiday Visa allows young people between the ages of 18 and 30 to work in Australia for up to six months with one employer. This visa, along with student visas, is the main pathway for young women to work as au pairs. A provision introduced in July 2015 allows young people on these visas working as au pairs to extend their stay with one employer to 12 months. This change was driven partly by the Productivity Commission's inquiry into childcare and early learning, and submissions detailing the inadequacy of current childcare options for many families. Thus, while significant pressures for policy change in ECEC are driven by the need to professionalise the sector, the Nanny Pilot programme and changes to the Working Holiday Visa are at odds with the trend towards high-quality ECEC provision.

United Kingdom

The UK was the last of the three study countries to introduce ECEC legislation and take on public responsibility for the regulation and funding of care and education services for young children. It was also the last to formally support in-home childcare, despite the fact that the hiring of nannies and domestic help is arguably embedded in British culture (see Gathorne-Hardy, 1972; Gregson and Lowe, 1994; Vincent and Ball, 2004). Prior to the Children's Act 1989, responsibility for funding and regulating ECEC services was primarily determined by local councils. Public funding was provided directly to centre-based services, while other care arrangements, particularly involving childminders and nannies, remained a private responsibility.

Since the 1960s, part-time nursery education has been promoted by the government and other sector interest groups as an extension to the education system. The Plowden report on primary education, published in 1967, recommended the expansion of mainly part-time nursery education and did not propose any full-time services to facilitate mothers' employment. The report informed sector discussion through the early 1970s, and helped to maintain the status quo and uphold the attitudes of government committees and civil servants in the Ministry of Health, and later Social Security (Lewis, 2013b). The 1972 White Paper on education signalled a debate between groups pressuring for expansion of education, opposed to care, for young children (Lewis, 2013b). This debate set the tone of early childhood education and care policy for the following two decades and, some would argue, still exists today.

There were still women's groups active in the childcare space, albeit there was some ambiguity about their demands. The Women's Liberation movement in the 1970s advocated for the expansion of full-day care for all children; however, such care was localised and varied considerably across the country. 'Self-help' playgroups were established by parents at the local level, often with council support. These playgroups were mostly organised and accessed by middle-class families (Finch, 1984). Full-time care in day nurseries was limited to children in need, particularly those in 'unfortunate' circumstances (Penn, 2009), while childminders were considered to provide the most appropriate care for the children of working parents. Faced with financial (and ideological) constraints, by the mid-1970s government's support for playgroups and childminders – opposed to more 'professional' nursery education and day nurseries – was identified as the way forward for the care and education of young children.

In 1976, a Department of Education and Science paper on nursery education declared that day care provision 'will have to be cheap in capital costs and trained manpower', and a conference on low-cost day provision for under-fives held the same year confirmed government's commitment to address the 'attainable', not the 'desirable' (cited in Lewis 2013b, p 265). This supported the preschool playgroup movement's approach that relied on the voluntary sector and expanded throughout the 1970s to meet the needs of, mostly, middle-class families. Part-time provision constrained mothers' labour market participation by the logistics of working around the short hours of care. The director of the National Children's Bureau, Mia Pringle, opposed women going out to work and viewed playgroups as complementary to the male breadwinner model. She contrasted this ideal with the alternatives: supplementary provision (nursery school), which was also acceptable; and compensatory/substitute family care (childminders, day nurseries), which should only be available to families with special needs (Lewis, 2013b, p 267). Through the 1970s, local day nurseries therefore became places of 'last resort for dysfunctional families' (Penn, 2009, p 118). In essence, while it was acknowledged that some women would continue to choose to work, the government's approach was to consider how to monitor private arrangements – such as day nurseries and childminders – rather than increase their involvement in the expansion of public services.

It was not until 1980 that a more united campaign for an integrated approach to education and care emerged. The National Childcare Campaign's discussion paper, *Childcare for All*, with financial support from the Equal Opportunities Commission, made a case for the development of community run nurseries delivered by trained staff, but maintained there should be parental involvement (Penn, 2009, p 119). There were disagreements about whether services should be publicly provided, or provided through a mixed economy in the form of community-based private providers. However, interestingly, both sides were 'uncomfortable about private childminders, which, they rightly recognised, tended to exploit working-class women' (Randall, 2002, p 231). A feminist-inspired childcare lobby grew in strength over the decade and there was increasing consensus that childcare was an issue for working mothers. This was in contrast to previous divisions between children's educational needs and the needs of socially disadvantaged families (Randall, 1996, p 180).

Reforms throughout the 1980s increased the regulatory responsibility of local authorities in childcare provision; however, financial expenditure and autonomy in funding decisions was limited. Due in part to the lack of publicly provided or funded services, there was a three-fold expansion in the number of private day nurseries during the 1980s (Randall, 2002, p 228). Most of the expansion of public provision was in part-time places (Randall, 1995, p 336). It is interesting to consider these trends in relation to broader childcare patterns. It was reported that in the late 1980s over two thirds of working mothers relied on relatives for their childcare arrangements. In 1986, it was estimated that childminders cared for approximately 70 per cent of children who attended some form of full day care and, after informal care by relatives, childminding was the second largest category of care used by children below school age. Owen (1988) also points out that there were likely large numbers of unregistered childminders who did not appear in official statistics. Furthermore, the mid-1980s is recognised as a time when there was resurgence in the use of nannies and au pairs. The increased demand for private nannies is attributed to the increase in mothers' employment, combined with a lack of public responsibility for day care and a dominant ideology that mothers – or a substitute – are the best form of care for young children (Gregson and Lowe, 1994).

The Children Act 1989 recognised that full-time care was a necessity for many families; however, the government maintained that it was still a private responsibility and continued to resist demands for greater public involvement (Lewis, 2013a). In the lead-up to the Children Act 1989, there were a number of pressure groups and committees that made recommendations for the increased regulation of private providers. For example, the Ministerial Group on Women's Issues announced a five-point plan in 1989, which included amendments to the Children's Bill improving childcare registration. The plan also encouraged 'employers and providers of childcare to adopt an accreditation scheme that would provide information about childcare facilities and guarantee their quality' (Randall, 1996, p 183). However, nannies were largely excluded from any discussion about the scope of arrangements that should be monitored for quality. One exception was the 1987 White Paper, which included a clause to bring nannyshare arrangements under childminder regulation (Owen, 1988). This was supported by the National Childminding Association (NCMA,[3] established in 1977), which pushed for increased centralisation and regulation of childminder networks during the late 1980s. The NCMA fought for greater regulation and staff training throughout the 1980s and 1990s, and sought greater recognition of the sector by focusing on employer interests and workplace sponsored childcare (Owen, 2003). Despite the NCMA's efforts to extend this regulation to nannies, it was not incorporated into the 1988 Children Bill and subsequent Children Act 1989 (Owen, 1988). Apart from the support for nannyshare arrangements to be included under the childminding regulation, nanny care remained quite separate from other forms of ECEC provision.

Initiatives in the late 1980s and 1990s, therefore, encouraged further private sector involvement, including from employers (Randall, 2002, pp 228-9). In 1990, the Equal Opportunities Commission published a report, *The Key to Real Choice* (Randall, 1996), which attracted the interest of employers, as well as that of organisations such as the Daycare Trust and Workplace Nurseries Campaign (Randall, 1996, p 182). The Ministerial Group on Women's Issues encouraged employers to provide childcare and encouraged tax relief for employers to do so. The report also encouraged employers to 'guarantee their quality' (Randall, 1996, p 183). Women's interest groups, too, began to draw on the market rhetoric of the Conservative government to promote an employment-focused agenda for the expansion of childcare provision. By the late 1980s, even the position of the National Childcare Campaign had evolved to 'accept the case for workplace nurseries' (Randall, 2002, p 231). The Conservative campaign for Tax Relief for Child Care was set up in June 1990 to secure tax relief on all forms of registered childcare. The Working Mothers' Association was a key supporter in this campaign (Randall, 1996, p 183).

Pressure groups advocating for more formal and regulated provision shifted their demands from public provision toward acceptance of public assistance to foster the demand side of the market. For example, the pressure group Employers for Childcare, formed in 1993, believed that aligning with the government's proposed demand-side approaches would achieve more for working mothers than fighting against them (Randall, 1995, p 328). In 1994, the government announced the introduction of a demand-driven voucher system for four-year-olds to facilitate parents' choice to use playgroups, childminders and day nurseries. The scheme was criticised by the state and private nursery groups alike, as well as the Pre-School Playgroup Association. Many groups were hesitant because of concerns that the voucher scheme would impede their own interests (Randall, 1996; Lewis, 2003), including the NCMA, which fought for inclusion in the Nursery Voucher scheme through its Childminders are Educators campaign (Professional Association for Childcare and Early Years, 2013).

Although the Liberal and Labour parties announced their commitment in the early 1990s to provide universal childcare, the agenda shifted in 1995 when demand-side funding measures (childcare vouchers) were introduced to increase private provision (Randall,

2002). In particular, the Childcare Voucher scheme was established through employers. This initiative offers vouchers to the parents of participating employers to assist with the cost of childcare, detailed further in Chapter Four. In 1997, the National Childcare Strategy expanded ECEC options for children and provided financial assistance for working families to help with the costs of childcare. This included the flagship programme, Sure Start, designed to address poverty in disadvantaged neighbourhoods. At the same time, Early Years Free Entitlement was introduced (since expanded in 2004), offering 15 hours of early years provision to three- and four-year-olds (and now some two-year-olds) (Lewis and Campbell, 2007). And, in 1999, the introduction of the childcare element of the Working Tax Credit allowed working families on low incomes using formal childcare services – namely nurseries and childminders – to claim up to 70 per cent of their childcare costs.

The initial introduction of the childcare element of the Working Tax Credit did not extend to families using nannies. The first introduction of government support for in-home childcare was through a pilot programme in 2004 and 2005, when the childcare element of the Working Tax Credit was extended to registered informal carers, including nannies and au pairs, through the Home Childcare Register. Overall, the register was designed as 'light touch' regulation to provide options for working parents. When the scheme was implemented, the NCMA also opened up membership to nannies to provide support and training similar to that available for childminders (Professional Association for Childcare and Early Years, 2013). The levels of government funding, means testing and regulation of in-home childcare continue to be debated today (Morton, 2012, 2014). The issues of funding and regulation and the intersection with migration policy and the hiring of au pairs are examined in later chapters, which analyse how the origins of the traditional nanny in the UK have shifted in recent years.

Canada

Canada stands out among these three countries for not having national ECEC legislation. Instead, responsibilities for regulating the care and education of young children are held by the provinces and territories. However, federal government support for in-home childcare exists through well-established tax measures and immigration policy. The Child Care Expense Deduction (CCED) was established in 1971 and is arguably a culturally accepted alternative to subsidies for regulated

ECEC. As in Australia and the UK, non-parental childcare in Canada was limited in the decades following the closure of wartime nurseries. Most mothers with young children remained at home with their children, or found alternative private arrangements (Bird, 1970, p 264). And, also similar to the other two countries, nannies and in-home childcare were only a reality for the wealthy.

Interestingly, and in contrast to Australia and the UK, the first major report (in 1970) calling for greater public involvement in childcare (other than as a purely welfare measure) proposed the inclusion of care provided in the child's home in the mix of care options. As Schlesinger (1971) states in his summary of the recommendations from the report by the Commission on the Status of Women in Canada, the 'commission envisioned day care as encompassing domestic workers and visiting homemakers as well as nurseries for full time, short term, and emergency care' (Schlesinger, 1971, p 254). This provision acknowledged that some women may need day care facilities at home because of parental or child illness or disability. The Commission's recommendations were not implemented, and opponents of the recommendations succeeded in making a case for lower-cost, private care. However, this detail illustrates that in-home childcare was regarded as a valid form of care for public subsidisation from the early 1970s. And while there was no national childcare programme that supported in-home childcare, the introduction of the 1971 Child Care Expense Deduction as part of the Income Tax Act laid the foundation for government's financial and ideological support for informal and private arrangements.

A decade later, in 1981, the Foreign Domestic Movement was established.[4] This programme reaffirmed government's belief that unregulated care in the child's home was an appropriate form of care for young children or – at very least – was the most affordable way to support the increasing levels of employment among mothers. Renamed in 1992, the Live-In Caregiver Program has been referred to as Canada's 'de facto' childcare programme (Cho, 2013). However, the focus has never been children; rather, it is the economic benefits gained through facilitating mothers' employment. As Daenzer contended (writing in the late 1990s), 'economic interests have been, and continue to be, the primary considerations that guided the opening up of the program to non-British and to non-white women' (Daenzer, 1997, p 104).

This should not, however, overshadow the advocacy efforts made by the federal (and provincial) childcare movements. From the 1970s to 1990s, feminists and childcare advocacy groups fought tirelessly for increased public responsibility for early childhood education and care (see Tyyskä, 1993; Friendly and Rothman, 1995; Prentice; 2001; Timpson, 2001; Mahon, 2004; Mahon and Jenson, 2006). Despite some optimism in the mid-1980s following the 1986 Liberal Task Force on Child Care, the Conservative government's report, *Sharing the Responsibility* (1987), reiterated the belief that:

> [T]he primary responsibility for child care must rest with the family … [and]…the community and wider society have important roles to play in assisting parents and providing supplementary forms of child care. (Martin, 1987, p 10)

The recommendations acknowledged a role for government to improve the quality of informal arrangements, such as unregulated day care homes; however, debate focused on the tax system to subsidise the (limited) options available and was justified in the name of parental choice. The report's recommendations were echoed in the National Strategy on Child Care announced in 1987, which proposed Canada's first childcare legislation (called Bill C-144). After Bill C-144 failed to receive Senate approval in 1988, the Conservative government indicated that it would reintroduce childcare legislation if it returned to office. However, the then Minister of Health and Welfare was quick to assert the federal government's priorities, indicating that Canadian tax dollars should not 'pay for the yuppie couple', but rather support families in economic need. The minister added that childcare 'is not simply a program designed to increase career opportunities' (cited in Teghtsoonian, 1995, p 423). Because these policies and tax measures were not officially part of a childcare programme, the federal government turned a blind eye to the regressive (CCED) and exploitive Live-In Caregiver Program (LCP) measures inherent in the mechanisms facilitating (middle-class) women's workforce participation. At the same time, many Conservative MPs believed that women should be encouraged to stay at home and look after the family.

Many women Liberal supporters also promoted the idea of tax credits and an employers' capital cost write-off for workplace day care, under the belief that it would provide more choice (Tyyskä, 1995, 152). Teghtsoonian identifies 'two strands of neo-conservative ideology' in Canada in the 1980s and 1990s – one that supported women in the home, and the other (more neoliberal) that supported their participation in the workforce to limit dependence on social assistance (Teghtsoonian, 1995, p 418). Both strands supported, albeit with different intentions, the use of tax measures to support private forms of care for young children (Harder, 2004). And, both strands opposed the feminist vision proposed by the 1970 Commission on the Status of Women and the 1986 Liberal Task Force on Child Care, which supported the expansion of publicly funded and regulated care outside the home. As one interviewee commented in this study on conservative ideology in the 1980s and 1990s, there was a belief that "if you had children you should pay for them and it's not a public responsibility... [it's] a private affair between a parent [and a business]... it's a service that they purchase the same way they buy a car" (provider organisation, Canada).

In the absence of a national childcare framework, it is the provinces that hold primary responsibility for childcare funding and regulation. As introduced earlier, the focus for Canadian analysis is the province of Ontario: it is the most populated province; its childcare advocacy groups have been historically influential in shaping federal movements (Mahon, 2013); and it is the province with the largest number of Live-In Caregivers (Human Resources and Skills Development Canada, 2013). At the provincial level, the mid- to late 1990s was a period of unravelling of progress for advocates such as the Ontario Coalition for Better Child Care (OCBCC). Following severe austerity cuts between 1990 and 1995 under the Liberals, the Canadian Health and Social Transfer (CHST) replaced the Canadian Assistance Plan (CAP) in 1995. This meant there was no funding designated for childcare – provinces now had discretion over where the money went. Exacerbating this problem in Ontario, the Conservative government released a report (by the then Minister of Community and Social Services, Janet Ecker), entitled *Improving Ontario's Child Care System*. This report recommended 'reduced access to government-regulated and funded child care', and that childcare should include 'as many different kinds of quality care as possible'. The report's recommendations were arguably influenced by the Association of Day Care Operators of Ontario, which represented private for-profit operators supporting 'parental choice' (Tyyskä, 2001, p 139).

In 1997, the province of Ontario gave more responsibility to the municipalities, which could opt to subsidise informal care. The OCBCC described this announcement as the 'birth of the voucher system and the collapse of regulated child care' (cited in Tyyskä, 2001, p 140). These policy defeats for advocates for universal childcare, such as the Ontario Coalition for Better Child Care, were reaffirmed with the OntarioWorks programme in 1998. The programme aimed to get welfare recipients into work and the provincial-municipal agreement allowed the cost of unregulated and informal arrangements to be covered – this was a change from the previous agreement, which was limited to regulated services (Tyyskä, 2001, p 141). The OntarioWorks programme was implemented to facilitate mothers' participation in the workforce as a means to address child poverty. However, a contentious point in the policy was that there was no right to quality care for the mothers and children. Instead the informal sector was promoted as the natural solution to mothers' work-related care needs (Mahon, 2007, p 72).

In the lead-up to the 1993 federal election, the Liberal party promised to expand regulated childcare dramatically and called for a 'more dedicated funding approach' (cited in Friendly, 2000, p 15). However, the 1995 budget revealed a very different approach to that promised in the so-called Red Book, or Social Security Review report. The budget announced the switch from CAP to CHST block grants. This new funding approach not only cut overall funds, it also lumped childcare together with health, social welfare and secondary education with no provision for guaranteeing that funds would be used for childcare specifically.

In addition to fiscal pressures and austerity measures, ideological preferences for private (including commercial) providers resulted in even greater disappointment for the federal and provincial advocacy bodies. The need for children's services was addressed through the National Children's Agenda (1999), which subsumed childcare as one of multiple strategies to improve child wellbeing and eliminate child poverty. Funding and policy initiatives under this strategy were therefore targeted to those in most need. Universal childcare was not viewed by government (at the federal or provincial level) as an appropriate solution to addressing mothers' demands for work-related gender equality. Instead, alternative solutions for supporting workforce participation – including the Live-In Caregiver Program – were promoted, while children's needs were addressed through targeted programmes and subsidies for low-income families. The National Children's Agenda represented a broader neoliberal shift that subsumed childcare 'under services for early childhood development' where 'the notion of childcare as a support for gender equality (or for employability) disappears' (Mahon and Phillips, 2002, p 208). In efforts to broaden support, many advocacy groups accepted this new discourse, despite the fact that it ignored the need for high-quality services for all children, and did not address gender equality in the home and the workplace.

Throughout the late 1990s and early 2000s, federal and provincial advocacy groups, including the Child Care Advocacy Association of Canada, fought for a national framework for ECEC. However, the momentum gained through the 1990s was suffocated in 2006, when the Conservative Harper government introduced the Universal Child Care Benefit (in addition to the CCED). This initiative was implemented as an alternative to the development of the Liberal government's Multilateral Framework Agreement on Early Learning and Care. The Liberals' proposed universal framework was scrapped for the Universal Child Care Benefit, in the form of $100 per month per child under six years. The Conservative government's discourse of 'choice' in childcare dominated the cash-benefit approach to childcare funding for almost a decade. The recent election in 2015 of the centre Liberal party ignites new opportunities to establish a nationally regulated system in Canada.

Restructuring support for ECEC: a new direction?

In all three study countries, similar debates took place regarding the role of care versus education across the public and private, and formal and informal spheres. Dominant ideas about the care of young children being the responsibility of the family hindered the success of advocacy efforts, particularly by the feminist movement, for regulated, centre-based ECEC. However, looking at the details of the debates, pressures and actors through the lens of in-home childcare, contrasting attitudes are revealed.

In Australia, competing interests for universal ECEC led to a greater role for the private sector in centre-based care and support for (lightly) regulated home-based care as part of family day care. In the 1970s, groups such as the Australian Pre-School Association (now Early Childhood Australia) and Community Child Care that supported different forms of non-profit, centre-based care provided by trained caregivers were challenged by new ideologies and financial pressures for targeted and 'cheaper' forms of home-based care. Lower employment rates among women and mothers (and high levels of part-time work) also arguably contributed to the limited demand for more flexible childcare options in the 1980s and 1990s. The community preschool movement, particularly in Victoria and New South Wales, was more in line with the child-centred needs of these families. Instead, in-home childcare originated in the late 1990s in response to the needs of families with illness or disability, and was naturally incorporated into family day care. As discussed in later chapters, this targeted approach to in-home childcare is arguably being pushed aside as greater attention is being given to the economic benefits of mothers' workforce participation.

In the UK, demand for traditional 'nanny' care increased in response to the lack of public responsibility for formal ECEC; however, such care remained largely outside the scope of debates regarding public and private care domains, until the late 1990s. Instead, advocacy movements were divided by demands for part-time education versus full-day care (mostly childminders) for mothers that needed to work, neither of which made a case for government support for care in the child's home. Demand for work-related childcare in the 1980s shifted responsibility for care from the private family to private organisations and employers. Pressures and movements (including demands by feminist groups) were divided in their demands for government involvement in the provision of childcare, and calls for universal care were weak. The care of young children remained a private matter until the mid-1990s, and therefore left in-home childcare outside the scope of ECEC debate. However, women's groups and employer groups continue to advocate for greater government support for childcare, and support for nannies and in-home childcare receive greater attention in early years sector debates. As Chapter Six discusses, recent debates about the subsidisation and regulation of nannies continue to reference class divisions and local care culture embedded in ECEC policy and practices.

In contrast to the situation in both Australia and the UK, in-home childcare in Canada was proposed as a valid form of formal and publicly supported care in the early 1970s, through the Child Care Expense Deduction. While advocates for in-home childcare did not demand greater government support, conservative and neoliberal governments ideologically favoured private care in the child's home. In the 1980s, the Child Care Expense Deduction continued to be supported by government as a solution to meeting demands for childcare in response to increasing female employment, while also providing parents a 'choice' about their childcare arrangements (Harder, 2004). Commenting on working families' needs for regulated childcare within a 'modern' economy, one interviewee affirms: "We [Canadians] still haven't evolved enough in terms of public policy and family policy to really enforce this" (peak organisation, Canada). Later chapters discuss the embedded assumptions about work and care that maintain a division between public and private responsibility for ECEC in Canada.

Analysis of the origins of in-home childcare in these three countries contributes to our understanding of care culture in liberal countries, including a more detailed explanation for why in-home childcare (and ECEC policy more broadly) differ in these three countries. Care cultures shape, and are shaped by, attitudes and ideas about appropriate forms of care for young children. And, therefore, patterns of in-home childcare use in the three countries can be explained in relation to policy developments and ideology, but may also shape policy demands in line with dominant forms of care. Later chapters give greater attention to how policy structures and ideas reflect assumptions about care responsibilities that contribute to variant care cultures. The next chapter takes a contemporary approach to analysis to compare the different ways that governments classify and promote different forms of ECEC, particularly in-home childcare, through funding, regulation and migration. It illustrates how recent policy structures arguably reproduce many of the origins of in-home childcare in each country. However, there are also examples of where government policy has sought to restructure patterns of ECEC and in-home childcare use.

Notes

[1] For comparative and country-specific accounts, see Tyyskä (1995), Randall (1996), Brennan (1998), Friendly (2000), Jenson and Sineau (2001), Timpson (2001), Baker (2006), Penn (2007), Mahon (2009) and Brennan and Mahon (2011),)

[2] 'Award wages' is a term used in Australia to refer to the "minimum wages and conditions an employee is entitled to". These are set out as 'awards' depending on the industry and work performed (Fair Work Ombudsman, 2014).

[3] The NCMA changed its name to the Professional Association for Childcare and Early Years in 2013. NCMA is used throughout the chapters because the name change occurred after fieldwork and most analysis was conducted.

[4] The programme was replaced by the Live-In Caregiver Program in 1992, and recently renamed under the Temporary Foreign Worker Program in 2014. Under the Temporary Foreign Worker Program there are two pathways, one of which is called the 'Caring for Children Pathway'.

THREE

Policy structures in Australia, the UK and Canada

One way to analyse early childhood education and care (ECEC) policy is to measure and compare total government expenditure on ECEC as a proportion of gross domestic product (GDP). While most countries across the Western world have increased investment in ECEC services as a percentage of GDP over the past decade (OECD, 2015, PF3.1), the ways in which spending is structured has changed. In addition to spending as a proportion of GDP, comparisons of ECEC policy also include: expenditure per child; access to and participation in formal, centred-based services; the affordability of centre-based ECEC as a proportion of average or median family income; and the quality of different service models. Affordability of services often reflects the role and level of responsibility the public sector has for funding and regulating services. Ultimately, affordability across different social groups – including income levels – provides an indication of the division of responsibility between public and private sectors for funding and delivering *formal* and *regulated* services (Meyers and Gornick, 2003; Lloyd and Penn, 2012; Gambaro et al, 2014). We know less about how policy mechanisms and funding structures can support the use of different types of ECEC, especially *informal* and *unregulated* care, including care in the child's home. The dynamic between these different types of services matter because, as Jenson and Sineau indicate, it is the 'details of the services, the eligibility rules and forms of delivery' that have an impact on the types of services accessible to families, and the quality of these services (2001, p 5).

Government involvement in the funding, delivery and regulation of ECEC affects families' early education and care options. Families' ECEC decisions about whether to use formal/informal and regulated/unregulated care are therefore shaped by individual and socially embedded preferences (Vincent and Ball, 2006), but also by government policy structures and supports. As discussed in the previous chapters, policy developments and government' positions towards in-home childcare have evolved alongside broader shifts in ECEC policy, which have included a shift from direct service delivery towards a marketised service environment led by demand-side funding. Funding and subsidies available for families using in-home childcare may or may not be contingent on services and individual providers meeting specific standards or regulations. This chapter elaborates on how *funding* and *regulation* for ECEC services are imposed (or not) on care provided in the child's home. It therefore focuses on how nannies and other forms of in-home childcare are situated within ECEC structures. In an innovative way, analysis also extends to broader policy domains, namely the rules and regulations surrounding the *migration* of care workers.

To begin with, ECEC terms and specific types of care that are pertinent to policymakers, and familiar to the public and service users (such as families), are revisited. In particular, it considers how different types of ECEC in these countries are situated across informal/formal, public/private and regulated/unregulated policy spheres. This information provides us with an understanding of the analytical approach taken in the remainder of the chapter. The next part of the chapter refers back to trends in policy restructuring outlined in Chapter One in order to offer a snapshot of the current funding, and regulatory and immigration mechanisms in each jurisdiction. This is followed by an in-depth analysis of how these three policy mechanisms pertain to Australia, the UK (with a focus on England) and Canada (with a focus on Ontario). Lastly, the chapter examines how these policies intersect in similar and different ways.

The first challenge to undertaking this analysis is to define and classify the different forms of informal/formal and regulated/unregulated ECEC. A simple comparison of trends across countries – for instance, the fact that children's participation in *formal* childcare services has increased over the past two decades – does not reveal the changing and inconsistent ways governments and service users classify different types or domains of care. Government policy, including funding and regulation, has implications for how ECEC services are classified, and in-home childcare holds a particularly precarious place: in-home childcare can describe a *type* of ECEC, but can also refer more broadly to the *setting* of care (Holloway and Tamplin, 2001; Land, 2002; Rutter and Evans, 2011). This is why we must first determine the scope and details of formal/informal and regulated/unregulated ECEC. Ultimately, these classifications shape our understanding of the boundaries between public and private responsibility for childcare and early education.

We know that young children have for over a century been cared for in different settings – in centre-based group care such as kindergartens and day nurseries, in other people's homes, including family and friends and other caregivers, and in the child's own home by grandparents, neighbours, friends or other caregivers. Policy reforms affect the way governments support each of these forms of care. In Australia, the UK and Canada, policy reforms have shifted the way in-home childcare is placed within broader ECEC and social service systems.

Overview of current ECEC systems

Legislative elements of countries' ECEC systems provide the overarching framework to analyse the funding and regulation of in-home childcare. Table 3.1 outlines the existing legislation, and accompanying regulations, for different ECEC settings in the each of the countries. In the UK and Canada, there is also a focus on the country level (England and Scotland) and provincial level (Ontario). The table summarises the different legislation and regulations as they apply to three broad types of ECEC – centre-based group settings, domestic group settings (in the provider's home), and domestic setting (child's home) – to refer to in-home childcare. Further detail of these settings is described in the country sections below.

Australia

The Education and Care Services National Law 2011 and accompanying Regulations provide the overarching framework for Australia's ECEC services. As noted in the Introduction, the National Law requires all states and territories to regulate long day care (LDC), family day care (FDC), preschool care, and outside school hours care (OSHC) to align with the standards set out in the National Quality Framework. While In Home Care (IHC) is a Commonwealth 'approved' service for receipt of Child Care Benefit (CCB) under the Family Assistance Law, it remains outside the scope of the National Quality Framework implemented as part of the National Law 2011. The Family Assistance Law prescribes operational requirements for services to be eligible for subsidy receipt, such as the number of hours per day and weeks per year that a service must be open. Families using Commonwealth-approved services (LDC, FDC, OSHC, IHC and Occasional Care) are eligible to receive the main funding streams for ECEC: the Child Care Benefit (which is means-tested) and the Child Care Rebate, or CCR, (which is activity-tested). These two funding mechanisms will be rolled into one Child Care Subsidy in 2018. Many states also fund free or low-

Table 3.1: Legislative framework of ECEC service types for children aged 0 to 5 years: Australia, the UK and Canada, 2015

Country/jurisdiction Legislation and regulation	Centre-based group setting	Domestic group setting (provider's home)	Domestic setting (child's home)
Australia *Education and Care Services National Law★*	National Quality Standards *Service types:* Long day care, outside school hours care	National Quality Standards *Service type:* Family day care	Interim Standards for In Home Care *Service type:* In Home Care
United Kingdom *Children and Family Act 2014*	Regulated at the country level		
England *Childcare Act 2016*	Ofsted Early Years Register (mandatory) *Service types:* Preschools, day nurseries	Ofsted Early Years Register (mandatory) *Service types:* Childminders	Ofsted (voluntary) Childcare Register (voluntary OCR) *Service types:* Home childcarers (nannies, au pairs)
Scotland *Regulation of Care (Act) 2001*	National Care Standards: Early Education and Childcare Registered with Scottish Social Services Council *Service types:* Nurseries, crèches, outside school hours care, playgroups, preschools[1]	National Care Standards: Early Education and Childcare Registered with Scottish Social Services Council *Service type:* Childminders	National Care Standards: Childcare Agencies Registration with Childcare Agency (voluntary) *Service type:* Nannies, other in-home childcarers

Country/jurisdiction *Legislation and regulation*	*Centre-based group setting*	*Domestic group setting (provider's home)*	*Domestic setting (child's home)*
Canada	No national legislation		
Ontario *Child Care and Early Years Act 2014*	License and municipal government operational standards *Service type:* Day nurseries	License and municipal government operational standards *Service type:* Private-home care (five children or more)	Not regulated *Service type:* All forms of home/in-home childcare for up to five children

★ The Education and Care Services National Regulations are monitored at the state level, which must align with the National Law.

[1] Shared responsibility with Education Scotland.

cost preschool to children in the year before starting school. This is separate to the Commonwealth subsidies.

ECEC service providers outside the Commonwealth-approved funding programme may apply for registration with the Department of Human Services. Registered childcare includes services that may, traditionally, fall into the 'informal' domain of ECEC, such as care provided by nannies, grandparents and other relatives or friends. Other types of registered care providers include some state-licensed preschools or kindergartens, playschools and mobile services. Some registered service providers are required to register with the government, while others (including nannies and grandparents) have the option to register so that families are eligible for receipt of a (reduced) subsidy. Registered childcare will, however, be abolished under the new Child Care Subsidy, expected to come into effect in July 2018.

United Kingdom

In the United Kingdom, the Children and Family Act 2014 legislation applies to all jurisdictions; however, separate legislation guides regulation in each jurisdiction – England, Wales, Scotland and Northern Ireland. The focus for this chapter is England, but also includes Scotland to illustrate how the structures differ across jurisdictions. The Children Act 2004 and the recently amended Childcare Act 2016 and accompanying Regulations provide the legislative framework for England (and Wales). The Childcare Act 2016 designates primary responsibility to local authorities, leaving regulation and standards to the independent body, the Office for Standards in Education, Children's Services and Skills (Ofsted). Ofsted's regulatory framework classifies ECEC (or children's services) into two broad types of care – *early years* and *childcare* – which set different requirements for providers. In Scotland, the Regulation of Care (Act) 2001 designates responsibility to the Care Inspectorate. The different regulations and standards in England and Scotland are elaborated later in this chapter. Families using services registered with Ofsted (in England) and the Care Inspectorate (in Scotland) are eligible for the same level of public funding – the childcare element of the Working Tax Credit and employer-sponsored childcare vouchers. However, the majority of public funding in England is delivered through the early years entitlement, which offers 15 hours of ECEC for three- and four-year-olds in most ECEC settings: nurseries, nursery classes, playgroups and pre-school, childminders, and at local Sure Start Centres. Disadvantaged two-year-olds are also eligible for the early years' entitlement (UK Government, 2014b).

ECEC funding is currently in flux in the UK. In the next two years, the proposed Tax-Free Childcare scheme (announced in 2013) is expected to be rolled out, and additional assistance to low-income families is included as part of Universal Credit (expected to replace the current Working Tax Credit). Tax-Free Childcare will allow parents on joint incomes up to £150,000, who do not already receive support through tax credits, to claim up to 20 per cent of their childcare costs, up to £10,000 per year for each child, receiving back up to £2,000 per year. At the time of writing, the funding formula for the Early Years Entitlement is also under consultation and changes are expected to be introduced in 2017.

Canada (and Ontario)

Canada stands out among these three countries for not having national ECEC legislation. Instead, provincial and territorial governments are responsible for regulating the care and education of young children. The federal government does, however, regulate some aspects of the provision of in-home childcare through immigration policy.

At the federal level, the Child Care Expense Deduction (CCED) and Universal Child Care Benefit (UCCB) provide financial support to families using any form of regulated or unregulated ECEC – neither programme distinguishes between regulated and unregulated childcare provision, although the CCED requires receipts. Alongside these financial supports for unregulated childcare, immigration policy (formerly called the Live-In Caregiver Program) also facilitates unregulated childcare in the child's home. This immigration scheme underpins much of the policy analysis of in-home childcare in Canada, as will be discussed in the next section.

At the provincial level, where Ontario is the focus for this book, the Child Care and Early Years Act 2014 (previously known as the Child Care Modernization Act) replaced the very out-dated Day Nurseries Act from 1989. One of the key pressures behind this reform was sector concern surrounding the provision of unregulated home-based childcare provided in the caregiver's home. While there have been some improvements surrounding compliance of home-based childcare in the caregiver's home (private home-based care), care in the child's home remains largely outside the scope of the legislation, although there is a complaints-based monitoring system. A capped number of subsidies for low-income working families are provided to families using centre-based and regulated home-based services licensed by Ontario's Ministry of Education.

Country summary

The ECEC legislative frameworks in Australia, the UK and Canada differ in various ways: in Australia, in-home childcare is included in the legislative framework, but excluded from national quality regulations; in the UK, in-home childcare in England is legislated, but regulated under a separate (and voluntary) registration scheme; and, in Canada there is no national legislation for ECEC, but in the province of Ontario in-home childcare is explicitly excluded from the recently introduced regulations. However, it is not only ECEC legislation and regulation that shapes the position of in-home childcare within the suite of childcare options. As the remainder of this chapter discusses, funding mechanisms and migration policies intersect in diverging ways in these three countries and jurisdictions. It is the details of policy mechanisms that shape the composition of the in-home childcare sector and its workforce, the quality of care of the services, the affordability and accessibility for families, and the working conditions of the caregivers.

Intersecting policies for in-home childcare

Governments' regulatory frameworks affect both *users* and *providers* of ECEC. For users, eligibility to access services and the generosity of funding is guided by legislation, whether at the federal or local levels. For providers, regulatory frameworks dictate the requirements of ECEC services – both organisations and individual workers – with respect to their operations and staff qualifications or standards. These policy mechanisms interact to create a complex picture of the intersection between providers and users. That is, government subsidies may be very generous and impose few eligibility requirements for families, but may be limited to users of specific types of services (for example, centre-based services where all staff have minimum qualifications). Conversely, subsidies may be less generous, with strict or minimal eligibility, but with no restrictions on the types of ECEC used (to include care by informal or formal carers). Various scenarios may exist depending on the interaction between:

- families' eligibility (income, work status, other family/circumstantial characteristics);
- generosity of subsidy or tax measure;
- types of care eligible for subsidy or tax measure;

- care workers' qualifications and criteria for registration/regulation (organisations and individuals);
- workers' rights/conditions (including immigration).

The intersection of these policy details affects the place of in-home childcare and, as it is argued, are reflective of different government priorities and approaches to ECEC. Policy mechanisms may facilitate families' use of in-home care and, at the same time, the lack of coherent ECEC policy structures, in turn, can push families to alternative forms of care arrangements, including informal and unregulated care provided in or outside the child's home (Sipilä et al, 2010).

The remainder of this chapter compares the policy details of in-home childcare in each country in relation to: ECEC quality regulation; financial support through subsidies and tax measures; and immigration policies that facilitate families' use of in-home childcare. First, Table 3.2 summarises these three areas of policy in each of the three study countries. It indicates the government department responsible for each area, as well as the name of the policy, programme or benefit relevant to each policy area. The remainder of the chapter compares the details for each of these policy areas, respectively.

Of course, there are various other policies and funding elements that intersect with the policy elements listed above. In particular, child and family benefits and tax measures affect the affordability of parental and non-parental childcare, and employment and labour laws govern the rights and working conditions of the in-home childcare workers. While these are no doubt important elements shaping in-home childcare, they are outside the focus on the intersection of ECEC and migration policy. This chapter delves into the detail of policies specific to in-home childcare to consider how quality regulation in ECEC, funding structures and migration rules and regulations contrast with other types of ECEC in their respective jurisdiction, and across jurisdictions.

Table 3.2: Elements of government intervention in in-home childcare: Australia, the UK and Canada, 2015

	Responsible governmental body (*policy, programme or benefit*)		
	ECEC quality regulation	*Subsidies, tax measures and cash benefits*	*Immigration policy*
Australia	Department of Education[1] *In Home Care programme*[2] *(Interim Standards for In Home Care)*	Department of Education[1] *Child Care Benefit*[3] *(CCB)* *Child Care Rebate*[3] *(CCR)*	Department of Immigration and Border Protection *(Working Holiday Visa)*
United Kingdom	England Office for Standards in Education, Children's Services and Skills *(Home Childcare Registry)* Scotland Care Inspectorate *(Childcare Agency Registry)*	HM Revenue and Customs *(Childcare element of Working Tax Credit, childcare vouchers)*	UK Visas and Immigration *(Youth Mobility Scheme)* EU regional agreements
Canada	*Canada N/A* Ontario Child Care and Early Years Act 2014 does not include care provided in child's home	Canada Revenue Agency *(Child Care Expense Deduction; Universal Child Care Benefit)*	Department for Immigration and Citizenship *Live-In Caregiver Program* (1982-2014)/ *Temporary Foreign Worker Program –* *Caring for Children Pathway* (2014-)

[1] In Australia, responsibility for childcare at the federal level was previously held by the Department of Education, Employment and Workplace Relations (2009-14), but was transferred to the Department of Social Services under the Coalition government in 2014, and then to the Department of Education in November 2015.

[2] The Nanny Pilot programme is being rolled out in 2016-18. This is a two-year trial programme. It is not subject to the national regulations or the Interim Standards for In Home Care.

[3] The Child Care Subsidy is expected to replace the CCB and CCR in January 2018.

Quality regulation in ECEC

In ECEC, regulatory frameworks set out the requirements for different types of services. Regulations are likely to include structural and operational requirements, including staff ratios and qualifications, and the curriculum. However, a set of regulations may apply different standards to different types of care. This means that, while centre-based care and home-based/family day care are regulated by government, standards, qualifications, curriculum and safeguarding differ. Across Australia, the UK and Canada, the set of rules and regulations for different types of ECEC offer interesting points of comparison for examining the detail and intersection of policy. While formal qualifications – especially early childhood degrees and diplomas – are increasingly recognised in policy regulations as critical to high-quality ECEC provision, debate continues surrounding the ratio of qualified staff to children and the level of qualification (certificate, diploma or degree). This debate extends from centre-based 'early education' settings to other forms of ECEC, including childminders and family day care and, more recently, in-home childcare.

Overall, the training and qualifications required for in-home childcare workers are relatively low and, in the UK and Canada (Ontario), even for regulated home-based childcare (childminders, licensed home-based childcare) caregivers are not required to hold any formal qualifications. With respect to qualifications, Australia is the exception, as the reforms introduced under the National Quality Framework require all staff (now called educators) in long day care and family day care to hold or be working towards a Certificate III. In long day care services with more than 30 children, there must be a degree-qualified educator within the setting (and one for every 30 children within a centre). Degree-qualified educators are also required for older children attending preschool programmes within long day care.

In England, Ofsted, under the Childcare Act 2016, sets the qualification requirements for staff working in registered early years and childcare settings. Nurseries, preschools and childminders are subject to mandatory registration on the Ofsted early years registry, while registration for home childcare is part of the voluntary childcare registry (Table 3.3). The standards and regulations set for different types of services are often reflective of the *purpose* or origin of the service, which is the focus of the next chapter. For example, Ofsted's voluntary childcare register was introduced in 2004 to recognise the need for more flexible arrangements and a broader demand for work-related ECEC. The quality of care was not a priority of the government at its inception. Criticism surrounding the register has centred on the lack of accountability and false sense of monitoring that parents and families are given in hiring an individual registered with Ofsted. All providers caring for children from birth to five years (except carers in the child's home) must register with the early years register, although the required qualifications across the settings differ. In group settings, the manager must hold a full and relevant level 3 qualification and half of all other staff must hold a full and relevant level 2 qualification. In early years group settings (nurseries, preschools and so on) with children three years and older, it is common practice for there to be a degree-qualified teacher or staff with early years professional status, as it allows the centre to decrease the ration from 1:8 to 1:13 children aged three to five years. In contrast, childminders (in home-based group settings) are not required to hold any formal qualification, but are expected to take an approved training course through their local authority and to hold a first-aid certificate (Ofsted, 2014b). Introduced in 2013, childminders may also choose to be registered with a childminding agency, rather than directly with Ofsted. Nannies and in-home childcare workers are required to have training in the document *Common core skills and knowledge for the children's workforce* or to hold a minimum level 2 qualification 'in an area relevant to child care' (Ofsted, 2014a). It should be noted that Ofsted's voluntary childcare register for in-home childcarers does not distinguish between qualified or trained nannies, and other forms of in-home childcare, such as au pairs.

In Scotland, staff working in centre-based nurseries and preschools must be registered with the Scottish Social Services Council (SSSC), and must hold certain qualifications based on the type of setting and position they hold. Practitioners in nurseries, crèches and playgroups must hold a qualification approved by the SSSC (SSSC, 2011). Lead practitioners and managers in nursery settings for three- to five-year-olds generally hold a teaching degree, even though, since 2003, they are not required to (Siraj and Kingston, 2015). The regulatory framework for staff working in a setting registered with the Care Inspectorate differs from those working in a preschool setting – which is subject to legislation by Education Scotland. In-home childcare workers must be part of a childcare agency that is registered with the Care Inspectorate in order for families to claim the childcare element of the Working Tax Credit. In-home childcare workers are monitored through approved childcare agencies. They are not required to hold any specific qualifications, but must meet the standards and guidelines established by these organisations.

Two elements of quality commonly assessed across ECEC settings are qualifications and curricula. Research shows that relevant qualifications are associated with high-quality ECEC provision. Curricula for particular settings or age groups of children also increase the consistency and standards of provision. Table 3.3 outlines the required qualifications and curricula in place for different types of ECEC settings, across the three study countries. It highlights the wide variation across and within these countries in terms of the level of qualification and application of curricula, including the ages of the children in question and whether in practice they are optional or governed by legislation.

Table 3.3: Qualifications and curriculum compared across ECEC settings: Australia, the UK and Canada

	Qualifications	Curriculum
Australia	Certificate III for all ECEC educators: ✓Long day care (*all staff*) ✓Family day care ✗In Home Care Degree-qualified staff for 4-year-olds in long day care.	Early Years Learning Framework (0 to 5 years) Legislated under the National Law and applies to: ✓Long day care ✓Family day care ✗In Home Care
United Kingdom		
England	Formal ECEC qualification required (Level 2): ✓Nurseries (*not all staff*) ✓Preschools ✗Childminders ✗Home childcare	*Early Years Foundation Stage* (0 to 5 years) Legislated under Childcare Act 2006 and applies to services on Ofsted's Early Years Register: ✓Nurseries ✓Childminders ✓Preschools ✗ Home childcare (part of voluntary childcare register)
Scotland	Qualification approved by Scottish Social Services Council: ✓Nurseries ✓Crèches ✓Playgroups ✓Preschools ✗Childminders ✗Home childcare The leading practitioner/ manager in each early years setting must hold an SCQF Level 9 (equivalent to a Bachelor's degree)[1]	*Pre-birth to Three Guidelines* (0 to 3 years) *Curriculum for Excellence* (3 to 18 years) Not legislated: Principles and recommendations for all children's services
Canada (Ontario)	Early childhood diploma or degree: ✓Licensed centre-based services (*not all staff*) ✗Licensed home-based services (caregiver's home) ✗Care in child's home (not legislated)	*Early Learning for Every Child Today* (0 to 8 years) Not legislated: Guiding principles for all licensed children's services, including kindergarten.

[1] Scottish Credit and Qualifications Framework (2015), http://scqf.org.uk/framework-diagram/Framework.htm

A limitation of qualification comparisons is that they do not capture the everyday practices of service settings, where individual workers may be qualified above and beyond the minimum requirements. For example, while it is not a requirement for the In Home Care programme in Australia,[1] educators are placed through service providers, and requirements for training and qualifications beyond the interim standards vary across service providers. Many services do require their educators to hold a Certificate III. Similarly, through interviews with peak organisations and service providers in England and Scotland, it was found that many agencies and services do provide in-home childcare workers with training and qualifications.

In addition, we must remember that qualifications do not capture the practices that guide service delivery by service organisations and by individual care workers across these settings. In particular, regulation can also establish and monitor the pedagogical principles, daily activities and relationships that are often set in national curricula or standards. Curricula may be legislated through regulation or, in other cases, they may be recommended but not necessarily practised in all settings. Each country (or jurisdiction) recently developed a curriculum for early years settings; however, the guidelines differ in terms of the target age, the particular ECEC settings that are required (or encouraged) to practise the curriculum, and the mechanism through which the sector is required to adopt the curriculum (Table 3.3).

Under the current regulatory frameworks in Australia, the UK (England and Scotland) and Canada (Ontario), there are minimal qualifications and standards for in-home childcare. However, wide variation still exists across the study countries, and between different service types within each jurisdiction. This is particularly evident in Canada, where early childhood teachers in Ontario must hold a diploma or degree, while licensed home-based[2] workers and support staff in centres are not required to hold any formal qualifications (Table 3.3). Ontario does not regulate in-home childcare as a form of ECEC provision; rather, care provided in the child's home is seen as a private arrangement and therefore not included in the definition of 'childcare' in the Child Care and Early Years Act 2014. It is, however, supported through immigration policy, under what was formerly called the Live-In Caregiver Program (but since 2014 this category falls under the Temporary Foreign Worker Program). This aspect of in-home childcare provision in Canada distinguishes it from Australia and the UK, where in-home childcare is overseen by ECEC authorities – even though the regulatory requirements are lower than for other ECEC settings. As Table 3.4 illustrates, the requirements for in-home childcare providers

Table 3.4: Regulatory requirements for in-home childcare provision: Australia, the UK and Canada

	Same standards as mainstream ECEC	Separate standards	Curriculum framework compulsory	First-aid certificate	Police/criminal records check	ECEC qualification	Other minimum training or experience
Australia[1]	✗	✓ Interim standards for In Home Care	✗	✓	✓	✗	✓
United Kingdom England[2]	✗	✓ Requirements of Ofsted Childcare Register (voluntary)	✗	✓	✓	✗	✓ Common Core or equivalent of Level 2
Scotland[3]		National Care Standards: Childcare Agencies	✓				
Canada[4] (Ontario)	✗	✗	✗	✗	✗ Cannot have a criminal record to migrate Canada	✗	✓ Completed Canadian post-secondary education or equivalent

[1] Refers to the In Home Care programme. The Nanny Pilot programme was introduced in January 2016 for a two-year trial period. It imposes fewer requirements than In Home Care. Nannies under the pilot are required to be 18 years old, to have completed a Working with Children check, to hold a first-aid qualification, and be an Australian citizen or permanent resident or have a relevant visa that allows employment on a continuous basis of 12 months or more, and be employed through an approved service provider.

[2] Refers to Home childcarers on the voluntary Ofsted register (voluntary OCR). Registered home childcarers must also be covered by their own insurance.

[3] Refers to home childcarers registered with a childcare agency with the Care Inspectorate.

[4] Refers to care workers under the Temporary Foreign Worker Program – Caring for Children Pathway. Eligible applicants must also be speak and read English or

differ across Australia, the UK and Canada, but, overall, the standards and required qualifications are low across these countries (also see Table 3.3 for comparison with different types of ECEC).

This brief overview of the ECEC regulatory frameworks in Australia, the UK and Canada illustrates the range of approaches governments adopt to establish and monitor the quality of education and care services for young children. While some countries are interested in ensuring minimum standards for all services and providers, through health and safety training standards, for example, others focus on the 'education' qualifications of staff in some settings.

Overall, in-home childcare workers are not bound by specific ECEC qualifications or standards in any of the three countries. Where there are guidelines or voluntary registration requirements for those workers, they are generally low – and lower than workers in licensed centre-based or group-based settings. However, the differential standards and regulations for in-home childcare are not consistently reflected in or linked to the eligibility or generosity of subsidies and other funding for users (families) of these different services.

Fee subsidies and tax measures

Fee subsidies and other forms of financial assistance, such as tax deductions and cash benefits, are a common component of ECEC systems across developed countries. However, the structure, scope and generosity of public funding vary immensely. While Australia, the UK and Canada are regularly grouped together for their common market-led approach to ECEC funding, the details of their funding structures are in practice very different. This is especially the case with in-home childcare.

In some cases, legislation requires that providers (organisations and individuals) meet a set of standards or criteria, or regulation in order for families using these services to be eligible for public funding. In other cases, legislative requirements are not directly connected to users' receipt of financial assistance, most often when fee assistance is delivered through reduction in costs via the tax system. To different extents in Australia, the UK and Canada, the relationship between regulatory frameworks and public funding is complicated by the federal systems (in Australia and Canada) and decentralised (UK) division of responsibilities. For example, in Australia, the Commonwealth government funds most ECEC services, while state governments are responsible for accrediting and monitoring them. Also 'childcare' as opposed to 'early education' programmes receive funding through separate policy mechanisms and sources. That is, states in Australia are responsible for funding preschool education (usually their respective Departments of Education), and the Commonwealth for childcare (through the Commonwealth Department of Education). Similarly, in the UK, while public funding for the early years entitlement for three- and four-year-olds is administered at the central level by the Department of Education, local government authorities have responsibility for setting subsidy rates and, until recently, have had considerable local autonomy surrounding service delivery. Funding for tax credits is administered separately through HM Revenue. And, in Canada, ECEC services are subsidised through the federal tax system and transferred to provinces, even though the provinces hold legislative responsibility for ECEC. At the federal level, the receipt of the CCED and UCCB is not contingent on using licensed or regulated services defined in provincial legislation. The complexities of ECEC funding arrangements are detailed next, with a particular focus on the mechanisms supporting regulated and unregulated forms of in-home childcare.

In addition to the complexities of governmental responsibility, there are also challenges to comparing the eligibility and generosity of public funding because of the different average incomes across these countries. The Organisation for Economic Co-operation and Development (OECD) reports that for a couple with two children the average annual net income is the highest in Australia ($46,344), followed by the UK ($41,451) and Canada ($35,471). The OECD uses these figures to calculate the gross and net costs of full-time childcare in an accredited ECEC service. Estimates show that, across OECD countries, the proportion of average wages spent on childcare range from 3 per cent (Austria) to over 60 per cent (Switzerland and Luxembourg), with an OECD average of 27.6 per cent of average wages. Canada, Australia and the UK are placed at the higher end of this spectrum, at 39 per cent, 49.2 per cent and 53 per cent, respectively. These figures are, however, calculated before government assistance. After assistance, the average net cost for a dual-earner (1.5 average wage) family in the OECD is 12.6 per cent. The three study countries all fall above the average: at 15.7 per cent in Australia, 22.2 per cent in Canada (Ontario) and 33.8 per cent in the UK. These figures must be taken with caution,[3] as they are based on 100 per cent average wage and we know that the part-time employment rate, especially for women, varies across these countries (OECD, 2013, Tables S.5 and S.6), as do the usage patterns (number of hours of care) for children. Despite these limitations, these figures offer an indication of the generosity of each country's ECEC funding system.

The high costs of accredited ECEC in these countries often lead families to look for more affordable arrangements in the informal

Table 3.5: Financial support for in-home childcare: Australia, the UK and Canada, 2015

| Country and type of care | Financial assistance mechanism | Family eligibility | | Generosity |
		Eligibility criteria	Income cut-off	
Australia *In Home Care* (approved IHC)	Child Care Benefit (CCB) Child Care Rebate (CCR) CCB (lower rate)	Child disability Family or guardian disability Rural or remote location Employment schedule that prevents use of mainstream service (that is, long day care or family day care) Three or more children under school age	**CCB** – max. rate paid for income up to $43,727 CCB – threshold for lower rate cut off at approx. $152,000 **CCR** – No income cut-off	CCB – up to a max of $208.50 per week (IHC) CCR – 50% out-of-pocket costs up to $7,500 per year (*only approved IHC*)
Registered childcare with Department of Human Services (DHS)		Working parents	No income cut-off	$34.80 per week (DHS-registered)
United Kingdom <u>England</u> *Home Childcare* (voluntary Ofsted register) <u>Scotland</u> Registered with childcare agency	Childcare element of Working Tax Credit Employer-sponsored childcare vouchers	Both parents must be working 16 hours or more per week to claim childcare vouchers or tax credits (same as other forms of registered childcare)	Approximately £35,000 (tax credits) Childcare vouchers – no income cut-off	Up to 70% of costs up to £122 per week (approx. £6,300 per year = approx. $10,000 per year)
Canada (Any informal or formal arrangements, including former Live-In Caregiver)	Child Care Expense Deduction	Receipt for any form of (informal or formal) care for children up to age seven by a non-relative	No	Deduct up to $7,000 per year (up to seven years), up to $11,000 for a child with a disability (maximum value approx. $1,500)

sector, including care by nannies and au pairs. To different extents in each country, subsidies or tax measures are available for users of in-home childcare. Table 3.5 outlines the details of each country's funding structures as they apply to in-home childcare, namely how the structure of public funding is shaped by the scope of *family eligibility* (income, workforce participation); the *generosity* of the subsidy, voucher or tax measure; and the scope of *service eligibility* (regulated, unregulated). It illustrates the scope of family eligibility and generosity, but does not detail the nuances related to the inclusion or exclusion of different types of regulated and unregulated ECEC settings. And, as was illustrated in the previous section, the scope of regulation and required standards and qualifications are not consistent across ECEC settings. The details of Table 3.5 are elaborated under each of the country sections.

Australia

In Australia, approval and regulation under the national legislation is not directly linked to receipt of subsidies. The Commonwealth is responsible for the majority of childcare funding through the CCB and CCR, while the states and territories fund (to different extents) early education (or preschool) programmes. Some services not covered under the national legislation are still approved by the Commonwealth under the Family Assistance Law for receipt of CCB and CCR, namely In Home Care and Occasional Care. Table 3.6 shows five common ECEC settings for children below school age, and summarises those that are included under the National Law (National Quality Framework), compared with those approved for CCB and CCR. In Home Care is one of two types of ECEC that does not fall under quality regulations, but is still approved for subsidies. Users of the formal In Home Care

Table 3.6: ECEC services for children 0 to 5 years, Australian (Commonwealth) regulation and funding approval arrangements

	National Law	Approved for CCB and CCR
Long day care	✓	✓
Family day care	✓	✓
In Home Care	✗	✓
Occasional care	✗	✓
Preschools	✓	✗

programme – those families that meet the eligibility requirements outlined in Table 3.5 – are eligible to receive the same level of subsidy as families using mainstream long day care and family day care, even though these services are not required to meet the same standards set out under the National Quality Framework.

For the majority of families who require or choose to use in-home childcare, parents are eligible for a reduced level of CCB. Grandparents and informal in-home carers – or nannies – are the most common form of registered care.[4] For families to be eligible for this reduced rate, the childcare provider must register with the Department for Human Services and the parents must have a 'work-related commitment' at some time during the week. Unlike approved CCB, there is no income threshold for receipt of registered CCB. Users of registered care are not eligible for CCR.

Overall, funding for in-home childcare in Australia is therefore generous for families eligible (and able) to access the formal In Home Care programme, while minimal financial assistance is available to families through the CCB where their caregiver is registered with the Department of Human Services, and only required to adhere to minimal requirements, namely a police check and first-aid certificate. The requirements for registered carers in Australia are comparable to Ofsted registration requirements in England, yet the scope of eligibility for families and generosity of public funding in England create different structures of support.

United Kingdom

Funding for ECEC in the UK is directed through three streams: part-time early years entitlement for all three- and four-year-olds (and some two-year-olds); the childcare element of the Working Tax Credit (WTC)[5] targeted at low-income families, and childcare vouchers,[6] which are primarily accessible to middle-income families with secure employment. Families with access to childcare vouchers are likely to request that their nanny register with Ofsted so that they can receive some assistance with the cost of childcare. If the home childcarer (or nanny) is registered, families are eligible to receive the childcare element of WTC, which covers up to 70 per cent of costs for families with an income under approximately £6,500, equal to a maximum of approximately £6,344 per year for one child. Families earning up to approximately £35,000 may be eligible for a lower amount. Families eligible for employer childcare vouchers can receive up to £2,860 per year (HM Revenue and Customs, 2013, 2014). The eligibility threshold for both the tax credit and vouchers were more generous when introduced in 1999. Table 3.7 outlines the relevant registration or regulation, and eligibility for WTC and childcare vouchers across four common ECEC settings in the UK: nurseries, childminders, playgroups and in-home childcare. These are detailed further in relation to in-home childcare.

Table 3.7: ECEC services for children 0 to 5 years, registration and funding approval: England and Scotland

Type of care	ECEC registration or regulation	Eligible for Working Tax Credit and childcare vouchers
Nurseries	Ofsted Early Years Register (England) National Care Standards: Early Education and Childcare (Scotland)	✓
Childminders	Ofsted Early Years Register (England) National Care Standards: Early Education and Childcare (Scotland)	✓
Playgroups	Ofsted Childcare Register (England)	✓
Nannies, in-home care/home childcare	Voluntary Childcare Register (England) National Care Standards: Childcare Agencies (Scotland)	✓

Funding for in-home childcare in England is therefore limited to families whose caregiver is voluntarily registered with Ofsted – often a request of the family for subsidy purposes. And, in Scotland, eligibility for the childcare element of WTC is restricted to families who choose to hire through a registered childcare agency. Critics of the system contend that this structure of subsidisation does not assist those families most likely to be using in-home childcare because the income threshold for the WTC is very low, and the receipt of childcare vouchers is contingent on working for an employer who is part of a voucher scheme. This has led to some pressures for childcare vouchers to be extended to all families using registered in-home childcare, rather than being employer-dependent. As mentioned earlier, new funding for ECEC in the UK is expected to commence in 2017. The incoming Tax-Free Childcare scheme will broaden the scope of eligibility for families in the UK, allowing more families to access support. In particular, it will reach families who are currently above the WTC cut-off, and do not have access to employer-sponsored childcare vouchers. Tax-Free Childcare will still, however, be restricted to families using a registered nanny or home childcarer – a stark contrast to the structure of support in Canada.

Canada

Funding for ECEC in Canada is administered and delivered through a mix of federal, provincial/territory, and local government responsibilities. However, unlike Australia and the UK, there is no national framework and federal transfers to provinces are not made accountable through regulation of services at the provincial or local levels. As Table 3.8 outlines, there is no registration or regulation required for in-home childcare at the federal or provincial level, even though the costs of this type of care can be offset through the main federal funding mechanism – the CCED. Since in-home childcare is not licensed in Ontario, users are not eligible for fee subsidies, with the exception of a small programme called OntarioWorks (described in more detail later in this section). Ontario is also the only jurisdiction of the three study countries where group home-based care can be unlicensed and still eligible for the CCED. However, it should be noted that unlicensed home-based group care is not allowed in all provinces in Canada.

Table 3.8: Public funding for childcare, children 0 to 5 years, Canada (and province of Ontario)

Type of care	ECEC registration or regulation	Child Care Expense Deduction (federal)	OntarioWorks subsidy programme (provincial)	Ontario fee subsidies (provincial)
Day nurseries	✓ Provincial	✓	✓	✓
Licensed Home based care	✓ Provincial	✓	✓	✓
Unlicensed home-based care	✗	✓	✓ Discretion of municipalities	✗
In-home childcare	✗	✓	✓ Discretion of municipalities	✗

There are two federal funding mechanisms: the CCED and the UCCB. The UCCB is a cash benefit to all families with children regardless of whether non-parental childcare is used; since UCCB is not tied to the use of childcare, it is excluded from Table 3.8. It was introduced under the Conservative government in 2006, currently provides $160 per month to all families with children from birth to six years, and $60 per month for families with children aged between six and 17 years. The rhetoric used by the Conservative government when it was introduced in 2006 supports the idea that the payment contributes to the cost of families' *choice* of ECEC arrangements – whether regulated/unregulated, formal/informal, public/private or parental/non-parental (Richardson et al, 2013).

The CCED enables working parents to deduct up to $7,000 in childcare costs per child (under seven years) from taxable income, regardless of whether the arrangements are regulated or unregulated (Table 3.5). In practice, the CCED offers a moderate sum, although the benefit is greater to high-income families. It is intended to offset the costs of childcare and so if families work more, earn more and pay for more childcare, they will also gain more from the CCED. A tax deduction is different from a credit and is more generous to high-income families (Harder, 2004). Unlike the UCCB, receipts must be kept to prove the use of childcare, although the costs covered are well beyond the scope of ECEC, and include sports classes, overnight camps and other extracurricular activities. Formal and informal care is eligible for the CCED, as long as the care provider is over 15 years and not an immediate family member (the idea being to exclude sibling and grandparent care from being deducted).

Additional fee subsidies for low-income families are funded by the provincial government (Ontario) under the Ministry of Education, and are administered and delivered by the municipal and regional governments, through agreements with Consolidated Municipal Service Managers and Regional Social Service Administration Boards. Eligibility is based on parents' participation in employment and family income. While childcare fee subsidies in Ontario do not support unregulated in-home care through any specific programmes or funding mechanisms, the Child Care and Early Learning Act 2014 gives municipalities autonomy and flexibility to provide assistance to families using unregulated and informal services if they so choose. In addition, the province's OntarioWorks programme and Disability Support programme (under the Ministry of Community and Social Services) facilitate parents' workforce participation through a number of financial and service supports, including financing assistance for informal and unregulated childcare. The Child Care Support component of OntarioWorks 'covers the actual cost of formal/licensed childcare, and informal/alternative childcare arrangements up to the established maximums' (Government of Ontario, 2010, p 2). However, it should be noted that these arrangements are rare and intended to for the short-term only.

While provision of unregulated in-home childcare is the most prevalent in Canada, compared with Australia and the UK, this cannot be fully explained by the ECEC regulatory and funding structures: the assistance received through the CCED and UCCB is by no means generous to families using any type of ECEC, including in-home childcare. At the provincial level, subsidies are restricted to fairly low-income working families, compared with Australia, where the CCR is not means-tested. What is distinctive about Canada's system is the facilitation of in-home childcare provision through a formal migration programme – formerly the well-established Live-In Caregiver Program, which in 2014 was renamed (with some adjustments) the Caring for Children Pathway under the Temporary Foreign Worker Program. In each of the countries, the high costs of accredited childcare (noted earlier) encourage families to look for cheaper care alternatives, including informal in-home childcare. Such flexible options may be especially worthwhile for parents with both school-aged children and younger children, where drop-offs and pick-up times often clash with a standard work day. In Canada, this includes caregivers recruited through the (former) Live-In Caregiver Program; however, to different extents in all countries migration policy allows pathways for (mostly) young adults to work as au pairs in private family homes to provide low-cost care and domestic work.

Immigration policy

Migration is rarely included in analyses of early childhood education and care policy. Understanding the different immigration policies

Table 3.9: Migration policy and formal schemes for in-home childcare workers: Australia, the UK and Canada

	Formal migration scheme for in-home childcare	Other visas and pathways enabling domestic work
Australia	No	Working Holiday Visa /Work and Holiday Visa (Subclass 417 and 462)
United Kingdom	No (Domestic Worker Visa for foreign temporary employers)	EU and EFTA (European Free Trade Agreement) nationalities Youth Mobility Scheme
Canada	Caring for Children Pathway (previously the Live-In Caregiver Program 1992-2014)	Working Holiday Visa

in each country reveals how the *details* of and *intersection* with the regulatory and funding approaches to different ECEC settings offers new insight into the circumstances through which government policy facilitates in-home childcare in different, and sometimes unintended, ways. Canada is the only one of the three study countries that has a formal migration scheme to recruit workers to provide care in the child's home. Table 3.9 outlines the current migration programmes that facilitate the recruitment of in-home childcare in each study country. While Canada is the only country with a designated programme, there are schemes in the other countries for working holidaymakers, or 'backpackers', wishing to work as au pairs.

The UK, in particular, has a significant proportion of migrant in-home childcare workers – often referred to as au pairs – a situation attributed to reforms in 2004 and 2008 that opened up travel and working rights to members of the European Union. In contrast, the only migration pathway for in-home childcare workers in Australia is through the Working Holiday Visa, available to young people (up to 30 years) and intended to allow working holidaymakers a way to subsidise their travel.

Australia: an outlier ... for now?

Recent developments in ECEC and migration policy debates indicate that Australia's position towards a migrant care workforce may be in flux. Until now, however, Australia's focus on skilled migration has limited the growth of migrants providing care in private homes. Submissions to the recent childcare inquiry by the Productivity Commission (2014a) put forward arguments that the recruitment of au pairs can help address demand for flexible, affordable, childcare (in Adamson et al, forthcoming). Presumably in response to these submissions and advocacy from au pair agencies, the Working Holiday Visa was amended in 2015 to allow visa holders working as au pairs to work for the same employer for up to 12 months, rather than six months under the previous rules.

The Working Holiday Visa attracts young women from Europe, particularly the UK, to work as au pairs for families. While it is promoted as a 'cultural exchange' programme, it is used by families as an affordable ECEC option (Au Pair World, 2014). Similar to the situation in the UK, and in contrast to that in Canada, au pairs apply for a different visa depending on their nationality. Families are not required to pay au pairs a minimum wage, but rather it is recommended they pay $6 per hour as 'pocket money', which usually works out at between $180 and $250 per week.

United Kingdom: a new class of nannies and au pairs?

In-home childcare is a traditionally accepted form of ECEC in the UK. However, anecdotal evidence suggests that the characteristics of nannies providing care and families using in-home childcare have changed. The hiring of in-home childcare workers is possible for more families because of recent migration from the European Union and European Economic Area (EAA) countries. This is because migrant workers (mostly women) are seeking employment in low-paid domestic settings, including as nannies and other domestic workers (Búriková and Miller, 2010). The demand for migrant nannies has been attributed to increased affordability and flexibility in the hours nannies are willing to work and duties they are willing to perform (Williams and Gavanas, 2008; Busch, 2013). While it is expected that employers abide by employment regulations, there is also evidence that the availability of a low-paid workforce and lack of availability of flexible and affordable regulated options makes informal in-home childcare the preferred arrangement for many families. However, it is important to note that all three- and four-year-olds are eligible for 15 hours per week of formal early education in a nursery through the early years entitlement and, therefore, most children in the year or two before formal schooling would attend formal ECEC at least part-time (see Table 0.2).

For individuals outside the European Union and other EAA countries, the Youth Mobility Scheme permits individuals aged 18 to 30 years from eligible countries to live and work in the UK for up to two years. Applicants seeking employment as an au pair through the scheme do not have worker or employee status, and therefore are not entitled to the National Minimum Wage or benefits and leave entitlements. Instead, au pairs are usually provided with room and board and 'pocket money' of around £100 per week (Cox and Busch, 2014a). Depending on how much pocket money au pairs are paid, they may have to pay income tax (UK Government, 2014a). Au pairs are allowed to register with Ofsted, provided they meet the criteria (Nannytax, 2014). As mentioned earlier, Ofsted registration enables families to receive the childcare element of the Working Tax Credit.

Reforms introduced in 2012 to the Domestic Worker Visa restrict entry of (non-EU) domestic workers.[7] The Domestic Worker Visa is also limited to six months and workers on this visa are not allowed to seek employment with another employer. Evidence of exploitation of these workers has led to calls by advocates, such as the community group Kalayaan, to reverse the reforms. Such claims for migrant care workers' rights and working conditions are familiar to migrant care workers and long-time critics of Canada's (former) Live-In Caregiver Program and Temporary Foreign Worker Program.

Canada's Live-In Caregiver Program: de facto option or cultural norm?

Canada's immigration policy has the most explicit approach to support unregulated in-home childcare. The Temporary Foreign Worker Program[8] (previously the Live-In Caregiver Program) enables overseas workers to apply to work in domestic settings caring for children, or elderly or disabled people, and offers an avenue for migrant workers (primarily women) to settle permanently in Canada. In November

Table 3.10: Specifics of the Temporary Foreign Worker Program (previously Live-In Caregiver Program), Canada

Requirements for caregiver CIC(a) and HRSDC(b)	Requirements for family (employer)	Caregiver obligations	Employer obligations	Eligibility for residency
Successfully completed the equivalent of Canadian high school education Completed at least six months of full-time training; or worked as a full-time caregiver for at least one year during the past three years Speak and read English or French	Proof that they or a dependant is in need of care (age of children) Proof of financial capability to pay Provision of suitable accommodation for caregiver	Provide care on a full-time basis (minimum 30 hours per week) to children under 18 years of age[2] Live and work without supervision in the private household	Pay minimum wage ($10.77 in Ontario) for a minimum of 30 hours Overtime (1.5 times wage) for 44 to 48 hours per week (deductions for meals and accommodation) Two weeks' vacation per year	Completed two years of live-in[1] work (with no more than two employers) Have up to four years to complete the employment requirement to be eligible to apply for permanent residency

[1] The live-in requirement for the programme was removed in November 2014.

[2] Also for elderly people and people with a disability.

(a) Citizenship and Immigration Canada

(b) Government of Canada (2016)

2014, the Live-In Caregiver Program (LCP) – which had existed since 1982 in Canada – formally ended with the announcement that migrants seeking to enter Canada to work as caregivers would now be incorporated into the Temporary Foreign Worker Program. The Caring for Children Pathway within this visa category essentially replaces the LCP. One major change is the removal of the live-in requirement. Until November 2014, the programme required caregivers to work in the home of their employer (family) for two years before permitting them to apply for permanent residency. This programme continues to be controversial because of the lengthy waiting times for caregivers applying for permanent residency, in addition to long-standing issues surrounding exploitation of migrant care workers (Kelly et al, 2011). Table 3.10 summarises the various requirements and obligations of the employer (sponsor) and migrant caregiver, as well as the process for gaining permanent residency. As the rest of this section describes, the overwhelming majority of caregivers come from the Philippines, often via Hong Kong or Singapore.

Overseas workers seeking to enter Canada as part of the Temporary Foreign Worker Program must have sponsorship from an employer (family). The employer must have sought and received approval to sponsor the caregiver, a process that is based on a set of criteria indicating the reasons why a caregiver is required in the family home, for example, to care for young children, or a frail or elderly person, and under the previous LCP, appropriate living arrangements and financial resources for the caregiver were a requirement for approval. Caregivers entering Canada under the programme are required to stay with their employer for a minimum of one year. At this point, they are able to look for another family (employer) in order to meet the two-year requirement before becoming eligible to apply for permanent residency.

While the programme is open to any overseas workers, the overwhelming majority of workers entering through the LCP are Filipino (Kelly et al, 2011). Employment and training opportunities are often not available in these workers' home country and so many 'transition' to Canada through Hong Kong and Singapore, where they gain the experience and/or qualifications required to apply for the programme, and also gain access to agencies to administer their application (Kelly et al, 2009). Agencies play a significant role in monitoring the eligibility criteria and brokering eligible caregivers and employers. In many cases, agencies have established partnerships in Hong Kong and Singapore where caregivers are currently living and working in order to facilitate the recruitment of potential workers.

Despite considerable criticism surrounding the exploitation of caregivers, the LCP (and the current Caring for Children Pathway) has been established as an acceptable ECEC arrangement, and reflects a government priority to retain ECEC in the private domain (Brickner and Straehle, 2010; Cho, 2013), rather than to increase the qualifications and status of ECEC professionals in the public sphere. While there are likely many caregivers in the LCP providing high-quality care to young children, the programme does not promote high-quality provision and provides limited protection of working conditions for caregivers (Table 3.10).

Contrasts and commonalities

The details of policy mechanisms create complex and often contradicting incentives and deterrents for using different ECEC arrangements. Cross-national comparison reveals that the regulations and standards of different forms of ECEC are not consistent across or within countries. Across these countries, inconsistencies exist with respect to the accountability of funding and quality regulation for different types of ECEC. These three policy elements intersect and shape the provision of *all* ECEC settings, although the differences in the affordability, accessibility and quality of care provided in the child's home are striking. These intersections have implications for parents seeking flexible employment, the quality of care the child receives, and the working conditions and status of the care worker.

In the UK and Australia, care workers must meet minimal criteria to register as approved providers to enable families to access financial support. The tensions between funding and quality regulation are most evident in Canada, where the CCED is purely a work-related expense deduction with no consideration of the quality of the care arrangements for children or the working conditions of care workers. Overall, in Canada the lack of government support for regulated, centre-based ECEC has provided families with few options to access quality ECEC. With no federal funding designated to regulated services (and limited availability), families resort to alternative unregulated arrangements, including unlicensed home-based childcare in Ontario (and other provinces), as well as in-home childcare facilitated through immigration policies.

Examination of migration policy for care workers reveals further divergences across the countries, with Australia, the UK and Canada having the least to most formal pathways, respectively, for recruiting migrant in-home childcare workers. However, the formality of migration policies for in-home childcare workers does not correlate with the formality of ECEC regulations governing in-home childcare. In contrast, while there is undoubtedly an informal market for in-home childcare in Australia, there are few policy mechanisms that actively support the supply of in-home carers through migration or demand through financial assistance. But what does this all mean for ECEC and in-home childcare? Which children and families are benefiting from these policies, and which are missing out?

The lack of public funding and limited availability of regulated ECEC – evident to different extents in all three countries – increases the cost of all care types. This pushes out many low- to middle-income families who may not be eligible for subsidies because of work activity tests, or (particularly in the UK), may have incomes above the eligibility threshold for the WTC. Low-income families therefore often look to more affordable informal and unregulated options. In Australia, it is widely recognised that the high cost of long day care and family day care push many low-income families out of formal ECEC. The rising costs of childcare in Australia are at the centre of policy and public debates about in-home childcare; however, because CCB and CCR are available only to users of approved services, there is less incentive for families to rely on unregulated care as their primary ECEC. This compares with Canada where the CCED and UCCB is available to families regardless of the type of care used.

In the UK (England), the childcare element of WTC is targeted to very low-income levels such that middle-income families cannot access assistance with the costs of ECEC unless they receive employer-sponsored childcare vouchers. The eligibility and generosity of the subsidies are the same for users of registered early years providers (nurseries and childminders) and families who use an Ofsted-registered nanny. However, families not eligible for WTC or childcare vouchers have little incentive to hire a registered nanny. Instead, there is demand for more affordable and flexible informal options, heightened by the influx of migrant workers from the EU.

In Canada, the UCCB and CCED are not linked to regulatory approval and therefore families using informal and unregulated care arrangements can access financial assistance similar to most families using regulated centre- and home-based ECEC. However, it should be remembered that there are a limited number of provincially subsidised places for low-income families in Ontario. Centre-based care is therefore used mostly by working families eligible for full or part subsidies, and by high-income families able to bear the market price. Unlicensed home-based care in the home of the care provider is an attractive option for many families who are not eligible or who cannot access a licensed centre- or home-based place. In-home childcare, on the other hand, is the default option for many middle- and high-income families. It is also an alternative for families when there is no availability in centre-based settings. There is evidently a large proportion of families across all income levels using potentially low-quality, unregulated care in Ontario and Canada (Sinha, 2014).

The intersection of these different policy elements undoubtedly shapes the options available to families and children, and the quality of these options for parents, children and care workers. Why, though, have such different policy approaches to in-home childcare developed in these three countries? The policy interventions aimed at in-home childcare – whether through regulatory support, funding or immigration – were established and promoted through various policy and public discourses and rationales.

The remaining chapters of the book (Part Two) give greater attention to the empirical data collected through interviews and other primary documents for the research. These data are analysed in relation to the earlier chapters (Part One), which have given detailed accounts of the conceptual trends, historical trajectories and policy mechanisms related to in-home childcare and ECEC more broadly.

Notes

[1] Approved and registered in-home care providers (with the Department for Human Services) must meet any state or territory legislation. Prior to the National Law, South Australia and Tasmania included in-home childcare (regardless of whether it was part of the In Home Care scheme) in regulations that required carers to be registered and to comply with minimal requirements, such as holding a first-aid certificate and undergoing a policy check.

[2] *Unlicensed* home-based care is provided in a caregiver's home for five children or fewer, and the provider is not required to meet any operating criteria. This is different from the situation in Australia and the UK, where such care is illegal, and care for a group of unrelated children in a private home must be licensed to operate.

[3] Nor does it account for purchasing power parity.

[4] The registered care category is being abolished in July 2017 when the new Child Care Subsidy system is implemented.

[5] The Working Tax Credit is being replaced by the Universal Credit.

[6] Childcare vouchers are being replaced by Tax Free Childcare in 2017. Tax Free Childcare will cover 20 per cent of childcare costs, up to a maximum of £2,000 per year.

[7] An exception is domestic workers accompanying foreign visitors (mostly diplomats).

[8] The Live-In Caregiver Program underwent changes in November 2014. It was renamed as the Caring for Children Pathway, under the Temporary Foreign Worker Program (which was titled the Temporary Foreign Domestic Movement between 1981–1992). Changes included the removal of the live-in requirement. Live-in arrangements can still be negotiated between the employer and employee. At the time of writing, it is unknown what effect this change in legislation will have on the live-in versus live-out arrangements of the programme.

Part Two
Policy intersections and inequalities

FOUR

Rhetoric and rationales for in-home childcare

Public spending on early childhood education and care (ECEC) is promoted by governments and advocates as a worthy investment for children's development and educational outcomes. It is also promoted as a way to facilitate mothers' participation in paid work, training and study. These reasons for investing in ECEC have, however, shifted over the past few decades. In the 1960s and 1970s, spending on ECEC and children's services was largely driven by governments' acknowledgement that some mothers needed to work. Advocates for the expansion of government investment were motivated by the principle that women and mothers should be supported to choose whether or not to work in or outside the home. Universal childcare would, as many advocated, promote mothers' choices and gender equality in and outside the home. In the 1980s and 1990s, the gender equality agenda that drove the women's movement's demands for publicly supported ECEC was gradually replaced with an economic agenda. An economic agenda emphasises the financial benefits gained through women's participation in the labour market. Under an economic agenda, women's labour market participation contributes to public revenue through taxes and also reduces spending on welfare. The prioritisation of an economic focus in Australia, the UK and Canada aligns with liberal ideas that promote individualism and labour market participation.

The rise of individualism and the promotion of active labour market policies are intrinsically linked to the reasons why governments support in-home childcare. In-home childcare can be designed to address a gap in services for children in families unable to use mainstream services. For example, children may have a disability that prevents them from leaving their house, or families may live in a location with limited access to local services. However, more often, in-home childcare is advocated for the increased flexibility it offers, especially the ability to offer non-standard and individualised hours of care. Parents working long or unpredictable hours, or with the need to travel for work, may feel that care in their own home is the best option to fit with their work patterns. The use of in-home childcare is therefore well suited to support a neoliberal agenda that promotes increased productivity by supporting a '24/7 economy'. The emphasis on employment, and investment in a 'knowledge economy' and productivity, is part of a neoliberal agenda that has been evident in Australia, the UK and Canada since the late 1980s and early 1990s; this agenda has been explained as a 'social investment' approach to social policy.

A liberal social investment approach is designed to achieve a variety of objectives. These objectives are focused on the gains from investment in human capital, which includes education, skills development and active labour market policies to support a productive economy. First, investment in human capital prioritises the earning capacity of *all* workers in the knowledge economy, which includes mothers with young children. Second, there is a focus on up-skilling and training for low-skilled workers to make them more employable in sectors with high demand. Foreign workers are often identified as potential sources of labour to fill workforce gaps. One sector with high demand is the care workforce. And, third, investment in early education to enhance children's development is central to a human capital approach to social investment. This is promoted through the future benefits gained from investment in the early years. These three priorities and policy areas are relevant to the development of in-home childcare, although they are not always supported simultaneously or equally.

A social investment approach prioritises mothers' workforce participation, and emphasises the economic gains for families able to work longer hours or take on additional shifts. Advocates of this approach have argued that government funding for flexible and individualised childcare arrangements, such as in-home childcare, can support increased workforce participation. In a market-led environment, in-home childcare – along with other types of ECEC – is increasingly supported through family cash benefits, childcare vouchers and subsidies and tax measures that are designed to promote individual choice for service users, or consumers. These mechanisms are designed to provide assistance to parents with the costs of care in order to help reconcile work and care responsibilities. With an emphasis on parents' choice and workforce participation, the implications for quality ECEC for children and the working conditions for care workers are often ignored.

This chapter explores the different objectives for, and interpretations of, policy support for in-home childcare in Australia, the UK and Canada, by looking at the discourses and debates surrounding government support for in-home childcare in these three policy contexts. Drawing on a mix of secondary and primary documents, plus data collected through interviews, this chapter examines the ways in which rhetoric and rationales for ECEC are interpreted and reflected in policy mechanisms that facilitate (or do not facilitate) regulated and unregulated in-home childcare (discussed in Chapter Three). In doing so, the focus of the analysis shifts from the previous chapter about *how* policy differs to provide insight into *why* policy differs. A social investment framework is used to explain, first, why policies towards in-home childcare were introduced and implemented in each country and, second, to analyse the differences across Australia, the UK and Canada.

The social investment approach

A 'social investment' approach to social policy emerged in the late 1980s and 1990s. As introduced in Chapter One, the concept was proposed by scholars to help explain the restructuring of government funding for social protection programmes and policies. The concept is characterised as a shift from policies aimed to protect individuals from the market through social protection towards 'productive welfare', reflected in active welfare measures, and a focus on skills, labour force participation and early education (Esping-Andersen, 2002; Morel et al, 2012). This shift to 'social investment' emphasises an economic frame that promotes women's participation in the labour market, and therefore adopts a productive view of women and children (Orloff and Palier, 2009; Williams, 2012a). In some settings, spending on high-quality childcare is recognised as an investment in children's 'education' and developmental outcomes (Dobrowolsky, 2002; Esping-Andersen, 2002; Lister, 2004; Jenson, 2008).

Since the 1990s, many countries have embraced the term 'social investment', and corresponding approach to social spending, as a way to advocate for increased public investment in ECEC programmes. At the beginning of the 1990s, public involvement in ECEC in Australia and Canada was wavering, while in the UK it was lagging behind that of many other European countries. The idea that spending in ECEC would bring benefits to mothers, children and the broader society made investment in early education and childcare an attractive policy commitment. 'Social investment' promised benefits in terms of both increased employment and better outcomes for children's futures. In principle, increased employment offers families higher earning capacity, and governments higher tax revenue. It is also argued that investment in human capital saves the government money, in the form of reduced spending on income support and social services for families and children. In addition, the rise of a social investment approach corresponds with new patterns of global migration and temporary work. Foreign workers are increasingly identified as a source of labour to fill skill gaps in the workforce, and are often in circumstances that give them less capacity than local workers to negotiate higher wages (Estévez-Abe and Hobson, 2015; Hellgren, 2015).

The adoption of a social investment approach reshaped governments' and the public's lens for thinking about ECEC. Previously, pressures for government involvement in ECEC rested on principles of gender equality and mothers' right or duty to non-parental care for their children (Randall, 1996, p 180; Brennan 1998, p 171; Phillips and Mahon, 2002). This frame of thinking about ECEC was pushed aside by a rhetoric that emphasised mothers' responsibility to participate in the productive economy. The new approach to investment in ECEC often fails to recognise children's right to high-quality care.

Scholars and other gender critics have identified a number of issues with the social investment approach to ECEC. Concerns have been raised about the risk of having a narrow approach to ECEC policy that focuses solely on mothers' workforce participation or, conversely, solely children's education. The frame for thinking about ECEC influences the type or structure of ECEC programmes. As Rianne Mahon suggests, if ECEC is solely framed as meeting developmental needs for the child, the response would be universal care part-day; if framed around child poverty, there would be a mix of educational and social services targeted towards low-income and other vulnerable children (Mahon, 2010b, p 203). These programmes may not necessarily address mothers' needs, such as flexibility of care. But, conversely, when ECEC rests only on a mothers' workforce participation rationale, 'babysitting and unregulated care may be considered sufficient' (Jenson, 2008, p 366). A narrow approach to social policy that focuses on mothers 'not only fail[s] to provide genuine ECEC' they also do not necessarily offer good quality employment for care workers (Mahon 2010a, 181).

This narrow approach is contrasted with a more holistic view that promotes universal, high-quality care. A more holistic social investment approach has been used in developed countries outside the liberal welfare regime. The child development focal point of social investment arguably led to a degree of convergence in policy rhetoric between neoliberal countries (Canada and Australia) and Nordic countries (Finland and Sweden) (Mahon et al, 2012). The liberal social investment approach, however, is focused more on investment in ECEC as a way to boost human capital in the future. This contrasts with Nordic and other European countries, where social investment in ECEC encompasses more than children's future outcomes. Here, social investment is characterised by a more holistic approach to children's rights to good quality care to enhance their wellbeing in the present, as well as future, where government involvement in ECEC is also underpinned by principles of gender equality in the home, which is less apparent in policy rhetoric in liberal countries. As mentioned above, a more holistic approach to social investment in ECEC also gives greater attention to the implications of policy for the care worker. As Linda White suggests, more holistic social investment approaches can and should 'extend beyond the argument regarding economic returns on investment':

> They need to rest on the fact of women's labor market participation, the damage that can be done to children exposed to poor quality programs, and the fact that so many of the workers performing these services are low-paid women. (White, 2011, p 303)

The concept of social investment has attracted significant attention in the ECEC policy context.[1] This concept has appealed to policymakers because it can be interpreted in different ways and therefore used to rationalise the restructuring of ECEC policies. The five objectives (or rationales) listed below are commonly referenced in relation to ECEC policy developments.

- *Child poverty* rationales are based on longitudinal research findings showing the importance of early intervention services, and the short- and long-term benefits to children in the form of higher educational attainment, decreased school drop-out and crime rates, and higher employment. Focused on disadvantaged, or 'poor' children, the child poverty objective argues that ECEC provides children with a 'head start'. A child poverty objective usually promotes a targeted approach to services.
- *Workforce participation* rationales have, in the past, been part of claims for gender equality. More recent workforce participation rationales emphasise a human capital approach, which supports activation measures to move individuals into paid employment. Paid employment is seen as an economic benefit for families in the form of financial independence, cost savings to government, and a contribution to the wider community and economy. A workforce participation rationale is closely linked to the alleviation of child poverty, as parental employment is viewed as a solution to children living in disadvantaged families.

- *Child development and early learning* rationales are supported by research showing that children who attend high-quality childcare and early education programmes have better cognitive and socio-emotional outcomes. This rationale supports the developmental benefits for all children; however, children from disadvantaged backgrounds are identified as benefiting more than children from middle- and higher-socioeconomic backgrounds.
- *Rights and child wellbeing* rationales focus on the wellbeing and citizenship of the child and draw on legal requirements established by the United Nations Convention on the Rights of the Child. This rationale emphasises the benefits of ECEC for children in the present, opposed to other child-centric rationales focused on their future outcomes and returns. It is closely linked to research supporting the holistic view of the child, which supports children as important participants in research on child wellbeing.
- *Gender equality* rationales draw on feminist literature that calls for equal opportunity for men and women, with respect to both employment opportunities and caring responsibilities. Second-wave feminism and the women's movement demanded childcare as a means to social justice that exemplifies a more holistic notion of gender equality. It is argued that few countries' ECEC policies currently rest on this rationale.

In Australia, the UK and Canada, these rationales have shaped policy developments and debate about in-home childcare and ECEC more broadly. As will become evident in the remainder of this chapter, some rationales in this list are more or less salient in the different national and regional contexts.

What is missing from this list of social investment objectives is the promotion of employment for low-skilled workers. As mentioned earlier, low-skilled and low-paid employment is implicitly linked to government policy that promotes mothers' employment in the knowledge economy: when market mechanisms facilitate users' individual choice to use in-home childcare, the hiring of low-skilled workers in the, largely, informal market is also supported. The promotion of a low-skilled care workforce is rarely recognised as part of the social investment approach to ECEC, yet is critical to reconciling the work and care demands of mothers with care responsibilities. The recruitment of migrant care workers also fits well with a social investment approach because these workers support the knowledge economy by providing low-paid care and domestic services for families working long hours outside the home (Morel, 2012; Williams, 2012a).

Rhetoric of in-home childcare: rationales for investment

Governments in Australia, the UK and Canada use distinctive policy mechanisms to support in-home childcare. In Australia, regulated in-home childcare (In Home Care) is an approved and targeted programme that is delivered through provider organisations, including family day care schemes. In the UK, formal care by nannies falls under the same regulatory body, but under separate (voluntary) rules and regulations. And, in Canada, in-home childcare is outside the scope of the formal ECEC sector, which comprises centre-based day care and smaller group care in the provider's home. The set of policies and programmes surrounding in-home childcare is situated within distinct policy contexts. These policy contexts are characterised by different policy structures (Chapter Three), as well as by different discourses and debates. In-home childcare is supported by a common social investment approach, yet the rhetoric and underlying rationales have shaped the position of in-home childcare within each country's (or jurisdiction) suite of ECEC policy.

Australia

Australia's In Home Care programme developed in response to pressures and rationales for targeted support for at-risk children and vulnerable families – a key tenet of a social investment rationale, yet very different from the rationales for in-home childcare in the UK and Canada, discussed later. The In Home Care programme originated in the late 1990s, around the same time that a 'social investment' discourse was becoming prominent across the other liberal welfare states. Although an explicit discourse is not identified in the late 1990s in Australia, the Howard government shifted spending to 'special needs childcare' through targeted programs (Lee and Strachan, 1998; Hill, 2006). Policy mechanisms expanded work-related childcare and, together with targeted programmes, aimed to address the needs of at-risk children (Hayden, 1997; Baker and Tippin, 1998; Brennan, 2002; Sumsion, 2006). The Stronger Families and Communities Strategy introduced more parenting support for vulnerable and disadvantaged children. The strategy was rationalised as a means to address child poverty. One of these programmes was In Home Care.

Origins and pressures for In Home Care: 1999 to 2007

The In Home Care programme in Australia evolved over a number of years 'as ministers and departments became aware of families ... unable to access mainstream services'(RPR Consulting, 2005, p 2). During this time, the provision of In Home Care required ministerial approval, which was given only 'in exceptional circumstances' (RPR Consulting, 2005, p 2). In June 1999, responsibility for streamlining the service was given to the then Department of Family and Community Services and, shortly after, the Family Day Care Handbook was amended to allow family day care workers to provide in-home care to families in particular circumstances. The Family Day Care Council of Australia and the Australian Federation of Child Care Services were commissioned to research the needs of families working shift work and with sick children (RPR Consulting, 2005). Findings from this research confirmed that there was an 'additional need', which supported the introduction of the In Home Care pilot sites in Tasmania, Queensland and South Australia.

In 2001, the In Home Care initiative was formalised and rolled out nationally under the Stronger Families and Communities initiative and allowed family day care workers to provide care in the child's home under family day care approval. When the programme expanded, additional eligibility criteria were added, including families with multiple (three or more) children under school age, and families living in rural and remote areas and other locations where there was no access to mainstream services. The criteria for accessing In Home Care were established to recognise that some children – because of child or family characteristics – face barriers to accessing mainstream services. As one government representative confirmed in an interview, In Home Care was "intended to be kind of the safety net [...] if your circumstances are such that you can't get into a long day care centre or whatever then that was the last resort really" (government representative, Australia).

There is still confusion over the purpose and principles of In Home Care. It is not clear whether the scheme was intended to facilitate employment, *or* whether the programme aimed to improve child and family wellbeing for at-risk and vulnerable families. Findings from a 2005 evaluation undertaken on behalf of the federal Department of Families and Communities found that the 'purposes and policy objectives of IHC have been difficult to ascertain' because, while (at the time of the evaluation) the IHC programme was administered by the Child Care Branch, which aims to 'provide access to quality childcare for children, families and communities', its funding objectives under the Stronger Families and Communities Strategy were to provide 'choice and flexibility in childcare' in disadvantaged communities (RPR Consulting 2005, p x). The ambiguity in policy and discourse evident during the early years of the In Home Care scheme remain today.

Under the Howard government, which came to power in 1996, a Senate inquiry into balancing work and family revived debate about extending financial assistance to families using registered in-home childcare outside the approved In Home Care programme, such as care by nannies. The resulting report (Standing Committee on Family and Human Services, 2006) proposed that mainstream services (that is, Long Day Care) were not providing adequate childcare and families were resorting to black market care because of the low rate of subsidisation under the registered scheme. The committee recommended that extending assistance would remove incentives to use black market care, and argued this through the rhetoric of parental choice and workforce participation. This focus on parental employment ignores the implications for children and care workers.

A new agenda for ECEC ... but what about In Home Care?

The Labor government's Investing in the Early Years Strategy (2007) was the first explicit use of a social investment discourse in ECEC in Australia. Stakeholders interviewed as part of this research identified that since the implementation of the National Early Childhood Agenda, the "rhetoric ... [is] more cohesive ... and there's a general agreement that early education is important" (peak organisation, Australia). This increased focus on quality early education is driven by a social investment rhetoric, which exposes further contradictions to the purpose of In Home Care. It is not clear whether the In Home Care programme is expected to provide ongoing 'educational' programming, or to provide temporary solutions to meet families' needs as laid out under initial objectives of the programme in 2001. While the National Early Childhood Agenda appears to take a holistic approach to children and family services for children aged 0 to five years, the details of the policy reveal a distinction between the purposes of different types of ECEC services. Regulations and rhetoric confirm the 'educational' focus of preschool and kindergarten and, as discussed in Chapter Three, the National Quality Framework applies to long day care, family day care and outside school hours care, but not In Home Care. This further complicates the sector's understanding of the purpose of In Home Care.

For some stakeholders, In Home Care is viewed as a 'vital' service to meet children's educational needs, particularly those in rural and remote areas "where the educators might live on the property" (peak organisation, Australia). A government representative agreed that IHC should "provide quality care that includes some element of early learning [because] that's the government's child care agenda" (government representative, Australia). Stakeholders also identified that parents' perceptions have changed; for families living in remote areas the purpose of In Home Care has shifted from "just going out and babysitting" to an understanding the "carers going out there are doing educational activities and their children are learning, etc. and actually getting them prepared for kindy and school" (provider organisation, Australia). These different perspectives expressed by ECEC stakeholders reflect the influence of a social investment approach to ECEC, particularly through the National Early Childhood Agenda and the emphasis on quality learning. However, for many stakeholders, In Home Care retains its original intention, that is to relieve families from non-standard working schedules and additional needs associated with having illness or disability in the family.

Pressures for flexible, after-hours ECEC resurfaced in a 2009 inquiry into childcare. Submissions proposed more flexible care in the name of parental choice and workforce participation (Education Employment and Workplace Relations References Committee, 2009), which was also raised in the 2006 inquiry into work and family balance. The 'nanny debate' was brought to the policy agenda in 2012 by the opposition Liberal National party at the time, which announced its intention to explore options for the subsidisation of nannies and in-home childcare if elected. The current Coalition government discourse focuses on parents' choice and workforce opportunities, while the (previous) Labor government (2007-13) emphasised the need to give parents confidence that all care choices have minimum standards and 'pretty basic features like police checks' (Karvelas, 2012). Thus, while the previous Labor government also acknowledged the need for more flexible options, the approaches of the two parties differed. The Labor government's Education Minister at the time, Kate Ellis, acknowledged the challenges of families needing flexible childcare and said the Labor government 'would work to clean up the nanny industry' to introduce minimum standards but that it 'is a long road to regulate nannies' (cited in Karvelas, 2012).

When elected to office in 2013, the Coalition government under Tony Abbott undertook a Productivity Commission inquiry to improve Australia's 'childcare system to enhance participation, to boost productivity' (ABC News, 2013). The commission's report recommended that subsidies be extended to families using nannies, provided they held qualifications under the National Quality Framework (Certificate III). In April 2015, the Coalition government announced that it would introduce a two-year Nanny Pilot programme. The two year Pilot commenced in January 2016, and a formal evaluation of the programme is expected following its completion in 2018. The policy announcement emphasised the need to enhance the flexibility of the current ECEC system. The government pointed to the increase in mothers' workforce participation and shifting employment patterns. Support for the Nanny Pilot comes primarily from groups representing dual-earner couples and middle-class professional women who work long hours. The rationale for subsidising nannies rests explicitly on women's workforce participation and the potential for increased productivity, consistent with a human capital approach to social investment. It also promotes the individualisation of services through the rhetoric of choice and flexibility (Adamson et al, forthcoming).

In contrast, under the previous Labor government, the consideration to extend subsidies for families using nannies was first and foremost made about the safety and wellbeing of children. In both instances, there has been a shift away from the original objectives of In Home Care in 1999. These shifts in policy rationales create tensions and contradictions, discussed later in this chapter.

United Kingdom

The United Kingdom's 1997 Childcare Strategy adopted an explicit 'social investment' discourse, which placed children and families at the centre of New Labour reforms. The Childcare Strategy formed part of New Labour's 'new' approach to social policy. This platform emphasised skills development, education for young children, and the eradication of child poverty through parental employment and early intervention (Lloyd, 2008). Various accounts of ECEC policy development in the UK confirm the prominence of a social investment approach in the 1997 Childcare Strategy (Fawcett et al, 2004; Dobrowolsky and Jenson, 2005; Lister, 2006; Wincott, 2006). For example, Lloyd notes how the expanded investment through the tax credits and other initiatives under the Childcare Strategy in 1997 'ignored the implications for poor children ... [it] prioritised the economic benefits of women's labour market participation over the redistribute function' of ECEC (Lloyd, 2008, p 483).

However, less attention has been given to how the Childcare Strategy, and its focus on women's workforce participation, opened up debate about government support for in-home childcare and nannies. While it is difficult to estimate the number of families using in-home childcare in the 1990s, previous studies confirm a resurgence in the hiring of nannies and other domestic labour throughout the 1980s and 1990s (Gregson and Lowe, 1994; Cox, 2000). This resurgence fuelled debate among the sector about the balance between the promotion of mothers' employment and the need for regulated care to protect the needs of children and care workers.

Developing support for in-home childcare

The announcement of a Home Childcare Approval scheme in 2004 came after years of sector debates and consultation regarding the safeguarding of children in different forms of care. An examination of sector debate since the late 1990s identifies alternative rationales driving advocacy support for in-home childcare. Debate about nannies and in-home childcare evolved around the same time that changes to immigration policy resulted in an influx of au pairs from Eastern European countries. These debates, and the relationship to immigration policy, are central to the broader restructuring of care, characterised by the marketisation, commodification and individualisation of services – facilitated by both care and migration policy.

Shortly after announcing the 1997 National Childcare Strategy, the government published a number of reports looking at the funding and regulation of different forms of childcare and early education. One of these, the 1998 Better Regulation Taskforce report, did not support the registration of nannies, stating it was the parents' responsibility to protect children (Better Regulation Task Force, 1998). According to one expert, the Labour government "ignored the situation of nannies" because it "did not want to touch … the enormous tradition in the UK" (key informant, UK). Instead, the Labour government focused policy attention on services for more disadvantaged families, such as Sure Start, Neighbourhood Centres, and childminders. Support for these forms of care fit well with policy objectives to eradicate child poverty and support child development. But women's workforce participation was also central to the policy agenda.

The 2002 consultation paper, *Supporting the cost of home-based childcare* (DfES, 2002), recognised the challenges for working families and put forward the option for families to hire registered childminders as in-home childcarers. However, this proposal did not open up a new scheme, but rather required nannies to register as 'childminders' to be eligible for subsidisation. The consultation document cited the need for affordable care for children with additional needs and the large proportion of families working non-traditional hours as the target groups for the proposal. The proposal states that home childcarers would be 'professional childcarers, offering children safe, good quality care and providing them with play and learning opportunities that contribute to their development' (DfES, 2002, p 8). The Home Childcare scheme piggybacked on existing childminder regulation, and was implemented in April 2003 to allow childminders (already registered with Ofsted) to voluntarily register to provide care in the child's home.

Following sector pressures and a government review into the costs and benefits of a nanny register (for nannies opposed to childminders), the Children and Families Minister, Catherine Ashton, announced that the government would not introduce a nanny register or extend tax credits and vouchers to families using nannies. Instead, she stated, the 'job of government was to encourage parents to use approved carers' (cited in Tweed, 2003a). However, by 2004, a new consultation was announced by the recently appointed minister, Margaret Hodge, to consider extension of financial support to families using forms of unregistered childcare (DfES, 2004). The 2004 consultation document, *Childcare: Extending protection and broadening support*, signalled a shift in focus from support for 'quality', regulated, in-home childcare (as noted in the 2002 consultation paper) towards 'light-touch' regulation to facilitate families' choices. The document stated that the new scheme 'does not attempt to intervene in or override a parent's judgement when they choose who cares for their child', but rather is intended 'to help inform their choice ... [and is] backed up by access to financial support to make it affordable' (DfES, 2004, p 1).

The announcement of the Home Childcare Approval scheme in the 2004 Budget asserted that the government was not taking responsibility for safeguarding or ensuring minimum standards; instead, the scheme was 'designed to be non-intrusive and to leave responsibility firmly with parents for determining the nature and quality of the care' (DfES, 2004, n.p.), reflecting ambiguity in the role of government to regulate the quality of ECEC services and, at a minimum, ensure the safeguarding of children.

Concerns about the quality of care, particularly safeguarding for children, were raised shortly after the announcement. The head of the National Day Nurseries Association (NDNA) at the time stated:

> It is ironic that while childminders, nurseries, playgroups and out-of-school care are heavily regulated and inspected by Ofsted, a 'light touch' register is thought to be sufficient

for nannies working alone in the parents' home. (In Tweed, 2004)

Debates surrounding the introduction of financial support for families using in-home childcare, referred to as nannies or home childcare in the UK, have been part of broader ECEC developments, namely the 1998 and 2004 Childcare Strategies. Government and sector advocates' push for the registration of nannies danced around different social investment goals. Early initiatives appeared to be child-focused through a commitment to ensuring that home childcare was of high quality; however, the eventual implementation of the scheme in 2004 – despite paying lip service to the notion of 'quality' – was largely parent-focused, with objectives to boost workforce participation through increasing options for affordable ECEC arrangements.

While nannies, and governesses, have been a tradition embedded in the UK since the 19th century, the ultimate inclusion of nannies and in-home childcare workers under the regulatory framework represented a shift in the UK's thinking about responsibility for *care*. In particular, New Labour's focus on mothers' workforce participation as part of its social investment approach opened up opportunities to expand public financial support for women's workforce participation. This emphasis on mothers' employment shifted childcare from a purely private matter to the public interest. At the same time, policy at the EU level simultaneously promoted mothers' employment in the formal labour market and facilitated the movement of migrant workers, and the hiring of au pairs, from Eastern Europe to the UK after 2004, many of whom sought employment as care workers in private homes.

Nannies and a new agenda for the early years

Policy reforms and consultations since 2004 have opened up space for nanny associations to demand inclusion in the early years sector. However, the competing government objectives of education and workforce participation have complicated the political space in which they operate. While the voluntary 'light-touch' registration process includes nannies under the government's workforce participation agenda, they are excluded from most discussion about education and delivery of the Early Years Foundation Stage and Early Years entitlement.[2] Policy developments in 2012 brought quality early education to the forefront with the Nutbrown review (Nutbrown, 2012) and introduction of Early Years entitlement for two-year-olds. Both of these policy developments leave in-home childcare out of the scope of sector consultation for improving education services for young children. At the end of 2012, representatives from the nanny sector joined forces to campaign for inclusion in the early years workforce. Their goal is to 'promote quality in early years care to benefit all children and families' (Regulation Matters, 2015). To achieve this, the Regulation Matters campaign

> ... calls for the registration of all childcarers in the UK, so that nannies and other home childcarers are brought under the same regulatory umbrella and held to the registration standards currently required of childminders in order to safeguard children, improve childcare standards, and create consistency in the childcare industry. (Regulation Matters, 2015)

However, while there is a general consensus among stakeholders in the nanny sector about minimum standards and safeguarding, some sector representatives interviewed for this research expressed reservations about the educational potential of nannies, stating that "when children are three or four they should go to preschool" (nanny association, UK). These views are consistent with the government's separation of objectives for spending through tax credits and childcare vouchers from Early Years entitlement. As a government representative indicated, spending on vouchers and tax credits is designed to encourage parental employment, while the "rationale for the free entitlement is fundamentally an educational one and a child development one" (government representative, UK).

Support for in-home childcare through migration pathways also supports parental employment. Migrant workers provide a source of low-paid labour to support the knowledge economy *without* having to increase public investment in childcare subsidies. This is of course not an option for, or desire of, all families, although the demand for au pairs in London and the surrounding areas has experienced a surge in the past decade (Nannytax, 2015). The opening up of the EU to Eastern Europe since 2004 has further fostered the hiring of low-paid, and often untrained, migrant domestic workers or au pairs. The nature of this category of migrant workers changed through the 2004 and 2008 reforms, and creates further tensions with a social investment approach.

Canada

Canada's Liberal government explicitly announced its commitment to a social investment approach to ECEC in its 1997 Throne Speech.[3] This was not the first time the federal government framed childcare in economic terms. Since the 1980s, the promotion of women's employment has been viewed in policy discourse as an economic contribution, rather than a commitment to gender equality. The 1984 Royal Commission on Equality in Employment promoted employment equality, which was very much articulated through the 'productive potential' of women's employment (Timpson, 2001, pp 97 and 171). Furthermore, support for mothers' workforce participation was closely linked to the national focus on the alleviation of child poverty in the 1980s and early 1990s.

Reforms in the 1980s pushed single parents into work, yet the federal government made 'no commitment to formalised, professionalised, or "quality" oriented child care' (Hayden, 1997, p 5). The Liberal government made an early commitment to develop a national childcare programme. However, national policy reforms through the mid-1990s continued to prioritise the needs of vulnerable children and families, in the name of child poverty. The link between childcare and gender equality, or even children's rights to quality childcare, had faded from federal policy debate. The National Children's Agenda (NCA) (1997) was an umbrella concept that incorporated the National Child Benefit (NCB) and other child development initiatives (McKeen, 2007). Overall, the NCA represented a targeted approach to child wellbeing and development. The two goals of the NCB were to reduce child poverty and to 'promote attachment to the workforce by ensuring that families were always better off as a result of working' (Dobrowolsky and Jenson, 2004, p 171).

Demand from families with stable and well-paid jobs led to the growth of private centre-based services. With the lack of public subsidies for middle- and higher-income families (with the exception of the Child Care Expense Deduction), families also looked to more affordable childcare solutions, such as in-home childcare. By 1992 the Live-In Caregiver Program (previously called the Foreign Domestic Movement) was established, and offered a real option for families with adequate space and income.

De facto childcare: the Live-In Caregiver Program

In 1992, prior to being appointed the Minister for Employment and Immigration, Lloyd Axworthy, declared that the 'Domestic Workers program is an important part of the childcare system in this country' (cited in Cho, 2013). The Live-In Caregiver Program fit well with Canada's neoliberal agenda in the 1980s and 1990s: it facilitated women's workforce participation and productivity and, at the same time, aligned with the federal Conservative government's agenda to minimise spending. Over two decades later, the situation has barely changed. While many provinces have made progress towards expanding the availability of ECEC, the previous federal government (under Conservative leadership from 2006 to 2015) made no commitment to expanding options. As representatives from nanny agencies interviewed for this research explained, the lack of public investment in regulated ECEC contributes to demand for live-in caregivers (nanny agencies, Canada).

Ongoing demand for migrant caregivers (now part of the Caring for Children Pathway) has been attributed to high maternal workforce participation combined with a shortage of affordable and regulated childcare. Due to the lack of regulated and affordable childcare, dual-earner families in Canada face challenges to balancing work and family. As early as the 1980s, the Live-In Caregiver Program 'certainly provided one solution to the pressures' these families faced (Arat-Koç 1989, p 36). Scholars in this area point to the implications for care workers and inherent racial inequalities (Arat-Koç, 1989; Pratt, 2003; LeBaron, 2010; Gilliland, 2012). Less attention has been given to the rationales behind government and stakeholder support for in-home childcare, particularly as a deliberate policy alternative to regulated centre-based ECEC.[4]

The Live-In Caregiver Program, and the current Caring for Children Pathway under the Temporary Foreign Worker Program, facilitates forms of cheap labour that align with conservative ideology for private home care. It serves neoliberal and social investment objectives to increase workforce participation. In doing so, it replaces some of the demand for non-parental childcare options by middle- and high-income working parents, who are able to afford this type of childcare. In 1997, Patricia Daenzer argued that the '[e]conomic interests have been, and continue to be, the primary considerations that guided the opening up of the program' (Daenzer 1997, p 104). The rationale for the Live-In Caregiver Program aligns closely with an economic agenda that is tied to a neoliberal discourse that promotes productivity and mothers' participation in the knowledge economy. However, this rationale is in tension with the rise of a child-centred discourse in the 1990s that emphasised the economic benefits of investing in *children*.

Overall, the federal government's focus on women's employment is arguably not matched with appropriate attention to children. ECEC stakeholders interviewed for this research expressed concern about the lack of policy attention given to children in ECEC. As one representative from a peak organisation explained, "people need to go to work ... but [we also need] to make sure that what's going on with kids is the right thing" (peak organisation, Canada).

Social investment in Ontario and Canada: the education–care divide

Canada's previous federal Liberal government (1993-2006) pushed for a national Early Learning and Childhood Framework. But, progress towards this national goal unravelled when the Conservative government took power. The federal Conservative government (2006-2015) prioritised a rhetoric of parental 'choice' through the introduction of the Universal Child Care Benefit (Thériault, 2006; Richardson et al, 2013). Despite the ultimate demise of the national Early Learning and Childhood Framework in 2006, it is argued that the social investment discourse united stakeholders 'by a confidence in good returns [...] from investing in children'. This economic frame was identified as an 'investing-in-children paradigm' (Prentice 2009, p 690).

Provinces across Canada have taken initiatives to expand ECEC for young children, particularly in the year or two before school. The province of Ontario also recently initiated reforms to improve the quality of early learning and education across the province's regulated settings. The emphasis on quality early education was driven by new research and knowledge about child development (for example, McCain and Mustard, 1999; Bertrand et al, 2007). This emphasis on early education was symbolised by the transfer of ECEC services from the Ministry of Children and Youth to the Ministry of Education. As one key informant interviewed for this research stated, the shift "signals a philosophy that [...] childcare is an extension of [...] publicly funded education" (key informant, Canada), and "really puts [childcare] in that continuum of young learners" (Ontario government representative, Canada).

This educational rhetoric at the government level arguably shapes families' perceptions of different types of ECEC, including in-home childcare. For example, one local government representative interviewed believed "there's been a generational shift" where parents are choosing licensed childcare over nannies and, while "it's costing them as much", it reflects their choice about the "value of education" (local government, Canada). However, within the constraints of the childcare market, many families cannot access a regulated, high-quality space. Families hiring nannies are also "looking for more child educators, versus the housekeeper component" (nanny agency, Canada). But this may not be true for all families. For some, help with the everyday domestic tasks performed by a 'traditional' nanny is still sought after. For these families, the extra help to allow parents to work longer hours and earn more money might be as important. As one nanny agency affirmed, "a lot of people don't want a trained nanny" because they "want more help with the house" (nanny agency, Canada).

For the most part, the Live-In Caregiver Program has sat outside the scope of ECEC policy debate. As a result, the place of children – and the lack of quality regulations – have been absent from any discussion of the Live-In Caregiver Program. Yet, as described above, there is ongoing support for migrant workers to fill a gap in the provision of childcare services. Advocates and critics of the programme alike attribute the popularity of the 'de facto' programme to the lack of public responsibility for ECEC. The government acknowledges the gap the Live-In Caregiver Program fills in the absence of such public responsibility for childcare. As the quote below illustrates, the previous Conservative government relied heavily on the economic contributions made by migrant caregivers and were quick to assert their commitment, at least in rhetoric, to continue to support their recruitment. As stated by the Department of Immigration and Citizenship:

> The Conservative government recognizes the contributions of live-in caregivers to Canadian families and our economy, and the immigration department will continue to ensure live-in caregivers are safe and protected. (Mas, 2013)

There is no doubt that in-home childcare fills a gap in demand by meeting some (middle-class) working parents' needs for flexible care. However, Magkaisa Centre, a group advocating for the protection and improved rights of migrant care workers, argues that 'any initiative to create a national childcare program is not complete until the Live-In Caregiver Program is scrapped' (Rabble.ca, 2010).

Converging ideas and policy tensions

In Australia, the UK and Canada since the late 1990s, policy agendas have tended to emphasise investment in education and early development for young children and workforce participation for mothers. The justification and implementation of social investment-inspired social policies can sometimes lead to trade-offs, or unintended consequences, between different groups. Policy that prioritises mothers' employment can lead to trade-offs for both the quality of children's early education, and the quality of care workers employment.

Early education versus mothers' employment

The most obvious tension of the social investment discourse is the distinction between early education and mothers' employment. This is evident in all three countries in relation to rationales for in-home childcare and also the policy mechanisms that support this type of care. In Australia, rationales for the In Home Care programme bounce around between workforce participation, improvement of child and family wellbeing, and the provision of education and developmental opportunities for children. In Home Care was initially funded as part of the Stronger Families and Communities Strategy, which targeted disadvantaged families needing flexible childcare solutions. However, the programme has since moved to the childcare portfolio, which aims to improve the quality and affordability of ECEC (RPR Consulting, 2005, p 50). A government representative confirmed the tensions in the In Home Care programme by stating:

> 'There are probably families using it, and using it for the wrong purpose like respite care [...] but at the end of the day you've got very vulnerable children and very vulnerable families who need care and who need support. So it's a very difficult issue.' (Government representative, Australia)

Tensions also exist with respect to the broader ECEC push for education, and confusion about the underlying intention of In Home Care. For example, there was broad consensus among the study interviewees that in-home carers are "not babysitters [a]nd they have a role in the early developmental years of the child" (nanny agency, Australia); however, another stakeholder argued that because of the unusual patterns of In Home Care, including when children are sleeping, there is "always going to be a struggle to have In Home Care fit an ECEC model" (peak organisation, Australia).

The Nanny Pilot, which commenced in 2016, introduces a new complexity to the provision of in-home childcare in Australia. It shifts the objective of government support for in-home childcare in both rationale and policy design. The Nanny Pilot is explicitly focused on workforce participation, with no mention of the needs of the child or care worker. When Tony Abbott first proposed a review of childcare before the election he said it was

> [p]art of the Coalition's plan for a stronger economy. A more flexible and responsive childcare system will lift workforce participation and is part of the Coalition's plan to deliver a strong and prosperous economy and a safe and secure Australia. (Cited in Bryant, 2013)

This statement clearly prioritises women's workforce participation over high-quality ECEC for children. The facilitation of mothers' employment was not the central aim when In Home Care originated in the late 1990s. Similar contradictions between care and education exist in the UK's promotion of in-home childcare. The UK early years initiatives introduced in the late 1990s identified the need for 'high-quality' child-centred services, yet the rationale for extending funding to Home Childcare was explicitly employment-focused. The early years reforms during the 2000s emphasised standardised quality ECEC provision through the Early Years Foundation Stage and expansion of universal ECEC through the Early Years Entitlement. A government representative made clear the distinction between policies designed to address care and education goals:

> 'The rationale for the free entitlement is fundamentally an educational one and a child development one ... [whereas] the Working Tax Credit ... it's very much the idea of encouraging parents back into the workforce.' (Government representative, UK)

The government's line is perhaps in tension with many nanny associations and representatives campaigning for inclusion within the early years sector. There is, however, varying scope in the extent to which it is believed nannies should be required to fulfil an 'educational' role. There are also concerns in the UK about public funding and monitoring of in-home childcare. All families using Ofsted-registered ECEC services are eligible for the childcare element of the Working Tax Credit (if their incomes are below the cut-off point) and childcare vouchers provided by (some) employers. However, the level of monitoring of services and care workers is not consistent for all types of care. Representatives from nanny agencies pointed out that the current voluntary registration gives parents a false sense of quality (nanny agencies, UK) because there is little monitoring or enforcement of the, already low, standards. Nannies are only required to have undergone a police check and hold a first-aid certificate.

The Canadian experience differs from the situation in Australia and the UK in the fact that there is little federal government[5] interest or involvement in the quality and educational focus of ECEC. Despite increased rhetoric around parents' expectation for 'education' and 'early learning', there is little support by the sector to improve the quality of in-home childcare (particularly the Live-In Caregiver Program) to benefit the child. The Live-In Caregiver Program is viewed as a complement to centre-based preschools and kindergarten for three- and four-year olds. Therefore, while the federal government has claimed that the Live-In Caregiver Program is a key part of Canada's childcare system, the programme does not meet the quality standards articulated by many stakeholders in the sector.

At the same time, Ontario's (and other provinces') focus on education and child development is not consistent with the federal government's preference for private (and often unregulated) ECEC. Efforts by provincial advocates to expand government responsibility for ECEC are focused on research and evidence about child outcomes; yet federal rhetoric is underpinned by parental choice and a validation that informal arrangements with relatives, friends and neighbours is the most appropriate. In addition to ignoring the place of the child, the promotion of mothers' workforce participation and parental choice also often fail to consider the position of the care worker.

Working mothers versus care workers

Another tension exposed in the analysis of government in-home childcare policy, and ECEC more broadly, is the mismatch between the promotion of mothers' workforce participation and investment in the care workforce. Families (including children and parents) are regularly identified in public discourse as valuable investments – children for their future productivity and mothers for their financial contribution to the economy. Care workers, including in-home childcare workers, receive less attention in rhetoric and policy. In all three countries, a social investment approach promotes and funds childcare as an enabler for parents' (especially mothers') participation in paid work. In particular, the Child Care Rebate (Australia), Working Tax Credit and childcare vouchers (UK), and Child Care Expense Deduction (Canada) are all designed to facilitate parents' workforce participation. There is much less attention to funding to sustain a skilled and well-remunerated workforce.

When attention is given to the ECEC workforce, it tends to be limited to the centre-based workforce. For example, in Australia, campaigns to improve the wages of ECEC workers often distinguish qualified long day care workers from generally less-qualified family day care workers. In the UK, the push for professional status and qualifications of ECEC teachers focuses on centre-based settings, and rarely extends to investment in forms of home-based care, including nannies and in-home childcare. And, in Canada, there is a clear distinction in the province of Ontario between qualified early childhood educators (through the Ontario College of Early Childhood Educators) and untrained care workers. In-home childcare, particularly that provided by nannies as part of the Live-In Caregiver Program, is not viewed as a potential area for investment in training or up-skilling. In-home childcare workers are often portrayed in public discourse as a means to facilitate mothers' contribution to the knowledge economy and as a way to improve work–life balance. Mothers' employment and earnings in the knowledge economy are often prioritised above care workers' rights to fair wages and working conditions. As Chapter Five discusses, this is especially apparent when migrant workers are recruited to fill the care gap in these countries.

The line between care work and domestic work is often blurred as in-home care workers are expected to take on tasks that once were part of working mothers' unpaid work in the home. In some countries, the formalisation of such domestic and care work also contributes to governments' social investment approaches to increase employment rates and reduce expenditure on social assistance.

However, there is a trade-off in the promotion of both the knowledge economy and the care economy in the home. The primary focus on mothers' employment aligns with government objectives to achieve equality in the workforce. This focus ignores the underlying gender imbalance between men and women in the home; the gender inequalities experienced by low-paid earners, including women performing paid (and unpaid) care work; and especially the class and racial inequalities apparent within a growing migrant care workforce.

Situating tensions within a broader social investment context

It is evident that government support for in-home childcare rests on a range of social investment rationales; and we can see that, even where in-home childcare is underpinned by common rationales, programme and policy designs can operate very differently in practice. The two dichotomies discussed above – mothers' employment versus early education, and working mothers versus care workers – reflect broader tensions associated with liberal welfare policy and the social investment approach that is evident in the three study countries. These dichotomies are closely linked to ideas about workforce activation, individual choice and the reduction of public service provision. These are all features of a liberal social investment approach to policy, which are underpinned by the restructuring of care and welfare state policies.

The social investment approach emphasises workforce participation and productivity, yet, to different extents in each country, governments at the same time suggest that parents should have a choice about whether to stay at home or seek paid employment. In all three countries, the dominant workforce participation rationale is at odds with a neoliberal rhetoric of 'individual choice'. In theory, parents are actively encouraged to participate in the labour market and to increase their earnings, yet the reality is that there are not the childcare systems in place to address rising maternal employment rates. Governments therefore present informal childcare – including forms of in-home childcare – as a flexible way to meet the childcare gap. Migrant workers, especially, are viewed as a good source for affordable care labour. In-home childcare is also promoted as a means to facilitate parental or individual choice in work and care arrangements. But, as will be discussed in the next chapter, the ability for families to make real choices, and to find quality care that meets the parents and child's needs, is divided along income and class lines.

Liberal ideas about government responsibility for the care and education of young children are evident in the development of in-home childcare, and broader ECEC policy, in Australia, the UK and Canada. Social investment is identified as a strand of liberal and neoliberal thinking about the best way to spend public funds to reach government objectives. However, the discussion here shows that ideas of social investment are interpreted and adopted in different ways across countries and policy domains. In-home childcare is one policy area where the tensions and inconsistencies identified as part of a social investment approach are magnified through both rhetoric and policy design. These tensions exist, albeit to different extents, within and between the care and migration domains. As the next chapter discusses, the intersection of these policy domains creates new inequalities for different groups of families (parents, mothers and children) and care workers.

Notes

1. For conceptual and empirical analysis, see Dobrowolsky (2002), Esping-Andersen (2002), Lister (2004, 2008), Dobrowolsky and Jenson (2005), Jenson (2008), Prentice (2009), Mahon (2010a), Peng (2011), Penn (2011a), Williams (2012a) and Adamson and Brennan (2014).

2. As detailed in Chapter Three, the free Early Years Entitlement provides 15 hours of ECEC for three- and four-year-olds (and a targeted group of two-year-olds). The entitlement can be taken in centre-based settings, and by some childminders (subject to local variation). It cannot be taken by registered nannies.

3. A speech by prepared by the Prime Minister's office that outlines the priorities for government for the upcoming session of parliament.

4. Instead, research and advocacy surrounding the Live-In Caregiver Program has centred on global care chains, the rights of workers, citizenship and the inherent racial and gender inequalities of the LCP (Bakan and Stasiulis, 1994; Pratt, 1999; Hodge, 2006; Fudge, 2013).

5. It should be noted that at the time of writing, the federal Liberal government had recently replaced the Conservative government. The Liberal government agenda for early childhood education and care is unknown.

FIVE

Intersecting inequalities

Early childhood education and care (ECEC) policies universally have expanded and transformed over the past few decades. The funding objectives for public and private investment in ECEC services have shifted in various ways, often with intentions to achieve specific outcomes for different groups of the population. Broadly speaking, ECEC services have been designed for children and for parents (that is, mothers). As outlined in Chapter Two, spending on childcare before the 1960s was largely viewed as a philanthropic service for children from disadvantaged families – particularly children in families where it was a necessity for mothers to work. During the 1960s and 1970s, early 'education', opposed to 'care', services were developed for preschool-aged children and were designed to enhance children's development and school readiness. Such early education services were used mostly by middle-class children whose mothers did not work outside the home. They were not designed to encourage mothers to participate in the workforce. Calls for expanded public spending on childcare services in the 1960s and 1970s were underpinned by the idea that ECEC should be expanded and available to all mothers as a means to address gender inequities in the workplace and the home.

In the 1990s, new research demonstrated the benefits of high-quality ECEC services for disadvantaged children and families. Under this new 'human capital' rationale, targeted investment in ECEC services for vulnerable families was promoted as a strategy to address inequities in children's learning outcomes and give them a 'head start' before starting school. Mothers have also been at the centre of policy design. The availability of childcare services enhances mothers' ability to participate in the paid labour force and, in principle, helps balance the division of unpaid childcare in the home. However, research shows there is still a far way to go to realising gender equality, particularly in the home (Craig and Mullan, 2011; Craig and Powell, 2013).

Women around the world have increased their participation in the paid labour market. Women from some countries, however, increasingly seek opportunities outside their home country. For women from developing countries, care work in more developed countries is often regarded as a pathway to a better life. For many women (and men), the opportunity to undertake paid work in more developed countries is viewed as a way to earn money to be sent back to their families in their home countries. Although migrant workers may have higher earning capacities in developed countries than in their home countries, many recent migrants are willing to work for lower wages than locally born workers (Stiell and England, 1999; Williams and Gavanas, 2008). The tendency for migrant care workers to accept lower wages than the local care workforce occurs within an already devalued market for childcare labour (Pratt, 2003).

Independently, childcare policy *and* migration policy structures produce social inequalities among families and care workers. A significant body of research in the ECEC field identifies how policy structures affect the affordability, accessibility and quality of formal ECEC services for young children (for example, Meyers and Gornick, 2003; Penn, 2012; Gambaro et al, 2014). Other research has examined the dynamic between formal and informal ECEC services and identified patterns of care use by families. For example, parents who work atypical hours are more likely to use a mix of formal and informal childcare (Bryson et al, 2012; Rutter and Evans, 2012a; Brady and Perales, 2014). This may be because families choose to work longer or atypical hours and cannot find formal care to match their needs; because they cannot find work during standard hours; or because they cannot find childcare during standard hours. Moreover, some families may prefer informal care and therefore choose to work atypical hours that match the availability of care. As mentioned, the use of informal care can be a positive choice for families, which lends support to the argument that informal childcare should be subsidised. However, the subsidisation of informal care can have consequences for care workers (Land, 2002).

The subsidisation of informal childcare can lead to a 'race to the bottom', as families seek value for money from the subsidy they receive. This issue is compounded when migration policy facilitates the recruitment of lower-paid care workers. For example, studies illustrate how migration policy shapes inequities and poor conditions for caregivers providing live-in childcare (Bakan and Stasiulis, 1997; Brickner and Straehle, 2010; Busch, 2013). However, limited attention has been given to how these two policy intersect with ECEC funding and regulation. It is only recent research that has highlighted the significance of migration (Williams and Gavanas, 2008; Busch, 2013) and employment (Morgan, 2005) policies for the provision of childcare. This body of research has pointed to the inequalities produced through employment and migration policies. In particular, the absence of accessible formal childcare has led to demand for low-cost informal care options, often available through migration schemes (Cox, 2006a). Migration policy, too, therefore contributes to the affordability, accessibility and quality of childcare in some national contexts. And the intersection of policies has implications for gender, income/class[1] and race/migration. These intersecting issues of gender, income/class and race/migration are experienced by families (mothers, parents and children) and by care workers.

Restructuring of inequalities

The restructuring of care responsibilities – including the movement of care workers across borders – raises complex policy issues related to gender, class and race. In the childcare domain, there can be a trade-off between policies that enhance the affordability for families and those that support quality provision for children. And in the migration domain, policies to increase the availability of flexible care for families may have adverse effects on care workers and children. That is, policies designed to increase mothers' workforce participation to address gender equality in the workplace often overshadow the working conditions and inequities experienced by women performing the care work, and the quality of care for children.

As described in earlier chapters, the introduction and expansion of public funding, registration and regulation, and migration pathways have all contributed to the restructuring of care responsibilities. The restructuring of childcare, in addition to other social policy areas, has been promoted through a discourse of social investment. A social investment discourse can open up opportunities for some groups, and simultaneously close down opportunities for other groups to articulate their needs. As explained by Fiona Williams, policy restructuring has tended to address the inequalities of some social groups (namely working mothers) while, sometimes unintentionally, producing 'new forms of inequality' that can have consequences for in-home childcare workers (Williams, 2012a, p 113). Within an environment of economic productivity, mothers are often seeking longer hours of work to overcome gender inequities in the workplace. To accommodate longer working hours, families often require more flexible childcare options. Mothers from dual-earner and high-income families often choose to work longer hours to progress their career and to increase their earning capacity. Mothers from low-income or single-earner households may be working non-standard or unpredictable hours because they may have few other employment opportunities.

In a commoditised market for childcare (see Busch, 2013), families with greater financial resources tend to have greater choice in the quantity, quality and flexibility of care they purchase. Low-income families may look to informal options with friends or family, putting together a patchwork arrangement. Middle- and high-income families also seek 'value for money in a low-paid care work sector', as they search for care providers that will provide more care and domestic work for less money (Williams, 2012a, p 112). Migrant women often fill this gap in demand for longer hours and more flexible care, and sometimes this requires the nanny to live in the home of the family. Whether living in or out, migrant workers recruited to perform care and domestic duties in private households may not be protected by (or aware of) the industry rules and regulations. This can, in effect, lead to exploitation and can reinforce gendered, class and racial inequities in the home. In some countries, the recruitment of migrant in-home childcare workers is facilitated through specific migration policies. Migration pathways and working visas can be designed to promote increased workforce participation among middle- and high-income families by decreasing the cost of non-parental childcare. While much has been written on issues of access and affordability associated with market-led ECEC systems, the literature[2] often ignores the controversial space in which in-home childcare exists within countries' ECEC sectors. This chapter explores the intersection of these policy domains for in-home childcare through the lens of gender, class/income and race/migration status.

The chapter also examines the different ways funding and regulatory mechanisms affect issues of gender, class/income and race/migration for families and care workers. Similar to other chapters in Part Two, primary data collected from interviews for this research is used to complement and enrich the analysis of structural policy mechanisms, described in Chapter Three. It considers how policies addressing inequalities experienced by one social group can, in practice, have negative implications for other social groups involved. This issue is exacerbated for in-home childcare, where care workers are often subject to few regulations and their work is largely invisible, in the private and informal domain.

Families versus care workers

Care and migration policy both shape the supply and demand of in-home childcare. Issues of gender, class/income and race/migration cut across all three groups involved – mothers, children and care workers. However, the gender, class/income and race/migration framework is used to identify the most salient issues for care users (families) and care providers (in-home childcare workers); gender and class/income are most significant for care users and the intersection of race/migration with existing gender and class/income inequalities are most relevant for care providers, particularly in the UK and Canada. The class/income inequalities that affect care users extend to parents and children. As mentioned, there are, of course, other potential implications for children. In particular, policy design affects the *quality* of the care provided.

Gender: the undervaluation of women's (care) work

Gender is inherent in any policy analysis of care, including ECEC. Care work is gendered as women's paid and unpaid care work and continues to be undervalued and poorly recognised. Within this context, in-home childcare policy produces gender inequalities in relation to mothers and care workers. Care policy, in particular, is designed to help families (primarily mothers) reconcile their care and work responsibilities and therefore promotes gender equality in the workforce. At the same time, migration policy that allows families to hire domestic workers arguably allows women in the receiving countries greater employment opportunities. Some might argue that migration pathways provide opportunities for women from sending countries to find better-paid work than in their home countries. But these care and migration policies create new inequalities for care workers and do not address gender inequalities between men and women in the home. In each of the national contexts discussed, the intersection of care and migration policies creates different dynamics, which affect the experiences of families and care workers in complex ways.

Australia's formal In Home Care scheme, implemented in 2001, was designed to assist families in certain circumstances to access regulated ECEC. The In Home Care programme is part of broader support from the federal government to cover care-related costs associated with working outside the home. It currently provides care to approximately 5,600 children. In relation to gender equality and work–care balance, the employment criteria are designed to assist families with precarious employment patterns, such as those working shifts and non-standard hours. It therefore allows many women in vulnerable situations to participate in employment and, at the same time, offers an affordable and adequate standard of care for their children. As outlined in previous chapters, the current Coalition government has introduced funding for in-home childcare beyond the targeted In Home Care programme.

Under the Nanny Pilot programme (being trialled between 2016 and 2018), subsidies are available to approximately 3,000 families.[3] The extension of subsidies to more users of in-home childcare can potentially benefit dual-earner and high-earning single mothers; however, this would be at the expense of deeper class inequalities among low-paid women working in precarious and female-dominated employment. The Nanny Pilot further degrades the value of ECEC because qualifications are not required. The government explicitly recognises that in-home childcare can enhance mothers' employment opportunities, but with no recognition of the value of the care work provided by the nannies. The devaluation of childcare resonates with the broader ECEC sector. One peak organisation explained how the low wages of ECEC workers

> 'enables [sic] women to participate in the labour force off the backs of another female workforce that is earning poverty wages and that is not sustainable and is completely unacceptable ... have middle-class women banging on about needing more childcare, never mind the fact that the women looking after her children can't pay for her own, can't afford to live.' (peak organisation, Australia)

Similar to the situation in Australia, care policy in the UK aims to open up opportunities and encourage mothers with young children to participate in the workforce. Tax credits and childcare vouchers do assist eligible parents with the cost of in-home childcare, provided their nanny/carer is registered with Ofsted. Voluntary registration with Ofsted crosses the boundary of care and work/employment policy in that it fails to protect (mostly female) care workers from the vulnerabilities of working in a low-paid and unprotected work sector. This, of course, also has implications for the quality of care for children. Changes to migration policy in the UK also encourages the hiring of care workers into the informal, in-home care sector, which can act to push down wages within an already under-valued and gendered workforce (Busch, 2012, 2013).

In Canada, demands for equal opportunity for mothers to enter the workforce were central to the decision to introduce the Child Care Expense Deduction in 1972 and the Live-In Caregiver Program in 1992. The interaction of these care and migration policies, in addition to the relatively low minimum wage, prioritises professional women's contribution to the knowledge economy. This has implications for gender equality between men and women in the home as well as for the value of work done by lower-skilled and more vulnerable women, including migrant care workers. This is consistent with broader findings of Canadian social policy (Arat-Koç, 1989; Brickner and Straehle, 2010), where policymaking and policy discourse under neoliberalism 'treats gender inequality as a problem solved for white Canadian women, and an ongoing ... problem for immigrant and racialised women' (Arat-Koç 2012, p 7).

In all three countries, care policies for in-home childcare are focused more on mothers' employment and their contribution to the economy than on the achievement of gender equality at home. Australia's In Home Care scheme is the only programme that pays some attention to the needs of vulnerable families. Yet, the Nanny Pilot signals a shift away from the targeted approach to in-home childcare in Australia to one that prioritises mothers' employment with little regard for the value of care work provided by the nannies. Migration policy, particularly in the UK and Canada, also contributes to the deepening of gender inequalities among unemployed and low-skilled women and those unable to reconcile work and care responsibilities. In sum, the alleviation of time pressures and care responsibilities for some mothers through the subsidisation of in-home childcare can in practice create new inequalities for other groups of working mothers and care workers. The extent to which policy addresses or embeds intersecting inequalities – namely income/class and race/migration – is discussed next.

Class and income: stratification among care users

ECEC, migration and work/employment policies shape class and income stratification for both families (mothers and children) and care workers. Usage patterns of home-based (group and nanny) care and centre-based childcare are often divided along class lines. In the UK and Canada, in particular, certain types of care were designed for certain groups of families. For example, in the UK there were class divisions across childminding and nannies, where poorer low-skilled women were more likely to provide care for a similar class of women. And, with in-home childcare, wealthier families tended to hire young women from a class similar to their own (Gregson and Lowe, 1994; Owen, 2003, Vincent et al, 2008; Penn, 2009). More recently, in the UK, an expert in the field interviewed as part of this research suggested that lower-income families prefer to use nurseries than childminders, while for "middle-class parents, home-based childcare from a nanny or a relative is ideal for babies" (key informant, UK).

While care by nannies and au pairs is increasingly common for Australian families, national census data and anecdotal evidence indicates that full-time in-home childcare is only a reality for middle- and high-income families (Australian Bureau of Statistics, 2015). According to one Australian stakeholder, families "on lower salaries do find it acceptable to have a nanny [...] it's not a social status thing anymore", but because of the cost it does "push it into that high-income earning bracket" (nanny agency, Australia). There was consensus among most key stakeholders interviewed in the UK that nannies were still only accessible to middle- to upper-income families. There was agreement among many stakeholders that more middle-income families are accessing nannies now than even five years ago, although nannies are still concentrated in wealthier areas and among higher-income families. It was suggested that "you still need to be earning quite a good salary to have a nanny because nannies' salaries are very competitive" (nanny association, UK). A 2011 survey confirmed that almost 75 per cent of families with nannies had incomes over £100,000 per year.[4] Asked about the changing place of nannies as a childcare arrangement, one representative agreed that nannies "are almost a parallel to the childminder position, but the reality is it's a fairly privileged position" (peak organisation, UK).

However, it should be noted that, in both Australia and the UK, there is more demand for part-time nanny arrangements, or 'nannyshares' for people who "aren't very high earners" (nanny associations, UK). So, while more average earners are seeking in-home childcare, they can only afford a nanny part-time (nanny association, Australia). Similarly, 'nannyshares' are identified as "one of the best businesses [...] for families that want a nanny but can't afford the costs" (nanny agency, UK). Nannyshares are not as common a pattern in Canada, where live-in caregivers are only allowed to work for one family and are required under the immigration policy to work a minimum of 30 hours per week. In addition, full-time employment is more common among mothers with young children in Canada, compared with the UK or Australia (OECD, 2005; Rammohan and Whelan, 2007). It appears that for the most part, while nannies are more culturally accepted, and desirable, among middle-income families in all countries, full-time nannies are not accessible to the majority of families. In addition, wealthier families are most able to negotiate high-quality care, for example by hiring nannies with more experience and qualifications. There are some exceptions to this general trend, particularly through programmes in Australia and the UK.

Australia's In Home Care programme is perhaps the one exception in the three countries where care policy is designed to mitigate class/income inequalities in terms of families' access to in-home childcare. The In Home Care (IHC) programme offers affordable in-home childcare to families who otherwise would be unable to negotiate their work and care responsibilities. However, the targeted and capped design of the programme means that many families who would benefit miss out. A 2005 evaluation of the IHC scheme found that the formal scheme is still unaffordable for many families eligible under the In Home Care criteria. Stakeholders with knowledge and experience delivering the In Home Care programme believed that the system must be changed to make it affordable for one-child families where there is an identified need, particularly a disability or family circumstances putting the child at-risk (RPR Consulting, 2005). Currently, service providers (including family day care schemes and private organisations) determine eligibility, and there is room for interpretation of the eligibility criteria. Providers may be "looser or stricter [sic] depending on their own personal point of view" (government representative, Australia).

This Australian policy model is unique among the three countries in that in-home childcare is targeted to families on the basis of need. Policy thus distinguishes between publicly supported 'in-home childcare' and private nannies. However, the introduction of the Nanny Pilot in 2016 is likely to create new social cleavages between those who can afford a nanny and those who cannot. Families eligible for a subsidy will still have significant out-of-pocket costs. The exceptions are likely to be middle-income families with multiple children (three or more) under school age.

Innovative models of in-home childcare have been adopted in parts of the UK, but not embedded in national policy. One model in particular is provided by a service called @HomeChildcare. The service, based in north-west England, employs Ofsted-registered childcare workers to go into the homes of families (many of which are on low incomes) that need flexible, in-home childcare. The founder was "interested in removing [cost] barriers and making it affordable and more accessible to just ordinary families ... who couldn't find childcare for later in the evenings and early mornings" (provider organisation, UK). Apart from such standalone service providers, the childcare element of the Working Tax Credit (WTC) and childcare vouchers reproduce existing class divisions among families using nannies. Even if families are using an Ofsted-registered nanny – therefore making families eligible for WTCs – the high cost of in-home childcare and low level of generosity and strict eligibility criteria of the benefit makes in-home childcare out of reach for most low-income families. At the same time, migration policy has contributed to an influx of migrant workers willing to do the same job as local workers but for lower wages, an issue that is explored further below. Despite access to subsidisation through tax credits and vouchers, most families in the UK hiring nannies are still middle- and high-income earners. The traditional income disparities among users of in-home childcare are contended by critics and confirmed by data.[5] This type of care work is still undervalued, as the wages and working conditions of (largely) female workers are not increasing (Social Issues Research Centre, 2009).

Class/income stratification in the use and provision of in-home childcare is most apparent in Canada, and the findings based on data collected for this research are consistent with those of other scholars (Arat-Koç, 1989; Bakan and Stasiulis, 1997; Stiell and England, 1997; Brickner and Straehle, 2010). The federal government's limited involvement in funding and regulating ECEC, in addition to culturally embedded ideas about private responsibility for childcare, means that it is common (and acceptable) for families to resort to unlicensed care in the provider's home and child's home. The Child Care Expense Deduction further embeds income inequalities among families (Harder, 2004), in contrast to subsidies designed to redistribute public funds to the most disadvantaged. The limited number of provincially subsidised spaces in licenced services means many low- to middle-income families resort to unregulated, informal care. In Ontario, it is also suggested that licensed home-based childcare is stratified along class lines, where women from lower socioeconomic classes are deemed the solution to addressing the needs of a similar class of children and families (key informant, Canada).

Middle- and high-income families, on the other hand, negotiate their options within a mixed market for childcare. Outside of the formal immigration programme, a number of nanny agencies cater to the needs of wealthy families, with one representative stating they "only take the cream of the crop because [they're] trying to simulate what [their] clients want" (nanny agency, Canada). This suggests that only the wealthiest families can afford high-quality care. Even advocates for high-quality, universal care acknowledged that "if you can afford it then you can have a nanny who does the washing as well as mind the kids; I guess that's what people of wealth do" (key informant, Canada).

In-home childcare has become the default option for many families in professional dual-earner households. Patricia Daenzer explains how the ideal of in-home childcare (especially live-in) has been embedded in Canada for a number of decades:

Historically, middle-class women and affluent families have found the live-in arrangement of the domestic work program convenient to their life styles and needs. The increased advocacy against the subjugation of domestics heightened at a time when many middle-class women were quite dependent upon the program to support their own occupational and status mobility. (Daenzer 1997, p 104)

According to one agency, changes to the Live-In Caregiver Program in 2008 and 2009 drove up the price of employing a nanny by about 32 per cent, which "literally knocked out the middle-class, it's only the upper and upper-middle class that can afford nannies" (nanny agency, Canada). However, other stakeholders interviewed suggested nannies "aren't just a thing for the rich" (nanny agency, Canada), but rather if you have more than two children "it makes sense for families" (provider organisation, Canada). As one representative from a nanny agency observed:

'The problem with the lower-middle class is that with two parent workers finding day care can be extremely expensive if they have two or more children. There's a shortage of day care in Canada … and if you have two or more children it's more economical to have a nanny than to put your children in day care.' (Nanny agency, Canada)

The inadequacy of the ECEC system in Canada (outside Quebec) therefore drives greater demand for migrant live-in caregivers – but this form of care is only a reality for middle- to high-income earners. And, for many families, in-home childcare is only an option because of the availability of low-cost migrant care workers.

Race and migration: a compounded struggle for care workers

Race and ethnicity are often identified as a priority area in ECEC policy reform. In particular, targeted programmes and funding tend to focus on marginalised children and families such as children from minority ethnic backgrounds and recent immigrants. Families' race and ethnicity have also been found to play an important role in shaping their childcare decisions (Vincent et al, 2008). ECEC and care policy less often address race and migration inequalities in relation to the care workforce. However, as introduced earlier, the intersection of policies is significant to gender and racial inequalities for in-home childcare and other domestic care workers. Care and migration policy in Australia stands out from the UK and Canada for its *lack* of support for the recruitment of low-paid, migrant domestic care workers (but see Meagher, 2000 with reference to domestic work more broadly). While anecdotal evidence suggests there is a market for informal in-home childcare (Berg, 2015), the lack of government facilitation mitigates the potential exploitation of low-paid, migrant care workers. This may, however, be set to change. In 2015 the Department of Immigration and Border Protection amended the Working Holiday Visa to allow working holidaymakers to apply for an extension of employment with a single employer from six months to 12 months. This change was called for by families and au pair agencies in the submissions to the government's 2014 Productivity Commission. It was promoted as a way to enhance the flexibility and affordability of childcare options for families with young children (Productivity Commission, 2015). In the UK and Canada, by contrast, migration policy designed to recruit low-paid in-home care and domestic workers is not new. In Canada, in particular, migration policy has for decades reinforced intersecting gender, class/income and race/migration issues that are inherent in the hiring of in-home childcare and other domestic workers. Migration policy alone might not necessarily embed these issues; however, European research finds that cash benefits, tax measures and vouchers contribute to this process (Morel, 2012).

In the UK, migration from Eastern Europe reinforces intersecting gender, class and racial inequalities among migrant care workers. Data from tax surveys in the UK show that the majority of nannies are British-born (Nannytax, 2015); however, these figures are more representative of 'professional' or career nannies, and do not account for the grey market driven by migrant care workers, or au pairs, from Eastern Europe (Williams and Gavanas, 2008; Busch, 2013). Au pairs are generally cheaper to employ than formal nannies because they live-in the household and are supposed to work a maximum of 25 hours per week. However, research confirms that many au pairs work longer hours for no or little pay (Cox 2000, Williams and Gavanas 2008, Busch 2013, 2014). The willingness of migrant care workers to accept low wages and work flexible hours means that families increasingly seek value for money (Williams, 2008). As one stakeholder stated, migrant nannies "will do jobs that … British nannies won't do" (nanny association, UK). The opening up of the EU in 2004 expanded the market for nannies in the UK and, with the removal of the au pair visa in 2008, migrant workers from the EU can work in the UK without a visa. However, this arguably contributes to more informal arrangements and fewer protections than existed under the au pair visa (Busch, 2012).

The influx of migrant workers has created complex class and racial hierarchies among nannies (and those who previously might have identified as au pairs). For example, Busch argues that migrant women from the Eastern European countries that joined the European Union in 2004 are often regarded as better value and preferable to British women from low socioeconomic classes. With the influx of migrant care workers pushing wages down, one stakeholder explained a contrasting dynamic whereby local nannies search for opportunities in other countries:

> 'With the EU opening up … a lot of nannies, British nannies, go abroad [to] Russia [where there is] huge amounts of money. [In] Arabic countries […] they want English as a mother tongue. So that's where the demand for [British nannies] is at the moment.' (nanny association, UK)

The impact of migration policy on race/migration inequality is also significant in Canada, where care and migration policy, and the relative informality of the domestic labour market, facilitate the hiring of migrant nannies (mostly Filipinos). The Live-In Caregiver Program has embedded class divisions among families (discussed earlier) and racial hierarchies between care users and care providers. Racial hierarchies imposed through the Live-In Caregiver Program compound existing gendered and class inequalities associated with care work, particularly in the domestic sphere where (traditionally unpaid) work is undervalued. The Live-In Caregiver Program has been criticised for prioritising the employment of middle-class mothers at the expense of migrant care workers, which deepens class *and* racial dimensions of inequality (Arat-Koç 1989, p 53). As Sedaf Arat-Koc argues (2012), the gender inequalities of 'white' women have become invisible in Canadian discourse; however, the 'problems' of immigrant women have become 'hyper-visible' along racial and class discourses.

Families who can afford a local nanny are considered "lucky", according to one interviewee (nanny agency, Canada). The rules of the (former) Live-In Caregiver Program required care workers to live with the family and, as one participant interviewed explained, "because the caregiver is so tied to the family they often get taken advantage of, doing extra housework and overtime" (nanny agency, Canada). This means that middle- and high-income families are able to purchase childcare and domestic services on the backs of lower-class and migrant women. As Judy Fudge's research argues, the structure of the Live-In Caregiver Program effectively "subsidises the costs to families who resort to live-in domestic workers to meet their childcare needs by ensuring that these workers remain overworked and underpaid" (Fudge 1997, p 140). Middle- and high-income families negotiate care in the private market where there is a 'race to the bottom' for families to find the cheapest option, often provided by migrant care workers. This is argued elsewhere in the context of the US (see Tronto, 2002; Duffy, 2005).

In the early 2000s, there were large numbers of migrants arriving in Canada to take up non-existent jobs, having been charged considerable amounts of money by employment agencies. One stakeholder interviewed suggested that, by 2004, people coming from China[6] were paying $10,000 to get an employer family and by 2006 about half the people "were paying money to get into the country, not to get that job" (nanny agency, Canada). Reforms were implemented in 2008 to eliminate the ability of agencies to charge these fees, and to limit the number of migrants sponsoring family from the Philippines. Supporters of these reforms acknowledge that "there's been so much abuse, but … it's not all agency abuse … it's agencies, employers, caregivers…." This interviewee went on to say that "if people just followed the guidelines", it would have the potential to benefit families who really need in-home childcare, such as nurses and doctors (nanny agency, Canada).

Once Live-In Caregivers have been "released" (nanny agency, Canada) from two years of living with a family,[7] they are eligible to apply for permanent residency, which allows them to seek employment outside the sponsored family's home. However, after gaining permanent residency in Canada, many care workers continue to work in domestic settings (childcare or aged care). One nanny agency interviewed suggested that "because they are so used to involving the housekeeping they don't mind doing that" (nanny agency, Canada).

The hierarchy among nannies is complicated because they are segregated by both their nationality and migration status. Under the former Live-In Caregiver Program rules, once they gained permanent residency rights, they are no longer required to live in the home, yet they still risk experiencing exploitation, particularly because many work for cash and are no longer covered by immigration regulations. One representative from a nanny agency suggested that this may even push down wages further because the employer no longer needs to show their capacity to pay the minimum wage to the caregiver:

'If you [employer] make $300 a week and can still pay
for your nanny, that doesn't matter, that doesn't matter to
anybody. But if you're making $300 a week … through
the Live-in Caregiver Program there's requirements that
need to be met and you wouldn't be able to hire a live-in
caregiver.' (nanny agency, Canada)

Apart from the Live-In Caregiver Program, the lack of government
involvement in ECEC funding and regulation has shaped racial/ethnic
divisions among home-based care workers, particularly in Ontario.
Licensed home-based childcare in Ontario is predominantly delivered
by migrant women living in disadvantaged socioeconomic areas,
providing care to children of a similar background. This pattern was
established in the 1980s when welfare programmes were designed to
encourage women living on social assistance to work as private home
childcarers to eliminate their dependence on welfare payments. As a
long-time researcher in this area stated:

'[It's the] notion that you've got the regulated people living
in really disadvantaged … circumstances … because they're
often new immigrants to the country.… [T]hey're women
whose professional occupations are not recognised here.'
(key informant, Canada)

This anecdote gets to the centre of the issue of devaluation of care,
and the restructuring of care responsibilities from an unpaid family
responsibility towards commodified, low-paid work provided by
vulnerable women. The recruitment of women from overseas to
provide care in the child's home is similar in that it shifts childcare
responsibilities to low-paid, usually migrant, women. In the UK and
Canada, migration facilitates the recruitment of in-home childcare in
the private home with limited oversight and regulation.

In the case of Canada, the Live-In Caregiver Program (and current
Caring for Children Pathway under the Temporary Foreign Worker
Program) formalises in-home childcare as form of employment, but
not as a form of ECEC provision. The lack of regulation for in-home
childcare in Canada also means there is no standard for in-home
childcare set at the national or provincial level. Most in-home care
workers (outside the former Live-In Caregiver Program and current
Temporary Foreign Worker Program) are likely to be employed on low
wages with little employment protection. Migration policy can work
to formalise such arrangements and provide protections in principle for

care workers (Busch, 2013, 2014; Howe and Reilly, 2015). However, there are competing pressures and tensions at play that act to further devalue care work and create new racial inequalities for many migrant in-home childcare workers.

This phenomenon of formalising care in the home to provide care and assist with domestic work is evident in a number of Western countries today. The availability of cash benefits, care vouchers and tax measures provide financial incentives for dual-earner middle-class families to hire in-home childcare to help reconcile their employment and domestic responsibilities. However, it should be emphasised that, with the exception of Australian In Home Care, even generous subsidy systems do not help low-income working families to access in-home childcare. When migration policy allows families to actively recruit care and domestic workers from other countries, the supply of affordable options increases and becomes a reality for middle-class families with time pressures (Morel, 2012). While these policies may help achieve women's (and governments') aspirations for workplace participation, new issues emerge for care workers – many of whom are low-skilled,[8] vulnerable, migrant women. The recruitment of women from less developed to more developed countries to provide care (and other domestic labour) therefore contributes to embedded hierarchies among childcare workers that are shaped by gender, class and race/migration status. As the next chapter discusses, the compounding issues of gender, class and race are often ignored, or sidelined, in policy debate. The ways in which these issues are framed in national and local contexts further embeds structural inequalities to produce distinctive cultures of care.

Notes

[1] While it is acknowledged that there are differences between 'class' and 'income', the two are merged for analytical purposes, although they are often used differently within the context of the discussion. For example, 'class' is used more in the UK than in Australia.

[2] For example, see Arat-Koç (1989), Bakan and Stasiulis (1994), Sipilä et al (2010), Williams (2008, 2012a), Williams and Gavanas (2008) and Busch (2013).

[3] It should be noted that six months into the Pilot, take-up of this programme has been low.

[4] The Nannytax annual survey (2011) found that 22 per cent of families earned between £100,000 and £150000, 19 per cent between £150,000 and £200,000, 10 per cent between £200,000 and £250,000, and seven per cent between £250,000 and £300,000K. Sixteen per cent earned £300,000 or more.

[5] This information is provided from an interview with nanny representative and is based on data from 2011 Nannytax survey (www.nannytax.co.uk/wages-survey).

[6]   Many migrants (mostly Filipino) entering Canada as part of the Live-In Caregiver Program (LCP) spend a year (or more) in China or other Asian countries. They work for families in these countries to attain the minimum experience (one year) or training (six months) to make them eligible for the LCP. Agencies in China and Hong Kong work closely with agencies in Canada to recruit migrants for the LCP (nanny agencies, Canada).

[7]   Under the Caring for Children Pathway under the Temporary Foreign Worker Program, migrant care workers are no longer required to live in the home of their employer, but are still required to work as a home childcarer for two years.

[8]   Or their qualifications are not recognised in their new country.

SIX

Cultures of in-home childcare

The provision of in-home childcare has shifted in recent decades. It has shifted as a result of welfare state restructuring, which is attributed to both changes in policy mechanisms and ideas about the objectives of social policy. The policy structures and discourses that shape in-home childcare differ across countries, and also over time, to create distinct cultures of in-home childcare. As with other countries around the world, in Australia, the UK and Canada, these cultures of care are reflective of ideas about the most appropriate forms of care for young children. These include both who should provide care, and how it should be provided.

This chapter brings together findings from earlier chapters to understand the dynamic of these distinct care cultures. To do so, it considers the embedded norms and assumptions about the objectives of, and responsibility for, early childhood education and care (ECEC), and the role of migration policy in facilitating childcare in the home. The distinctive cultures of care are linked to the histories of childcare policy (Chapter Two), policy systems and practices (Chapter Three), rhetoric and rationales for different forms of ECEC (Chapter Four), and the reinforcement of inequalities in the provision of in-home childcare (Chapter Five). In each of the study countries, the 'problem' of in-home childcare is represented in different ways in policy debate and discourse, and this analysis is informed by both publicly available policy documents and statements as well as interviews conducted with key stakeholders in each county. Policy debates revolve primarily around the three inequalities explored in the previous chapter: gender, class/income and race/migration. Consistent with recent contributions to the field of gender, ideas and inequality (Béland, 2009; Orloff and Palier, 2009), this chapter draws on policy debates about inequality in order to identify discourses that reflect distinct cultural ideas about the provision of in-home childcare.

First, the chapter discusses the concept of 'care culture', how it has been used in other cross-national research, and its potential to explain differences in care policies and practices. There is a need to go beyond traditional comparative welfare state theories to understand variation in in-home childcare in the study countries. Most important, the concept of 'care culture' focuses on cultural dimensions of the welfare state, although it does not ignore the importance of structural factors shaping outcomes, including gender and class inequalities produced through different care regimes (Kremer, 2007; Williams, 2010b). The second part of the chapter draws on discourses from secondary sources and interviews with key stakeholders in the study countries to identify how the prominent debates about in-home childcare in each country are reflective of embedded assumptions about gender, class/income and race/migration. The concept of care culture helps to explain these assumptions, and the intersection between care and migration policy in which these assumptions are embedded.

Concept of care culture

Welfare regime theory developed in the 1990s as a way to explain and classify the generosity and design of spending on social policy. As introduced in Chapter One, classifications of welfare states were based on the relationship between work and social protection policies. Early classifications offered a typology to better understand the extent to which labour was commodified across welfare states. Gender scholars have critiqued early welfare state classifications because, first and foremost, Esping-Anderson's (1990) typology ignored unpaid work and gendered divisions in the home. In response, gender scholars developed new classifications and typologies to account for the place of gender and care.[1] These classifications all tend to group Australia, the UK and Canada together, by highlighting the shared liberal tendencies and reliance on the market for delivering services, including childcare. Julia O'Connor and colleagues (1999) suggested that 'discussion of the liberal type has given little attention to those aspects of liberal ideology which refer to gender and the relation between state and family' (O'Connor et al, 1999, p 43). These authors identified different gender logics within liberal welfare countries, with governments' policies supporting gender neutrality in Australia, gender difference in the UK and gender sameness in Canada. While these logics are not directly transferable to the case of in-home childcare, they do illustrate the distinctive pathways of liberal countries' work and care policies.

The concept of 'welfare culture' is increasingly used as a way to capture the complex and dynamic interaction between policy and norms, or attitudes (Van Oorschot et al, 2008), that are central to recent care typologies (Pfau-Effinger, 2005b; Kremer, 2007). The care regime typologies developed by Bettio and Plantenga (2004), Williams and Gavanas (2008), Mahon et al (2012) and others embrace the broad scope of policies and practices, norms and discourses. As introduced earlier, Williams and Gavanas define care culture as:

> ... dominant national and local cultural discourse on what constitutes appropriate child care, such as surrogate mothers, mothers working and caring part-time; international help; shared parental care, or professional care. (2008, p 16)

'Care culture' emphasises the importance of identifying cultural norms in caring roles constituted through gender, class, place and ethnicity (Duncan et al, 2004; Duncan, 2005; Williams, 2010b). Thus, the concept of care culture cannot be separated from a set of assumptions about embedded inequalities that are reflected in countries' social policies.

Previous chapters in this book have explored policy histories, structures, discourses and inequalities through the lens of in-home childcare. Through this analysis, it has become evident that in-home childcare is situated at the crossroads of different policy domains (informal/formal, public/private, regulated/unregulated) and at the intersection of policy areas (childcare and migration). In some policy contexts, the precarious position in which in-home childcare sits creates new and intersecting inequalities for families and care workers. But the inequalities in the three study countries have generated different policy debates. These different responses and debates are reflective of distinct care cultures.

Inequalities and policy debates

In-home childcare is central to ECEC debates about promoting mothers' employment and enhancing children's education and care. Debates about in-home childcare also extend to migration policy and employment regulations relating to the hiring of domestic workers. In Australia, the UK and Canada, debates about in-home childcare are concentrated in different policy domains. The separation of policy domains, into silos, can lead policy stakeholders to focus on issues experienced by one group of stakeholders at the expense of others. In each of the study countries, the problem is represented in different ways and arguably reflects different understandings of inequalities experienced by mothers, children and care workers, which are conceptualised in different ways in relation to gender, income/class and race/migration. The discourses portrayed in policy documents (historical and contemporary) and articulated by stakeholders help to explain why issues of gender, class/income and race/migration are manifested differently in each of these countries.

Care and migration policies shape the types of childcare accessible to children across different socioeconomic groups, and they also shape and create gendered, class and racial inequalities among parents and the care workforce. As discussed in Chapter Five, hierarchies among in-home childcare workers that exist across class and racial divides are superimposed on an already undervalued feminised workforce. However, the nature of these inequalities and hierarchies within the in-home childcare workforce differ across countries as a result of ECEC and migration policy. Policymakers, advocacy groups and the broader public have responded to these inequalities and hierarchal structures in various ways. These different responses and debates are reflective of distinct cultural acceptances of – and challenges to – these inequalities, which are embedded in societal perceptions about the division of responsibility for childcare across gender, class and racial lines.

Australia

Historically, Australia has directed funding for childcare to a range of regulated ECEC services. During the 1970s and 1980s, these were largely community-run centres and council- or government-supported family day care schemes. In the 1990s, the sector experienced a dramatic shift to private (and commercial) services. However, the policy design has, until recently, restricted government involvement in funding unregulated childcare. Although it has unravelled under recent reforms,[2] there has been a culture of equity in Australia that sets it apart from the UK and Canada. This was evident in the availability of subsidies for all children using approved ECEC services, regardless of their parents' workforce participation.

More recently, debate about in-home childcare has focused on women's participation in the workforce, promoted under the principle of equal opportunity for women in the workplace. A content analysis of public responses (published in the media) to the proposal to extend subsidies to nannies identified four main themes: the role of women; middle-class welfare; the role of nannies; and the pressures of modern living (Garvis and Pendergast, 2013). These authors illustrate that the issues and debates surrounding nannies and in-home childcare in Australia centre on the need for flexible childcare associated with long and non-standard working hours; and on class-based perceptions about who should receive government support for nannies, and childcare more broadly.

As discussed in previous chapters, the In Home Care programme, established in 2000, was intended to assist families who faced barriers to accessing mainstream services. Recent debate about the expansion of the In Home Care programme has centred on the need for increased numbers of spaces of flexible childcare. For example, Susan Ley, former Assistant Minister for Education in the Coalition government states that the current government-supported in-home care is a niche product, mainly for disadvantaged families: 'What I want to see is an assessment (of) whether it should, or can, be expanded to complement mainstream childcare options for modern working parents (cited in Uren, 2013).

The group of 'modern working parents' is not defined, but the implication is that the current programme is inadequate because it is limited to disadvantaged families. There are indeed many groups of women, families and businesses that have for over a decade promoted the subsidisation of nannies, either through tax breaks or through the extension of the childcare subsidy system (see Standing Committee on Family and Human Services, 2006).

Debates about nannies in Australia have centred around two main themes: first, equity in access to subsidies (or other financial assistance) for families who use nannies or other in-home childcare; and, second, the appropriate qualifications and standards for nannies. A representative from an established nanny agency explained the embedded perception about class-based inequality in Australia:

> 'When I first started in the late 1990s it was all the families that were very high income, higher socioeconomic groups, and that's not necessarily the case any more. And the government's terrified of being seen to support wealthy families.' (nanny agency, Australia)

This sentiment has been at the centre of opposition to extend subsidies for families using nannies; however, the idea or principle of 'equity' has been used in contradictory ways in Australian discourse. Principles of equality and equity are used to promote the extension of funding for nannies, but, at the same time, these principles are used in opposition to the nanny agenda. Proposals for reform (put forward in the 2005 and 2009 Senate inquiries and in submissions to the 2014 Productivity Commission in 2013-14) argue that families should receive equal levels of financial support for centre-based and in-home childcare. But there are also groups of commentators who disagree, under the argument that public support for nannies is regressive and jeopardises the quality of ECEC provision for children (Adamson et al, forthcoming). The contentious use of equality and equity are evident in responses to the Productivity Commission's inquiry into childcare and early childhood learning and the recently introduced Nanny Pilot programme, which commenced in 2016. Groups promoting the extension of funding for nannies claim that the subsidy system should allow families (primarily mothers) equitable access to subsidies for different types of ECEC. That is, they believe that a family choosing to use a nanny should be eligible for the equal levels of funding as users of long day care and family day care (Jha, 2014). Proponents of government-subsidised in-home childcare suggest that the lack of flexible options discourages women from re-entering the labour force when their children are young and therefore, they argue, has a negative impact on women's employment opportunities and gender equality in the workplace (Standing Committee on Family and Human Services, 2006; Education Employment and Workplace Relations References Committee, 2009; Australian Women Chamber of Commerce and Industry, 2013). Occupational groups working non-standard hours and shifts, such as police officers and nurses, are often identified as the target group, but it should be noted that these groups are covered (in principle) under the current approved In Home Care scheme.

The promotion of government support for families using nannies has been explicitly linked to gender equality in relation to mothers' workforce participation (Australian Women Chamber of Commerce and Industry, 2013; Jha 2014). This agenda prioritises mothers' economic productivity, as discussed in Chapter Five. In 2013, prior to the announcement of the Nanny Pilot, the President of the Australian Nanny Association stated that assistance should be extended to users of in-home child because the 'lack of childcare options is excluding a large group of people from the workforce and that is affecting the economy and productivity' (cited in Militec and Browne, 2013). The large group of people affected are those who, presumably, cannot access mainstream services, either because childcare services are not open, there are no places available, or the service is not affordable for the family.

Submissions to the Productivity Commission on childcare and early childhood learning that supported the extension of the Child Care Rebate to in-home childcare tend to prioritise gender equality in relation to mothers' employment over care workers' or children's needs. However, it must be noted that many key stakeholder groups in the nanny and in-home childcare sector also support the increase in standards and qualifications for care workers (Australian Nanny

Association, 2014, 2015; National In-Home Childcare Association, 2014).

Gender equality in the workforce and equity in access to subsidies have therefore been central to support for public funding for nannies. At the same time, equity is central to claims against the expansion of subsidies for families using nannies, which rests on claims about class/income inequalities. That is, it is argued that providing subsidies to families using nannies will redistribute more public funding to wealthy families, which should be directed to the most disadvantaged families. Those who oppose government support for nannies argue that, under the current system, the extension of subsidies to all families using nannies would favour middle-class families (E. Cox, 2011). For example, one stakeholder interviewed opposed subsidies for nannies, stating that "in practical terms what it means is people on high income who currently pay nannies will continue to be able to pay nannies ... so really what that's going to do it it's just more stratification" (provider organisation, Australia). And, as the former Labour party's Minister for Early Education, Kate Ellis, believed:

> Families should be free to choose whatever care works for their family, including nannies ... [b]ut the current debate is around if taxpayers should be subsidising an unregulated form of care that is the most expensive form of child care and outside of the reach of a vast majority of Australian families. (Cited in Uren, 2013)

While it is not explicit, the upper- and middle-class families are the exception to the 'vast majority of Australian families'.

As in the UK, there was also opposition from those stakeholders interviewed who had concerns that the extension of subsidies to unregulated in-home childcare could have implications for the quality of care provided to children and the working conditions and wages of care workers. This is consistent with the principle that public funds should be directed to regulated services with qualified educators, and should not be prohibitive to families at the lower end of the income scale.

Until the announcement of the Nanny Pilot in May 2015, nannies remained in the private and unregulated sector with limited subsidisation.[3] More recent resistance and opposition to the introduction of the Nanny Pilot has been fuelled by peak bodies, providers, families and the public. There is widespread agreement that nannies without qualifications (as proposed under the Nanny Pilot) should not fall into the same category of service provision as mainstream services, namely long day care and family day care, which require educators to hold a minimum Certificate III qualification. There is a strong tendency towards ensuring that public funds support professional and regulated ECEC services, opposed to unregulated and informal arrangements. This, in combination with Australia's 'egalitarian principles' (McNicholas, 2014), has perhaps closed off opportunities for a care culture that supports the recruitment of migrant care workers.

Policy debate about in-home childcare has until recently remained squarely in the ECEC domain. However, anecdotal evidence suggests that au pairs are increasingly used and are sought after to fill the gap in flexible and affordable childcare in Australia. The issue of migration also infiltrated childcare policy debates in submissions to the 2014 Productivity Commission inquiry into childcare and early childhood learning. Submissions to the Productivity Commission included a range of recommendations, from minimal registration requirements (for example, see Indonesia Institute, 2014) to standards consistent with the National Quality Framework (for example, see Australian Nanny Association, 2014; Dial-An-Angel, 2014; National In-Home Childcare Association, 2014). The Commission recommended an extension of the Working Holiday Visa to allow nannies to work with a family for 12 months, rather than the previous six-month limit. The Department of Immigration and Border Protection introduced this change in July 2015. Resistance has come from ECEC sector stakeholders and advocates for workers' rights who are concerned about the lack of safeguards for children, and the lack of employment standards and protections for au pairs, respectively. The proposition that government should support informal and unregulated childcare through migration has, until recently, not been given serious consideration in Australia. But the recent extension of the Working Holiday Maker visa for those working as au pairs has shifted Australian debates about the restructuring of care responsibilities closer to the UK and Canada.

United Kingdom

Debate in the UK regarding government involvement in the funding and regulation of nannies and in-home childcare surfaced earlier than in Australia, includes a broader advocacy base and focuses on different policy areas. Although advocates in the 1980s and early 1990s lobbied for increased regulation covering nannies, the issue did not gain much attention in public debate until New Labour expanded its commitment to ECEC more broadly in the late 1990s. For the most part, the principle of gender equality to enhance mothers' workforce participation, which has predominated Australian debate, has been in the background in UK policy discussions. Overall, there has been less resistance from the public and key stakeholders to exclude nannies from the suite of funded ECEC options in the UK. Instead, debate has focused on standards and regulations covering nannies. There was consensus among stakeholders interviewed that having a nanny has increased among middle-income families in the past decade and, even for those who cannot afford to have a nanny, it is identified as an ideal arrangement for many British families.[4]

Since New Labour increased government involvement in ECEC, representatives of the nanny sector have focused their advocacy efforts on the position of nannies within the childcare workforce. In particular, unions and groups training and representing nannies have sought equality for nannies in the early years sector. In recent years, efforts to professionalise the workforce have been complicated by increases in the numbers of migrant in-home childcare workers. New dynamics in the nanny and au pair workforce have ignited differential gendered- and race-based claims for equality.

As in Australia, mothers' opportunity to participate in the labour market equal to men has driven recent debates about ECEC funding structures in the UK. While government subsidisation of preschool has traditionally supported 'education', childcare vouchers and tax credits for nurseries, childminders and, since 2004, those working in registered home childcare (nannies) are designed to facilitate workforce participation among mothers. What is distinct about the debate in the UK, particularly in comparison with Australia, is the focus on the regulation of nannies as a means to improve their status, as opposed to the availability or generosity of subsidies for families using nannies and in-home childcare. As outlined in Chapter Three, the current registration for nannies is voluntary and imposes minimal requirements – police clearance, a first-aid qualification and common core skills.[5]

The government's 'hands-off' approach to regulating nannies is explained through class-based understandings of different types of care. It is suggested that the New Labour government "ignored" the issue of nannies because of the perception that they are only for the wealthy, and therefore not a priority for a 'socialist' government (key informant, UK). For example, even a staunch supporter of nannies and market-based care stated that "one of the frustrations in the UK … [is] the government doesn't like nannies, they think they're for middle-class people, so it's kind of like it looks after itself" (nanny agency, UK). Instead, government prioritises funding and regulation to "other forms of care not used by the most well-off" (key informant, UK), such as childminders and nurseries. The lack of regulation has attracted attention from across the early years and nanny sector.

There is support from nanny providers, early childhood workers and teacher unions, nanny agencies, and organisations representing nannies in the UK to extend regulations to nannies so that "the same rules should apply to everyone" (key informant, UK). In the UK, the emphasis is on the need for adequate regulation so that service providers – in this case nannies – are on a level playing field. Such regulation would benefit the nannies as well as the children receiving care. There was unequivocal support from the stakeholders interviewed in the UK that there should be basic protection for children in all ECEC settings, regardless of whether families receive financial assistance. Critique from the popular online source, NurseryWorld, suggests that the 'curious "hands-off" attitude towards nanny employment as a private matter for parents is not necessarily doing nannies, let alone children, any favours' (NurseryWorld, 2009). This differs from Australia, where the focus of the debate has centred on the principle that the users (parents) should be on a level playing field and have access to the same level of public funding for different service types – centre-based or home-based.

Stakeholders in the nanny sector have argued that current regulation is insufficient to protect the safety of children. The campaign Regulation Matters, initiated in 2012 by a group of organisations including nanny agencies, professional and training organisations, and a trade union, aims to make the registration of nannies with Ofsted compulsory. The campaign is 'a national movement calling for the registration of all childcarers in the UK in order to safeguard children, improve childcare standards and create consistency in the childcare industry' (Regulation Matters, 2013). A member of the campaign and long-time advocate for the improvement of standards to protect workers and provide safeguards for children and families argues:

> They [workers in nurseries and childminders] have to be required to work to a specific standard and […] they are subject to disciplinary procedures if they don't come up to those standards. Why are we saying that children cared for in their own home don't deserve the same protection? Don't they deserve the same high quality of care being provided? Why is that okay? (peak organisation, UK)

Calls for increased regulation in the UK can be attributed to the fact that the existing subsidy system – namely the childcare element of the Working Tax Credit – is targeted towards relatively low-income families, which reduces the class-based debate for users evident in Australia. But it is also arguably due to class-based debates surrounding the increase in the number of middle-income families hiring nannies that do not necessarily receive any public subsidies or assistance through childcare vouchers. Trends suggest that middle-income, dual-earner families increasingly hire nannies (and au pairs) and, stakeholders from across the early childhood sector believe there should be greater public responsibility to ensure the quality of this type of care. There is pressure to improve regulation because the traditional notion of nannies 'only being for the rich' is not the reality any more, as increasing numbers of dual-earner, middle-class families need the flexibility that in-home childcare provides. Having a nanny is, according to many nanny agencies and other stakeholders, becoming more acceptable and desirable across income groups and was described as an 'ideal' for families. One representative from a nanny agency in Australia compared her experience after moving from England, suggesting that in the UK the "traditional" nanny is "engrained in society" as quality care (nanny agency, Australia). This was especially the case for infants and young toddlers. Many stakeholders interviewed confirmed the suggestion that nannies were the 'ideal' in the UK. For example, a researcher on childcare use and patterns stated: "For middle-class parents, home-based childcare from a nanny or a relative is the ideal for babies, then moving on to nurseries when a child is two or three" (key informant, UK).

The announcement of changes to the childcare subsidy system, expected in 2017, has prompted speculation about the impact on families using nannies, as well as nannies themselves. Employer organisations welcomed the 2013 announcement of the Tax-Free Childcare scheme (Gaunt, 2013; Morton, 2013), but there has also been interest in the possible impact on the registration of nannies. Commentary from the Voice Union (representing nannies) suggests that:

> Although the tax-free childcare scheme still requires nannies and home childcarers to be part of the voluntary register, it will be interesting to see if this leads to an increase in the number of nannies seeking voluntary registration.... Our previous research indicates that nannies would welcome formal registration as part of the validation of their profession. (Cited in Morton, 2014)

The registration of in-home childcare is presented as a necessary step to improve the status of nannies and to recognise the value of their caring role in line with other early years workers. Calls for increased regulation of the nanny sector come from individuals and groups concerned about the quality of care for children as well as the employment conditions of the nanny. In the latter case, there are separate and distinct calls from, on the one hand, organisations advocating for greater recognition of local nannies and, on the other, from organisations representing migrant nannies and domestic workers. Lobbying for the recognition of in-home childcare workers in this way links debates about in-home childcare to workforce standards, and also fosters issues about hierarchies within the nanny workforce.

In the UK, debates about employment standards and the working conditions of the in-home childcare workforce have also been shaped by recent changes to migration policy. There has been an increase in the number of migrant domestic workers from Eastern Europe since the 1990s, which includes those caring for children, namely nannies and au pairs (Williams and Gavanas, 2008; Busch, 2012). While the majority of nannies are British, a large proportion (approximately 15 per cent) are from Eastern European countries (Búriková and Miller, 2010). Migration from the EU in 2004 increased the number of people available for au pair placements without visas and the later abolition of the au pair visa in 2008 meant that anyone providing care for children in private homes could call themselves an au pair (Cox, 2012; Busch, 2013). For workers with full employment rights (not on a visa), there was no clear distinction between nannies, au pairs and other migrant domestic workers. It is common for nanny agencies to distinguish between trained 'nannies' and more informal au pairs, but there is an increasingly blurred line between the two (Busch, 2012). Despite overlap in the tasks and responsibilities of nannies and au pairs, au pairs are generally paid less and therefore accessible to middle-class families.

The increasing number of migrants entering the UK and willing to accept lower wages has raised concern within the nanny sector. These concerns about migrant domestic care workers are framed in various ways. Some groups worry that nannies are not being protected, and therefore "may be used and abused as housekeepers and nannies" (peak organisation, UK). However, an opposite concern expressed by some nanny associations relates to the importance of distinguishing professionally trained nannies from informal migrant care workers. For example, one stakeholder explained that Eastern Europeans enter the UK as au pairs, and as soon as they see the wages the local nannies are on they call themselves nannies, "but they'll accept less than the experienced nanny, so it brings the wages down" (nanny association, UK). This is perceived as a problem because wages for professional, trained nannies are pushed down as families seek value for money, sometimes employing unskilled[6] au pairs willing to do the housework in addition to caring for children (nanny associations, UK). This combination of migrant vulnerabilities, racialised inequalities and misrecognition with exploitation and poor working conditions among in-home childcare workers has been identified in scholarly research and advocacy work in the UK (Cox, 2006b; Williams, 2008; Busch, 2013), particularly in relation to changing EU migration patterns.

Overall, arguments for improving the regulation of nannies stem from perceptions about class and race that are central to changes in patterns of service use, particularly the rise in demand from middle-income (opposed to only wealthy) families for nannies. Debates about in-home childcare therefore respond to traditional class-based understandings of nannies to lobby for improved regulation of the nanny workforce in line with the broader early years sector. At the same time, migration policy and the opening up of the EU creates debates about the domestic care workforce that draw on hierarchies among different types of in-home childcare workers. These point to intersecting issues of gender, class and race/migration that are central to the culture of in-home childcare in Canada.

Canada

In-home childcare is an accepted and embedded form of childcare for many Canadian families. In Canada, the term 'nannies' is used interchangeably with 'migrant caregivers' to refer to migrants who enter under the (former) Live-In Caregiver Program. Debate about the role and position of in-home childcare remains tied to migration policy, and sits largely separate to policy debate in the ECEC domain. The Live-In Caregiver Program has been viewed as a vehicle to support (mostly middle- to high-income) mothers' workforce participation. For dual-earner professional families in Canada, nannies and other forms of private in-home childcare are viewed as an acceptable, and even necessary, form of childcare. The absence of federal government involvement in childcare and resulting reliance on private care dominates discussions about the 'care culture' in Canada. One of the study interviewees, a long-time researcher and advocate for universal ECEC, tried to explain the attitude, by stating that "people in Canada accept that it's a private responsibility", and so "it's not a matter of waiting until there's a groundswell ... it's somehow related to what they see actually reflected" (key informant, Canada).

Many nanny agencies and service providers echoed this sentiment. Service providers and other stakeholders indicated that recent federal governments have "not even wanted to touch childcare" (service provider, Canada), which has meant that childcare is really seen as a business, as a "private affair" between parents and a service (service provider, Canada). Furthermore, one nanny agency explained the reliance on private childcare, specifically the Live-In Caregiver Program, by suggesting that the "shortage in Canada of quality day care" means that many families have "no other options" (nanny agency, Canada). This reliance on private nannies was reiterated in economic terms by another agency:

> 'There's a shortage of day care in Canada and the government hasn't really addressed that. So there's not a lot of support and if you have two or more children it's more economical to have a nanny than to put your children in day care.' (nanny agency, Canada)

The higher prevalence of full-time maternal employment in Canada, compared with Australia and the UK (OECD, 2005, p 73; Rammohan and Whelan, 2007; Roeters and Craig, 2014), also arguably contributes to higher demand for nannies. In-home childcare is likely more desirable for families with both parents (or a sole parent) working full-time, compared with the second (or sole) earner working part-time or not participating in the labour market. These work practices and cultural discourses about work and care help to explain the greater reliance and acceptance of in-home childcare in Canada. Discourses across the migration and ECEC domains are reflective of a cultural acceptance of private childcare provision, and the inequalities produced by the policies that support such forms of childcare.

As discussed in the previous chapter, the intersection of these policy domains has embedded inequalities, especially for care workers. Racialised assumptions about the worth of migrants' caring roles are entrenched through gendered assumptions about 'women's work'. While the entry of more women into the workforce enables privileged couples to pay for caregiving work, it does 'nothing to raise the social status of traditionally female occupations, especially caregiving' (Brickner and Straehle, 2010). Arat-Koç summarises this cultural acceptance when stating 'there is no longer a strong-enough and effective-enough political voice, from feminism or immigrant organisations to challenge the unacceptability of these conditions and to demand change' (Arat-Koç 2012, p 8). This rings true for both changes to migration policy and to ECEC policy.

Support for the Live-In Caregiver Program specifically comes largely from nanny agencies. The programme was justified through its flexibility and affordability for families with more than one child under school age. Supporters of the programme also make claims that the scheme offers immigrant women a pathway to better employment and citizenship in Canada. For example, the unequal relationship between families and caregivers reflects the dominant culture conveyed by nanny agencies, which supports the continuation of the Live-In Caregiver Program: "These girls [are given] an opportunity to come to Canada to work so they should be making some sort of sacrifices" (nanny agency, Canada). Furthermore, this interviewee suggested that:

> 'Unless they're in an abusive situation [they] should stay there for one year, because that's why [they] came to Canada ... why did [they] come to Canada? To be a caregiver. So it's not like they're changing from a secretary to a nanny.' (nanny agency, Canada)

Unregulated in-home childcare is accepted not only by families in Canada, but also by the broader in-home childcare sector, and even some ECEC sector representatives. One nanny agency explained: "[but] a nanny isn't like a registered nurse, like they can't pull the license, she's just a woman who offers childcare ... even if they have their ECE qualification they don't have a nanny card that can be taken away" (nanny agency, Canada). This interviewee considered the lack of regulation of the nanny industry, and ECEC more broadly, to be 'cultural' and 'habit-based', by suggesting that families have an attitude of 'it must be fine to leave my child with that woman because other people left their child with their women'. She went on to say that there might be too much trust and reflected that "perhaps that's where a nanny certification would be helpful to show a piece of paper" (nanny agency, Canada). When asked about the potential for the government to introduce regulation for nannies, one long-time advocate and researcher responded, "They don't even think about it" (key informant, Canada).

Thus, debate about funding and regulation of in-home childcare as a form of ECEC is largely off the radar. In-home childcare was viewed by interviewees as an option only for the privileged, and was not regarded as a priority for ECEC reform. For ECEC and government representatives, it was a reality for the wealthy, and varied across local areas. For example, one local government representative commented on the 'nanny culture in Toronto', stating:

> 'There are pockets in the city, where you go to a playground in the middle of the day … and you just see a sea of nannies. But these are people who … live in the home, with the family…. It's an option for people who can afford it.' (Government representative, Canada)

There was a reluctance by ECEC service providers and organisations to talk about the Live-In Caregiver Program because it was viewed outside the scope of ECEC policy. For example, when a provider of regulated home-based childcare was asked about the training and regulations they thought were appropriate for nannies, the response was that "no one seems to be talking about it in our circles" (service provider, Canada). This differed from the UK, for example, where ECEC providers believed that it was important to set minimum standards of training and regulation for all caregivers looking after children. Compared with the UK and Australia, there is little support in Canada to improve the regulatory oversight of in-home childcare and to recognise it as part of the formal ECEC sector.

Opposition to in-home childcare in Canada is concentrated in the migration policy domain, which rests on issues of gender, class and race for the migrant care workers providing the care. Compared with Australia and the UK, there is greater complacency toward the trade-off between gender, class, and racial inequalities embedded in government policy and social attitudes since the 1970s. Patricia Daenzer, for example, contends that when the Live-In Caregiver Program was introduced in 1992 (replacing the Foreign Domestic Movement) class inequalities were embedded (and accepted) as part of the programme:

> Eliminating the live-in requirement would have been an affront to the privilege of middle-class women. Thus, the 1992 policy was also the state's public affirmation of the preservation of class privileges. (Daenzer 1997, p 104)

Despite recognition that the Live-In Caregiver Program does not meet the needs of low-income families, there is little advocacy for reforming in-home childcare or broader ECEC settings to assist these families. This is in contrast to the UK and Australia where in-home childcare advocates and ECEC stakeholders believe ECEC policy should be designed to help families access in-home childcare and to ensure the safety and wellbeing of children using this type of care. The difference in attitude in Canada is arguably because in-home childcare is viewed as a private matter within the of migration and labour policy domains, outside the realm of ECEC debate.

Cultures of inequality?

An examination of the discourses and debates surrounding in-home childcare point to distinct attitudes about the division of responsibility for paying for, providing and regulating in-home childcare, and ECEC more broadly. These are reflected in debates about equity and equality for mothers, parents, care workers and, to a lesser extent, children. The debates play out differently in each study country, with varying attention to the inequalities experienced by working mothers, children and care workers. As indicated earlier in this chapter, these issues are situated within different historical and political contexts that shape, and are shaped by, individual, local and national assumptions about who should provide care and how care should be provided. When mothers are encouraged to participate in the workforce, it is assumed there is a non-parental alternative for childcare.

Governments support (or do not support) different forms of care through ECEC funding and regulation, migration policy and rules and regulations about the hiring of care workers in different settings. The previous chapter illustrated how care and migration policies create new gender and class inequalities in relation to families accessing in-home childcare, and also create hierarchies among in-home childcare workers across racial/migration lines, within an already gendered workforce.

Debates about in-home childcare cut across the ECEC and migration policy spheres and, to different extents in each country, actors lobby to improve options and the quality of care for children and families and also to improve the wages and conditions of care workers. Policy debates about in-home childcare are centred on different understandings of issues of gender, class/income and race/migration. The public discourses and advocacy claims made in response to these inequalities reveal different attitudes toward gender, class/income and race/migration. The current policy debates presented here reflect the establishment of institutional structures over time, in combination with reactions to recent policy initiatives that have shifted responsibility for ECEC and in-home childcare into new domains. These shifts have reproduced and sometimes compounded existing inequalities among families and care workers.

In Australia, in-home childcare is neither an embedded ideal nor a default alternative for families, as it is in the UK and Canada, respectively. Unlike the UK and Canada, Australia has no formal migration policy to facilitate the use of in-home childcare. The Working Holiday Visa allows au pairs to work for families for 12 months (extended from six months in 2015), but such care is regarded as complementary (rather than an alternative) to formal ECEC, and largely as an experience for au pairs, not a service for families (nanny agency, Australia). Australia's policy towards in-home childcare currently exists as a targeted ECEC programme, which stands out from Canada and the UK – and many other countries internationally – as it assists families who would otherwise face financial barriers to accessing flexible in-home childcare. The formal In Home Care scheme addresses many of the traditional class divisions that exclude access to in-home childcare. Evaluations have shown there is room for improvement (RPR Consulting, 2005), but the principle of providing targeted support for in-home childcare should not be abandoned. However, this is changing with the Nanny Pilot between 2016 and 2018. The outcomes and sector responses to the Nanny Pilot are unknown at the time of writing. While there has been general opposition from the ECEC sector, the Government will assess whether the programme is meeting its objective – to increase mothers' workforce participation – following an evaluation at the completion of the programme. The culture of part-time maternal employment in Australia may be just that – a culture that will not change through the introduction of new policies.

While there is undoubtedly an informal 'grey market' for in-home childcare arrangements, unregulated care in the child's home is not supported by government through funding or migration schemes. Recent debate about the extension of public subsidies to users of in-home childcare raises new issues about gender and class and potentially race, if new migration schemes for care workers are to be introduced. In particular, debate about the extension of subsidies to families using nannies has been framed around the principles of individual choice of ECEC type, and gender equality for mothers in the paid workforce. As in the UK and Canada, these discourses about 'choice' align with liberal ideas about individualism and a market-based model for ECEC in Australia. However, in contrast to the UK and Canada, policymakers and public attitudes in Australia have thus far resisted calls for care and migration policy that prioritise the demands of professional middle-class mothers over the needs of low-income families and workers in the ECEC sector. Current policy discourse and developments in migration debate suggest that Australia may be on the verge of reform in this area.

In-home childcare policy in the UK reproduces a tiered system of ECEC for families and care workers. The perception of nannies in the UK is embedded in ideas of domestic service and class-based divisions between employers and employees. Historically, it was a status symbol for the wealthiest families to have governesses and trained nannies to care for their children – not a necessity driven by mothers' participation in paid work. As one stakeholder commented, there "is still this myth ... that only the well-to-do and the rich and famous have nannies ... so therefore, it's not something a government is ever going to be sympathetic towards" (nanny association, UK). However, since the 1980s and 1990s, there has been an increase in the number of nannies and other providers of in-home childcare (especially au pairs) as mothers with young children have entered the workforce, with few ECEC options for families, except for the most disadvantaged. The in-home childcare sector – that was previously "left well alone" (key informant, UK) in the private sector – figured in public debates about government's role and responsibility in the lives of families and care workers. Since more middle-income families are using this form of care, it is argued, the government should take greater responsibility for ensuring basic quality for children and working conditions for care workers, especially when mothers with young children are being encouraged to return to the workforce to contribute to the economy.

Class-based divisions between public and private responsibility for care underpin the ideal of the British nanny. As ECEC and migration policy shifted through the 1990s and 2000s, the ideal of in-home childcare arguably remained, but now rests in new racialised assumptions about care responsibilities. Cultural preference for in-home childcare in combination with tax credits and vouchers for in-home childcare validates this form of care and figures show that, while users are still concentrated in the upper class, families are increasingly interested in a part-time nanny or a nannyshare. Nannies have become a more popular option (relative to centre-based care) for some middle-class families, with many stakeholders identifying nannies as 'the ideal'. The opening up of the EU expands the ECEC options for families seeking the ideal of flexible and affordable in-home childcare, but also poses new challenges as responsibility for the regulation of the quality of care for children and the protection of care workers sits across the private and public domains.

In Canada, financial assistance from the federal government supports any form of informal or formal, regulated or unregulated, care. The class-based divisions associated with users of in-home childcare are culturally accepted. This acceptance is shaped by neoliberal and neo-conservative views about the care of young children, and embedded policies and practices for hiring migrant care workers. Patricia Daenzer argues that these intersecting inequalities have been pushed away as 'cultural' issues, rather than being addressed as underlying structural issues affecting gender inequalities among all women (Daenzer, 1997). The Child Care Expense Deduction was introduced to overcome gender inequalities associated with women's return to work after having children, and allowed mothers to return to well-paid jobs while women from minority ethnic groups looked after their children. The principles underpinning the introduction of the Live-In Caregiver Program in 1981 (then the Foreign Domestic Movement) are embedded in the broader public's attitudes about the benefits for middle-class working families and the assumptions that the Live-In Caregiver Program offers migrant women opportunities that are better than those in their home country. These racialised hierarchies underpin assumptions about the value of care work, which in combination with the lack of public investment in ECEC, contributes to a care culture that promotes the hiring of in-home childcare as a 'win-win' situation for the family and the migrant care worker.

These comparative findings help to deepen understandings of the diverging intersection of in-home childcare subsidies and migration schemes. Access to affordable and high-quality ECEC is stratified across class lines and in-home childcare is no exception. At the same time, care and migration policy shapes issues of gender, class and race for care workers. At the simplest level, care and migration policy determines whether and how care workers are included or excluded from the formal ECEC sector. The dominant debates and issues in relation to inequality are reflective of the way these care policies and migration rules intersect, but also reflect broader differences in care culture that shape understandings of appropriate forms of care and division of responsibilities across gender, class and racial lines. These findings have particular implications for the status and recognition of in-home childcare workers and, ultimately, shape the value of high-quality services designed to address inequalities among families and ECEC workers.

Notes

[1]   For a discussion of gender regimes, see Lewis (1992, 1997), Orloff (1993) and Shaver (2000). For a discussion of care regimes, see Bettio and Plantenga (2004), Williams and Gavanas (2008), Mahon et al (2012) and Michel and Peng (2012).

[2]   Under the new Jobs for Families Childcare Package, subsidies (the Child Care Subsidy) will be tied to a parental activity test. With the exception of low-income

families and children at risk of abuse, children whose parents do not participate in work, study or training will not be eligible for a subsidised place in approved childcare services (Long Day Care, Family Day Care, Occasional Care, In Home Care, the Nanny Pilot).

[3]   As detailed in Chapter Three, under the Child Care Benefit families hiring nannies who are registered with the Department of Human Services are eligible for a much lower subsidy, equivalent to approximately $33 per week.

[4]   See Vincent and Ball (2006) for a class-based analysis of childcare choices in Britain.

[5]   *The common core* is a document that sets out the basic skills required for childcare and early years workers. For more information see Ofsted, 2010.

[6]   It should be noted that many domestic workers from Eastern Europe do have degrees from their home countries, including in teaching and nursing.

Conclusion

What has changed?

In-home childcare is not a new phenomenon in Western countries. For centuries, children have been cared for in their own home by relatives and non-relatives alike. Non-relative care in the child's home has, however, largely been limited to the upper echelons of society, or used as a temporary solution, such as care provided by babysitters and neighbours. Government involvement in early childhood education and care (ECEC) has been an issue for public and policy debate since the 1960s; however, until recently, both research and policy has largely focused on centre-based services and care based in the home of the provider (family day care, childminders). Care provided in the home of the child has largely been outside the gaze of public policy.

As Part One (Chapters One through Three) discussed, since the 1970s, governments have introduced various ways to support different types of childcare, originally as a means to assist mothers who needed to work. And, to some extent, governments have responded to the feminist movement's demands for childcare as a way to enhance gender equality. In recent decades, liberal (and other) countries have embraced a new approach to social policy, which has built on existing ideology and policy structures, but also emerged out of new discourses about the objectives of ECEC, and other care policies.

The new approach to social policy sits easily with liberal tenets of private responsibility, reliant on the market and individualism. In particular, the introduction and extension of a market-led approach to service delivery has repositioned care arrangements that previously sat squarely in the private domain. New payments and regulatory regimes blur the line between public and private care and, to different extents in each study country, impose contradictory processes of informalisation and formalisation. In many ways, the restructuring of payments and regulation are part of broader ECEC reforms; however, in-home childcare is, arguably, an exemplary case that highlights the tensions and inconsistencies involved in the restructuring of ECEC services. In particular, market mechanisms and immigration policy intersect to shape the commodification and informalisation of care services, yet at the same time, the introduction of registration and light-touch regulation of in-home childcare services points to the professionalisation of nannies, as they advocate for greater inclusion in the formal ECEC sector.

Changes to in-home childcare in Australia have taken place in two waves. The first wave of change occurred in the late 1990s. Early childhood education and care experienced significant changes through this decade. In long day care, subsidies for for-profit services were introduced in 1991, and this was followed by the removal of operational subsidies for not-for-profit services in 1996 (Brennan, 2007). At the same time, the family day care sector continued to evolve through processes of formalisation and professionalision (see Chapter Two). There were pressures from users and providers in the 1980s to impose standards for family day care to ensure accountability of public funds, and to recognise the work done by family day care 'mothers'. By the end of the 1990s, family day care was brought under the national accreditation system. This was a positive move, but some also believed the introduction of regulations changed the nature of family day care. In particular, it removed some of the flexibility that family day care once offered. At the same time, under the Liberal government elected in 1996, there was a new emphasis on at-risk children and families. These pressures culminated in the first major shift in in-home childcare in Australia: the establishment of the Sick Care Pilot and, following an evaluation, the In Home Care programme.

Australia is in the midst of its second major shift in in-home childcare. There have been various calls for subsidies or tax measures to subsidise nannies since the mid-2000s, but the issue gained real political and policy traction in the lead-up to the 2013 election. The Liberal leader, Tony Abbott, announced he would explore options to extend subsidies to families using nannies. Once he was elected Prime Minster, his Coalition government requested the Productivity Commission to conduct a review into childcare and early childhood learning. The extension of funding for nannies was at the centre of media and policy debate through this period. And, in May 2015, the Government announced the introduction of a two-year Nanny Pilot programme to deliver its promise of more flexible childcare. This programme rests firmly on the government's emphasis on productivity and workforce participation. The extension of the Working Holiday Visa from six to 12 months introduces a further complexity into the in-home childcare sector. At the time of writing, the outcomes and responses to the policy are yet to come.

Policy changes surrounding nannies in the UK have attracted less controversy than in Australia. This is arguably because the changes occurred during times when the early years sector, more broadly, was in flux. The National Childcare Agenda was announced in 1997, with major changes – such as the free entitlement to guarantee three- and four-year olds access to early education and Sure Start centres – being rolled out during the late 1990s and early 2000s. The decision to allow families using nannies to access the childcare element of the Working Tax Credit was piloted in the midst of this reform programme, in 2002, and formally rolled out in 2004 as the Home Childcare scheme. There have been minimal changes to the rules and regulations of in-home childcare since the voluntary register was established in 2006 for caregivers enrolled in the Home Childcare scheme. The Regulation Matters campaign has been pushing for a switch from voluntary to compulsory regulation for nannies in order to improve their professional status and ensure adequate safeguards for children. However, changes in migration policy are arguably pushing the nanny sector in the opposite direction. Since 2004, with the opening up of the European Union, increasing numbers of migrant workers have been entering the UK as home-based childcare and domestic workers. They are mostly working in an informal environment, with few protections available for the care worker or the child. It is yet to be known whether sector advocates, care workers and policymakers will support each other in the push for greater regulation and professionalisation for *all* in-home childcare workers, non-migrant and migrant alike.

Various policy changes have affected in-home childcare in Canada, with reforms occurring in both the childcare (through tax measures and cash benefits) and migration domains. The Child Care Expense Deduction, introduced in 1972, signifies the federal government's long-standing commitment to private, market-led childcare, reinforced through the Universal Child Care Benefit in 2006. The efforts and achievements of the childcare movement should not be forgotten; however, in-home childcare has largely been at the periphery of their campaigns. In the migration domain, in 1981 the Foreign Domestic Movement programme orientated government policy towards private in-home childcare. The scheme was renamed the Live-In Caregiver Program in 1992, and underwent further changes in 2014 to become the Caring for Children Pathway (as part of the Temporary Foreign Workers Program). Reforms have included the removal of the highly criticised live-in requirement. However, the migration programme as it stands continues to promote private, unregulated in-home childcare. Broader shifts to ECEC, in Ontario for example, have established new regulations for unregulated home-based childcare (in the home of the caregiver). Time will tell whether campaigns and interest groups across the ECEC and migration domain will come together to improve regulations in all settings.

Why has in-home childcare changed?

Evidently, the introduction of, and changes to, in-home childcare are distinct to each country, and reflect different social, political and cultural contexts. Yet, the changes to in-home childcare, and ECEC more broadly, in the three countries rest on similar trends and approaches to childcare and social policy. The reasons for these changes were touched on in Part One (Chapter Two), and analysed further in Part Two (especially Chapters Four and Six).

Most importantly, responsibility for childcare has remained primarily in the private domain. In the decades following the Second World War, private families were responsible for the majority of childcare provision. The government took some responsibility for children whose mothers needed to work. Since the 1990s, governments in these three countries have taken greater interest in investing in ECEC. The reasons for increased public spending have been driven by broader welfare state restructuring, in particular the shift to productivity, instead of protection, which is central to a social investment approach to social policy. A social investment approach fits well with public spending on ECEC: spending on childcare facilitates mothers' employment, which increases tax revenue and, in theory, alleviates the need for social spending on families, while investment in quality early learning programmes can enhance children's early development, and their outcomes in the future.

The increasing interest in in-home childcare from governments, employers and families is driven by changing demographic trends, in particular increases in maternal employment rates and patterns of non-standard work. In a '24/7' economy, governments are open to policies that promote longer work hours. Governments' promotion of women's and mothers' employment has implications beyond national care policies: demographic changes, namely increases in women's workforce participation, and also an ageing population, have driven demand for low-cost care as alternatives to familial and publicly delivered institutional care. A 'care crisis' is identified as a driver for women's migration from poorer countries to more developed countries to provide care for elderly people, people with a disability and young children. This pattern has perhaps been most significant in liberal countries[1] where governments tend to take less public responsibility for care provision. In the case of in-home childcare, longer working hours for parents are sustained through long working hours by an underpaid care workforce, in addition to a patchwork of informal care. With limited flexibility in the formal, regulated ECEC sector, families and governments have continued to use informal options, including in-home childcare, to meet their childcare needs. The inadequacy of formal ECEC services for working families has helped advocates to mobilise support for government subsidisation of flexible arrangements for families, previously in the private and informal domain.

Implications for families and care workers

The promotion of women's workforce participation to achieve equal opportunity in the workplace has (sometimes) unintended consequences for other groups of women. In particular, issues of gender, class and race are identified as central to debates about government involvement in in-home childcare policy.

It was illustrated in Chapter Five that policy to address the needs (and choices) of working parents may have negative implications for the care workers. In particular, responsibility for care has been restructured within the private domain. Historically unequal divisions of care between men and women persist today, and when care shifted from the unpaid to paid domain, there were further divisions across class lines – in relation to both care users' capacity to access childcare, and care providers' low status and poor working conditions. In recent decades, responsibility for childcare has been divided unequally across gender, class and racial lines. The division of these responsibilities for in-home childcare is partly explained by structural policy changes, but also by embedded care cultures surrounding appropriate forms of care for young children. To varying extents in each country, these assumptions reflect the undervaluing of care and domestic work as a productive contribution in its own right. Instead, it is perceived as a way to promote productivity through mothers' employment in the knowledge economy.

The issues and inequalities experienced by families and care workers differ depending on the intersection of ECEC, migration and employment policy. Funding and subsidies for families using nannies may, without proper design and regulation, reinforce gender and income inequalities for care users. This is evident in Canada, where the federal Child Care Expense Deduction (CCED) offers the most financial benefit to well-off families who can afford to pay for private childcare. Both the CCED and the Universal Child Care Benefit are directed at unregulated care arrangements. In the UK, the strict eligibility criteria for Working Tax Credit and the restriction of childcare vouchers to mostly middle-income earners does not encourage the hiring of Ofsted-registered nannies. Instead, in-home childcare is more affordable by hiring a migrant worker from the EU or through the Youth Mobility scheme. In Australia, the recently introduced Nanny Pilot has been critiqued on the grounds that it is only accessible to dual-earner professional families who can afford the high out-of-pocket costs expected as a result of the subsidy design. Early reports about the Nanny Pilot indicate very low take-up of the programme because of the high cost of the programme to parents (Gartrell, 2016). But what are the implications for care workers and children in the care of nannies? The absence (or low level) of standards for in-home childcare in all three countries also attracts concern about the safety and quality of care for children.

The inequalities experienced by care workers are also shaped by the intersection of policies. When nannies and in-home childcare workers operate within an approved ECEC structure, they are likely to have better working conditions and to be required to meet higher standards of care provision. Australia's In Home Care programme is the closest to this model. In contrast, the subsidisation of nannies in the absence of regulation can have a negative impact on care workers and the quality of care for children. It is by using this argument that sector advocates in the UK are campaigning for compulsory regulation for all nannies and other in-home childcare providers. In the absence of such regulation, formal migration pathways for care workers can increase the potential for exploitation of care workers, and potentially lower the standards of care for children.

To what extent should ECEC legislation intervene in migration policies in order to monitor childcare provision? In the UK and Canada, migration policy intersects with care policy to promote different forms of informal and private in-home childcare arrangements. Critique from the migration sphere relates to the working conditions and status of the care workers (Arat-Koç, 1989; Bakan and Stasiulis, 1997; Newcombe, 2004; Brickner and Straehle, 2010; Cox, 2012). Still, though, there is little attention given to what this means for the quality of care for children. As Búriková and Miller point out in relation to the hiring of untrained au pairs in the UK:

> Although it was said by some that they didn't want untrained *au pairs* looking after their very young children, the idea that the way they treated their *au pair* would or could rebound upon their own children seems to be both

unspoken and apparently an afterthought. This is one of the most striking conclusions of our research. After all, one might have expected that parents, devoted to the welfare of their children, are already, in choosing to have an *au pair*, opting for essentially untrained childcare. But at least they could help ensure a positive attitude toward their children by their own positive treatment of the *au pair*. After all, if they treat their *au pair* badly, how should they expect the *au pair* in turn to treat their children when they are alone with them – especially if the children are very young and unable to report back to their parents any ill-treatment? (Búriková and Miller, 2010, p 84)

This excerpt is written in relation to individuals' decisions to hire untrained au pairs, and the 'striking finding' is that many parents did not associate their own treatment of au pairs with the care their young children receive from the au pair. This finding can easily be applied to the way we, as individuals and society, treat care workers – enacted through care and migration policy and broader care cultures.

There is consensus across most developed countries that spending on children's education is a worthy investment and, also, that women should have a right to earn. And, as discussed throughout, governments increasingly promote women's participation in employment as a precondition for eligibility for childcare subsidies and other welfare benefits. As a result, governments and the public do increasingly recognise in policy rhetoric and advocacy campaigns that affordable ECEC is necessary for maternal employment. As presented previously, governments promote maternal employment as a valuable contribution to tax revenue and productivity. We, as individuals and society, must also then recognise the value of the care work that facilitates this participation in the knowledge economy. This involves proper remuneration, fair working conditions and investment in the care worker's skills and knowledge. This should be regarded as a right for the care workers, and also a right for the children being cared for. While workers' rights have long been advocated in the ECEC field, in-home childcare is often ignored in these debates when, in practice, these caregivers are often the most vulnerable and affected by competing and contrasting policy domains.

If in-home childcare workers are to be truly recognised for the work they do, there must be greater value given to care work in the home. As Fiona Williams states, the social value attributed to care is reflected in how society remunerates its care workers through practical support such as formal career paths, training for care work and developing accreditation frameworks (2012a, p 114). Increased emphasis should be given to addressing the hierarchies among the ECEC sector, and among the in-home childcare workforce. A first step forward would be to provide greater training and protection to in-home childcare workers, which is best achieved through linking them to service organisations, and preventing a direct employer–employee relationship between nannies (care providers) and families (employers or users).

Movements to integrate and restructure in-home childcare within the ECEC sector will likely face different barriers in the three study countries. These barriers are reflective of embedded assumptions about who should be responsible for childcare, and whether those who are responsible should be trained and remunerated equal to other ECEC workers, and recognised as professionals.

Policy lessons

Assuming that in-home childcare is here to stay as a necessary form of care for the 'modern economy', what can be done to improve the outcomes of policy for parents, children and care workers? How can in-home childcare policy be reformed or restructured to improve the affordability for parents, the quality of care for all children and the quality of work for caregivers? Drawing on best practice examples and cautionary tales, four preliminary issues for policy consideration for in-home childcare are presented below. It should be emphasised that further research, including consultation with the multiple stakeholders involved, is required to provide country-specific recommendations.

Equitable subsidy structures for families

Governments' financial support for in-home childcare blurs the line between the informal/formal domains and public/private responsibility for care. If governments increase spending to support in-home childcare, and ECEC more broadly, the details of the funding and regulation will be critical. Although many government reforms are put forward to support positive choices for parents, such policies must also consider whether there are positive outcomes for care workers and children.

Public subsidies should flow to *quality* ECEC services. Subsidy models must consider the implications for access to in-home childcare for families across different income levels. As the analysis in Chapters Three and Five indicated, current funding measures in Canada and the UK provide little assistance to low-income families requiring this type of care. Australia's In Home Care programme provides targeted assistance to the most vulnerable families and to those working non-standard and precarious hours. It is recommended that funding structures for ECEC ensure that all families requiring in-home childcare for employment or other circumstances do not face substantial cost barriers to access such a service. Service providers and nanny agencies in Australia and the UK provide good practice examples of service models that help low-income families to access and afford flexible care to meet their employment and family needs. These models involved means-tested subsidies for families that did not penalise families with one or two children.

Standards and training for in-home childcare workers

Financial assistance for families using in-home childcare should be contingent on standards and monitoring procedures consistent with other forms of approved ECEC. Directing subsidies to regulated ECEC arrangements, where care workers have minimum qualifications, ensures greater accountability of public funding. This would mean providing training programmes equivalent to the minimum qualification standards required in centre- and home-based settings. Levels of regulation and training in the three countries are in flux and generally regarded as fairly low and, therefore, further consultation with experts and the sector is needed. Training and qualifications specific to in-home childcare provision could also be considered. This would be consistent with the direction of some training programmes offered by nanny agencies, service providers and training organisations in the three countries. The training and regulation of in-home childcare workers will have a positive impact on their wages and conditions, and increase their status within the ECEC workforce. This, in turn, will have a positive effect on the delivery of quality ECEC to children and families.

Employment status of in-home childcare workers

In-home childcare is provided more effectively and equitably when care workers are employed by service organisations, not families. This approach to delivering in-home childcare differs from national policy and practice in the three countries included in the study, where most in-home childcare workers are self-employed (Canada, UK) or independent contractors (Australia). There is greater risk for these workers because they do not have control over their environment and often lack the resources to provide high-quality care to children.

Examples of good practice in Australia and the UK (discussed in Chapters Three and Five) support a move towards in-home care workers being employed by provider organisations, rather than directly by families.[2] These findings are supported by evidence from studies in Australia (Meagher, 1997, 2000), the UK (Newcombe, 2004; R. Cox, 2006b, 2011; Williams and Gavanas, 2008; Búriková and Miller, 2010; Busch, 2013) and Canada (Bakan and Stasiulis, 1997; Pratt, 2003), which have found the potential for exploitation when care workers are employed by families to work in the home.

Related to this, interviews with key stakeholders indicate that many families needing in-home childcare only require part-time hours (a day or two each week, for example, or care in the mornings and evenings to cover before- and after-school and outside mainstream ECEC service hours each day). Enabling parents to access in-home childcare through centre-based or home-based services and organisations has the potential to increase the flexibility in their childcare arrangements, and also improves accountability for the family.

This would mean that fees for services would be paid to the service organisations and, if eligible for subsidies, families would pay a reduced fee to the service provider based on their income. By being employed by service provider organisations, in-home childcare workers would have the right to join a union and have representation across the broader ECEC workforce.

Employment of migrant in-home care workers

Across Western countries, in-home childcare is increasingly provided by migrant women who are typically required to have only minimal (if any) training as ECEC workers, and have few protections as migrant workers. International experience shows the strong possibility of such arrangements resulting in the exploitation of care workers. The rights and working conditions of in-home carers need to be protected, through national legislation that protects carers' social rights as citizens and workers. Various national and international organisations (such as Kalaayan in the UK, INTERCEDE in Canada and the International Labour Organization through its Convention on Domestic Workers), advocate for these issues, including the right of workers to join a union and to the right to remove conditions that tie their working and citizenship rights to their employment. All in-home childcare workers should have access to the same training and professional support, regardless of their migrant status. We know that providing better conditions and training for care workers also has a positive impact on the quality of care provided to children.

Why do changes to in-home childcare matter for comparative social policy?

This is the first book to trace the emergence of in-home childcare, as part of policy development and debate about ECEC, in Australia, the UK and Canada. The book presents new empirical research about in-home childcare that has significant policy and political relevance across the three study countries, as well as Western countries more broadly. The findings contribute conceptually to scholarship and debate with relevance to ECEC and migration policy domains.

The book's innovative approach integrates care and migration policy into the analysis of in-home childcare. Early childhood education and care is at the forefront of political and public debate and, at the same time, the global movement of care workers from poorer to richer countries provides opportunities and challenges for government, employers, care workers and families alike. This book delves into the complexities and overlap of the care and migration policy domains through the lens of in-home childcare. Previous research has tended to focus on a single policy domain, or the implications for children and families (in the case of ECEC policy) or care workers (in the case of migration policy). The current integrated approach generates new empirical findings about the implications of these policies for both the family (parents and children) and care workers.

The book developed three themes or concepts that are intensely relevant to both policy debates and academic scholarship. The first theme or concept developed from a theoretical and policy relevant perspective is the *formalisation/informalisation* of care. The dualism of formalisation/informalisation of care is closely linked to the restructuring of welfare state policy through the privatisation and marketisation of care and social services. Informal care often refers to unpaid care or care by relatives. The process of formalisation in this context denotes the introduction of, or increase in, government regulation and oversight, often in combination with government subsidies. The informal/formal divide is often blurred where there is an increase in public funding for services in the absence of regulation or rigorous accountability of funds. The informal/formal divide is central to the book, in the way that the research traces the emergence and transformation of in-home childcare to illustrate how policy reforms can shift responsibility across the public/private domain and also across the informal/formal spheres. Drawing on previous research (Leira, 2002; Pfau-Effinger, 2005b; Kremer, 2007), this concept is applied specifically to the provision of in-home childcare and contrasts the tensions and inconsistencies that developed across these countries and across the provision of different types of ECEC. It therefore has policy relevance for ECEC policymakers and scholars as well as for welfare regime scholars and theorists.

The second theme is the analysis of *policy intersections*. This concept is not new to social policy research, but the use of the concept in this book advances knowledge about a specific policy area – in-home childcare – which has, until recently, largely been ignored. Thus, while scholars have analysed broader intersections of care, migration and employment policy (Morgan, 2005; Lister et al, 2007; Morel, 2007; Williams and Gavanas, 2008; Shutes and Chiatti, 2012), this book explores the detail of a specific policy, while also illustrating its relevance to broader ECEC and domestic work. In particular, it illustrates how policy intersections can be embedded in historical norms and structures, but also that the restructuring of policies or the introduction of new policy creates competing discourses and contradictions in national and local ideals of care.

Finally, the concept of *care culture* is adopted as a frame to analyse and explain the differences in government support for in-home childcare in the three countries. Care culture (Pfau-Effinger, 2005b; Williams, 2012b) and the related idea of 'ideals of care' (Kremer, 2007) are emerging as new ways of thinking about care responsibilities in ECEC. The concept of care culture draws on the design of care and migration policy, and also accounts for normative approaches to care, such as political and public values, norms and attitudes. As discussed, care culture refers to 'dominant national and local cultural discourse on what constitutes appropriate childcare' (Williams and Gavanas 2008, p 16).

Variation between countries is arguably explained by different assumptions in each country about who should care for children and how care should be provided. In all three countries there is a reliance on, and historical preference for, private responsibility for childcare. By looking specifically at in-home childcare, it is evident that ideas about private provision of childcare are constructed differently. In Australia, an increased emphasis on productivity and workforce participation has arguably caused this fabric to unravel through activity tests and programmes such as the Nanny Pilot that prioritise mothers' employment over children's or care workers' wellbeing. However, these changes are opposed by representatives of the ECEC sector and members of the public, who feel they are an affront to Australia's egalitarian approach to ECEC funding. The UK's previous reliance on private, mostly familial care, ceded way in the late 1990s and early 2000s. Increased investment in ECEC was followed by increased pressures for regulation and public recognition of traditionally private forms of care, such as nannies. In efforts to challenge the notion of nannies only being for the rich, nanny representatives are pushing for inclusion in the early years sector to make the British 'ideal' a quality care option. An influx of migrant workers from Eastern Europe has imposed challenges as the nanny and au pair sectors seek to disentangle new racialised divisions among the in-home childcare workforce. In Canada, early support for private home-based childcare, through both the Child Care Expense Deduction and Live-In Caregiver Program, led to a distinct care culture of private, unregulated and racialised in-home childcare. Although the childcare movement campaigned for universal ECEC, and advocacy groups within the foreign domestic worker movement struggled for citizenship rights, the separation of these policy domains created little resistance to broader societal acceptance that, in the absence of publicly funded childcare, in-home arrangements were the only option for many working families.

The conclusions from this study do not seek to propose a new typology for these countries; however, the findings illustrate the distinct care cultures in these three liberal countries. The concept of care culture captures the interaction between policy mechanisms, new policy ideas, and embedded assumptions about appropriate forms of childcare. These differences are apparent from other literature that examines ECEC policy in these three countries (Jenson and Sineau, 2001; Michel and Mahon, 2002; Baker, 2006; Brennan et al, 2012; Mahon et al, 2012; White and Friendly, 2012); however, by using in-home childcare as a lens through which to analyse and compare ECEC policy, and by incorporating migration policy into the analysis, the differences between these liberal welfare regime types are magnified. In particular, the findings reveal that the assumptions about who should provide care for children, and how the care should be provided, point to embedded ideas about gender, class/income and race/migration in relation to the provision of ECEC. These assumptions about the most appropriate forms of care can be linked back to the three identified aspects of care culture: policy origins embedded in both structural and cultural norms; policy details that dictate structural support for different types of care; and discourses that shape policymakers' and the public's ideas about who should care for children.

The book illustrates that the patterns, policies and cultures of in-home childcare in Australia, the UK and Canada differ in multiple ways. Government support for in-home childcare (or policy) differs in relation to funding (tax measures and ECEC subsidies), regulation (of care settings and care workers) and immigration (migration schemes and domestic employer regulations). At the same time, the culture of in-home childcare differs according to how the government and the broader public view women's workforce participation, the objectives of ECEC, and the most appropriate form of care for young children. Together, these findings contribute to the development of further research that gives greater attention to how policy structures and discourses shape families' and care workers' perspectives of in-home childcare and their claims for policy reform and improvement of the in-home childcare workforce. By giving greater attention to the structural and normative factors that shape care workers' and families' ideas about care for young children, policy can be developed to better recognise the value of in-home care workers and the needs of the families and children they provide care for.

Notes

[1] For a discussion of migrant care work in other welfare regime types, see Williams (2012b), and for analysis of how familial care is outsourced to other forms of private home care, see Bettio and Plantenga (2004), Michel and Peng (2012) and Shutes and Chiatti (2012).

[2] Practice examples and support for this approach were held by a number of key stakeholders (nanny associations and provider organisations) in Australia and the UK.

References

ABC News. 2013. 'Federal inquiry set up into child care, early learning accessibility'. Accessed 12 December 2013. http://www.abc.net.au/news/2013-11-17/government-establishes-productivity-commission-into-childcare/5097480

Adamson, E., Cortis, N., Brennan, D., and Charlesworth, S. Forthcoming. 'Social care and migration policy in Australia: Emerging intersections?' *Australian Journal of Social Issues*.

Adamson, E. and Brennan, D. 2014. 'Social investment or private profit? Diverging notions of "investment" in early childhood education and care'. *International Journal of Early Childhood* 46 (1): 47-61.

Anderson, B. and Shutes, I. eds. 2014. *Migration and Care Labour: Theory, Policy and Politics, Migration, Diasporas and Citizenship*. Basingstoke: Palgrave Macmillan.

Arat-Koç, S. 1989. 'In the privacy of our own home: foreign domestic workers as solution to the crisis of the domestic sphere in Canada'. *Studies in Political Economy* 28: 33-58.

Arat-Koç, S. 1999. 'Neo-liberalism, state restructuring and immigration: changes in Canadian policies in the 1990s'. *Journal of Canadian Studies/Revue d'Études Canadiennes* 34 (2): 31-56.

Arat-Koç, S. 2012. 'Invisibilized, Individualized, and culturalized: paradoxical invisibility and hyper-visibility of gender in policy making and policy discourse in neoliberal Canada'. *Canadian Woman Studies* 29 (3): 6-17.

Au Pair World. 2014. 'How to become an au pair in Australia'. Accessed 21 May. www.aupair-world.net/au_pair_program/australia/au_pair/visa.

Australian Bureau of Statistics. 2008. 'Childhood Education and Care'. Cat. 4402.0, *ABS Australian Social Trends*. Canberra: Australian Bureau of Statistics.

Australian Bureau of Statistics. 2009. 'Work, life and family balance'. Cat. 4102.0, *ABS Australian Social Trends*. Canberra: Australian Bureau of Statistics.

Australian Bureau of Statistics. 2015. 'Childhood Education and Care'. Cat. 4402.0. *ABS Australian Social Trends*. Canberra: Australian Bureau of Statistics.

Australian Government. 2009. *The Early Years Learning Framework*. Canberra: Department of Education Employment and Workplace Relations, Commonwealth of Australia Employment and Workplace Relations. Canberra: Commonwealth of Australia.

Australian Government. 2015. 'Nanny pilot programme'. Australian Government. Accessed 27 November. www.dss.gov.au/our-responsibilities/families-and-children/programmes-services/early-childhood-child-care/nanny-pilot-programme.

Australian Nanny Association. 2014. *Submission to the Productivity Commission Inquiry into Child Care and Early Childhood Learning.* Accessed 3 July 2016. www.pc.gov.au/inquiries/completed/childcare/submissions/initial/submission-counter/sub254-childcare.pdf

Australian Nanny Association. 2015. Media release: 'Response to announcement of a nanny pilot program'.

Australian Women Chamber of Commerce and Industry. 2013. 'Closing the gap on child care in Australia: An issues paper on how to strategically increase Australia's national productivity'. Sydney: Australian Women Chamber of Commerce and Industry.

Bakan, A.B. and Stasiulis, D.. 1994. 'Foreign domestic worker policy in Canada and the social boundaries of modern citizenship'. *Science & Society* 58 (1): 7-33.

Bakan, A.B. and Stasiulis, D. 1997. *Not One of the Family: Foreign Domestic Workers in Canada.* Toronto: University of Toronto Press.

Baker, M. 2006. *Restructuring Family Policies: Convergences and Divergences.* Toronto: University of Toronto Press.

Baker, M. and Tippin, D. 1998. 'Fighting "child poverty": the discourse of restructuring in Canada and Australia'. *Australian Canadian Studies* 17 (2): 121-40.

Barnes, M., Bryson, C. and Smith, R. 2006. *Working Atypical Hours: What Happens to Family Life.* London: National Centre for Social Research.

Baxter, J. 2013. *Child Care Participation and Maternal Employment Trends in Australia* (Research Report No. 26). Melbourne: Australian Institute of Family Studies.

Baxter, J. 2014. 'Maternal employment and childcare in Australia'. In *Submission to the Productivity Commission Childcare and Early Childhood Learning Inquiry.* Melbourne: Australian Institute of Family Studies.

Béland, D. 2009. 'Gender, ideational analysis, and social policy.' *Social Politics: International Studies in Gender, State & Society* 16 (4): 558-81. doi: 10.1093/sp/jxp017.

Berg, L. 2015. 'Hiding in plain sight – au pairs in Australia'. In *Au Pairs' Lives in Global Context: Sisters or Servants,* edited by R. Cox. Basingstoke: Palgrave Macmillan.

Bertrand, J., Bernhard, J., Blaxall, J., Burning Fields, J., Gordon, M., Goulet, M., Greenberg, J., Latulippe, J., Littleford, J., Maltais, C., Pelletier, J., Schmidt, B., Thompson, K., Varmuza, P. and Zimanyi, L. 2007. 'Early learning for every child today: a framework for Ontario early childhood settings'. In *Best Start Expert Panel on Early Learning*. Toronto: Ontario Government.

Better Regulation Task Force. 1998. *Early Education and Day Care Review*. London: Cabinet Office.

Bettio, F. and Plantenga, J. 2004. 'Comparing care regimes in Europe'. *Feminist Economics* 10 (1): 85-113.

Bird, F. 1970. *Report of the Royal Commission on the Status of Women in Canada*. Minister of Supply and Services Canada. Ottawa: Information Canada.

Bonoli, G. 2005. 'The politics of the new social policies: providing coverage against new social risks in mature welfare states'. *Policy & Politics* 33 (3): 431-49.

Brady, M. and Perales, F. 2014. 'Hours of paid work among single and partnered mothers in Australia: the role of childcare packages'. *Journal of Family Issues*. doi: 10.1177/0192513x14531416.

Brennan, D. 1998. *The Politics of Australian Child Care: Philanthropy to Feminism and Beyond*. Cambridge: Cambridge University Press.

Brennan, D. 2002. 'Australia: child care and state-centred feminism in a liberal welfare regime'. In *Child Care Policy at the Crossroads: Gender and Welfare State Restructuring*, edited by S. Michel and R. Mahon, 95-112. London: Routledge.

Brennan, D. 2007. 'The ABC of child care politics'. *Australian Journal of Social Issues* 42 (2): 213-25.

Brennan, D. and Mahon, R. 2011. 'State structures and the politics of child care'. *Politics & Gender* 7 (2): 286-93. doi:10.1017/S1743923X11000134.

Brennan, D. and O'Donnell, C. 1986. *Caring for Australia's Children: Political and Industrial Issues in Child Care*. Allen & Unwin.

Brennan, D., Cass, B., Himmelweit, S. and Szebehely, M. 2012. 'The marketisation of care: rationales and consequences in Nordic and liberal care regimes'. *Journal of European Social Policy* 22 (4): 377-91. doi: 10.1177/0958928712449772.

Brickner, R.K. and Straehle, C. 2010. 'The missing link: gender, immigration policy and the Live-in Caregiver Program in Canada'. *Policy and Society* 29 (4): 309-20. doi: http://dx.doi.org/10.1016/j.polsoc.2010.09.004.

Brind, R., Norden, O., McGinigal, S., Oseman, D., Simon, A. and La Valle, I. 2011. *Childcare and Early Years Providers Survey 2011*. London: Department for Education.

Bryant, L. 2013. 'Quality childcare creates manifold economic benefits for Australia'. *Sydney Morning Herald*, 19 November. www.smh.com.au/comment/quality-childcare-creates-manifold-economic-benefits-for-australia-20131118-2xr3w.html - ixzz30WFDly7v.

Bryson, C., Brewer, M., Sibieta, L. and Butt, S. 2012. *The Role of Informal Childcare: A Synthesis and Critical Review of the Evidence: Full Report*. London: Nuffield Foundation.

Búriková, Z. and Miller, D. 2010. *Au Pair*. Cambridge: Polity.

Busch, N. 2012. 'Deprofessionalisation and informality in the market for commoditised care'. *Transnational Migration, Gender and Rights (Advances in Ecopolitics)* 10: 53-75.

Busch, N. 2013. 'The employment of migrant nannies in the UK: negotiating social class in an open market for commoditised in-home care'. *Social & Cultural Geography* 14 (5): 541-57.

Busch, N. 2014. 'When work doesn't pay: outcomes of a deregulated childcare market and au pair policy vacuum in the UK'. In *Au Pairs' Lives in Global Context: Sisters or Servants?*, edited by R. Cox, 53-69. Basingstoke: Palgrave Macmillan.

Bushnik, T. 2006. 'Child care in Canada'. *Children and Youth Research Paper Series*. Ottawa: Statistics Canada.

Cassells, R., McNamara, J., Lloyd, R. and Harding, A. 2007. 'Child care affordability and availability'. *Agenda: A Journal of Policy Analysis and Reform* 14 (2): 123-39.

Cho, K. 2013. *The Status Quo? Unfinished Business of Feminism in Canada*. National Film Board of Canada.

Clasen, J., and Siegel N., eds. 2007. *Investigating Welfare State Change: The 'Dependent Variable Problem' in Comparative Analysis*. Cheltenham: Edward Elgar.

Cleveland, G., Forer, B., Hyatt, D., Japel, C. and Krashinsky, M. 2008. 'New evidence about child care in Canada: use patterns, affordability and quality'. In *IRPP Choices*. Montreal: Institute for Research on Public Policy.

Cleveland, G. and Krashinsky, M. 1998. 'The benefits and costs of good child care: The economic rationale for public investment in young children – a policy study'. Scarborough: The University of Toronto.

Cleveland, G. and Krashinsky, M. 2003. 'Financing ECEC services in OECD countries'. In *The Childcare Transition: A League Table of Early Childhood Education and Care in Economically Advanced Countries*. Paris: OECD.

Coote, A. and Campbell, B. 1987. *Sweet Freedom: The Struggle for Women's Liberation*. Oxford: Blackwell.

Council of Australian Governments. 2009. *Investing in the Early Years – A National Early Childhood Development Strategy*. Canberra: Council of Australian Governments.

Cox, E. 2011. 'Tax forum: should nannies for high income women be subsidised?' *The Conversation*. Accessed 13 December 2015. www.theconversation.com/tax-forum-should-nannies-for-high-income-women-be-subsidised-3582

Cox, R. 2000. 'Exploring the growth of paid domestic labour: a case study of London'. *Geography* 85 (3): 241-51.

Cox, R. 2006a. 'Minding the gaps: the crisis in childcare'. In *The Servant Problem: Domestic Employment in a Global Economy*, edited by R. Cox, 35-56. London: IB Tauris.

Cox, R. 2006b. *The Servant Problem: Domestic Employment in a Global Economy*. London: IB Tauris.

Cox, R. 2011. 'Competitive mothering and delegated care: class relationships in nanny and au pair employment'. *Studies in the Maternal* 3 (2): 1-13.

Cox, R. 2012. 'Gendered work and migration regimes'. *Transnational Migration, Gender and Rights (Advances in Ecopolitics)* 10: 33-52.

Cox, R. and Busch, N. 2014a. *Au Pairing After the Au Pair Scheme? New Migration Rules and Childcare in Private Homes in the UK*. London: Birbeck, University of London.

Cox, R., and Busch, N. 2014b. 'Findings from review of migration and employment data'. *aupairproject*, 22 November. https://aupairproject.wordpress.com/2014/10/22/findings-from-review-of-migration-and-employment-data.

Craig, L. and Mullan, K. 2011. 'How mothers and fathers share childcare: a cross-national time-use comparison'. *American Sociological Review* 76 (6): 834-61.

Craig, L. and Abigail P. 2013. 'Non-parental childcare, time pressure and the gendered division of paid work, domestic work and parental childcare'. *Community, Work & Family* 16 (1): 100-119.

Cultural Au Pair in Australia Association. 2014. *Submission to Productivity Commission into Childcare and Early Childhood Learning*.

Daenzer, P. 1997. 'An affair between nations: international relations and the movement of household service workers'. In *Not One of the Family: Foreign Domestic Workers in Canada*, edited by A.B. Bakan and D. Stasiulis, 81-117. Toronto: University of Toronto Press.

DfE (Department for Education). 2003. *Every Child Matters*. London: HM Treasury.

DfE. 2014. *Childcare and Early Years Survey of Parents 2012–2013*. London: DfE.

DfES (Department for Education and Skills). 2002. Supporting the cost of home-based childcare: a proposal to approve home childcarers, and so enable parents to access the childcare tax credit element of the Working Tax Credit'. London: DfES.

DfES. 2004. 'Childcare: extending protection and broadening support'. In *Proposals for a Voluntary Scheme for the Approval of Childcare not Required to be Registered by Ofsted*. London: DfES.

Dial-An-Angel. 2014. *Submission to Productivity Commission Inquiry into Childcare and Early Childhood Learning*. www.pc.gov.au/inquiries/completed/childcare/submissions/initial/submission-counter/sub135-childcare.pdf.

Dobrowolsky, A. 2002. 'Rhetoric versus reality: the figure of the child and New Labour's Strategic "Social Investment State"'. *Studies in Political Economy* 69 (0): 43-73.

Dobrowolsky, A. and Jenson, J. 2004. 'Shifting representations of citizenship: Canadian politics of "women" and "children"'. *Social Politics: International Studies in Gender, State & Society* 11 (2): 154-80.

Dobrowolsky, A. and Jenson, J. 2005. 'Social investment perspectives and practices: a decade in British politics'. *Social Policy Review* 17: 203-30.

Doherty, G., Friendly, M. and Beach, J. 2003. *OECD Thematic Review of Early Childhood Education and Care: Canadian: Background Report*. Paris: Organisation for Economic Co-operation and Development.

Duffy, M. 2005. 'Reproducing labor inequalities: challenges for feminists conceptualizing care at the intersections of gender, race, and class'. *Gender & Society* 19 (1): 66-82.

Duncan, S. 2005. 'Mothering, class and rationality'. *The Sociological Review* 53 (1): 50-76.

Duncan, S., Edwards, R., Reynolds, T. and Alldred, P.-. 2004. 'Mothers and child care: policies, values and theories'. *Children & Society* 18 (4): 254-65.

Education Employment and Workplace Relations References Committee. 2009. *Senate Inquiry into the Provision of Childcare*. Canberra: Senate Printing House.

Ehrenreich, B. and Hochschild, A.R. eds. 2003. *Global Woman: Nannies, Maids, and Sex Workers in the New Economy*. London: Granta Publications.

Esping-Andersen, G. 1990. *The three worlds of welfare capitalism*, Cambridge: Polity Press.

Esping-Andersen, G. 2002. 'A child-centred social investment strategy'. In *Why We Need a New Welfare State*, edited by G. Esping-Andersen, 26-68. Oxford: Oxford University Press.

Estévez-Abe, M. and Hobson, B. 2015. 'Outsourcing domestic (care) work: the politics, policies, and political economy." *Social Politics: International Studies in Gender, State & Society* 22 (2): 133-46. doi: 10.1093/sp/jxv011.

Fagnani, J. 2012. 'Recent reforms in childcare and family policies in France and Germany: what was at stake?' *Children and Youth Services Review* 34 (3): 509-16.

Fagnani, J. and Math, A. 2011. 'The predicament of childcare policy in France: what is at stake?' *Journal of Contemporary European Studies* 19 (4): 547-61.

Fair Work Ombudsman. 2014. 'Awards'. Australian Government. Accessed 18 November. www.fairwork.gov.au/awards-and-agreements/awards.

Fawcett, B., Featherstone, B. and Goddard, J. 2004. *Contemporary Child Care Policy and Practice*. New York, NY: Palgrave Macmillan.

Finch, J. 1984. 'The deceit of self-help: preschool playgroups and working class mothers'. *Journal of Social Policy* 13 (1): 1-20.

Fitzgerald, J. 2006. *Lobbying in Australia: You Can't Expect Anything to Change if you Don't Speak up!* Kenthurst: Rosenberg Publishing.

Friendly, M. 2000. 'Child care and Canadian federalism in the 1990s: Canary in a coal mine'. *Occasional Paper 11.* Toronto: Child Care Resource and Research Unit.

Friendly, M., Halfon, S. Beach, J. and Forer, B. 2013. *Early Childhood Education and Care in Canada 2012*. Toronto: Child Care Resource and Research Unit.

Friendly, M. and Rothman, L. 1995. 'Miles to go ... the policy context of child care in Canada'. *Child Welfare* 74 (3).

Fudge, J. 1997. 'Little victories and big defeats: the rise and fall of collective bargaining rights for domestic workers in Ontario'. In *Not One of the Family: Foreign Domestic Workers in Canada*, edited by A.B. Bakan and D. Stasiulis, 119-45. Toronto: University of Toronto Press.

Fudge, J. 2013. 'Women workers: Is equality enough?' *Feminists@ Law*, 2(2): 1-18.

Gambaro, L., Stewart, K. and Waldfogel, J. 2014. *An Equal Start? Providing Quality Early Education and Care for Disadvantaged Children*. Bristol: Policy Press.

Gartrell, A. 2016. Federal election 2016: Turnbull government's $185m nanny scheme pays out just $9000. *The Age*, 1 July.

Garvis, S. and Pendergast, D. 2013. 'Perceptions of rebates for nanny care: an analysis of an online discussion'. *Australasian Journal of Early Childhood* 38 (3): 105-11.

Gathorne-Hardy, J. 1972. *The Rise and Fall of the English Nanny.* London: Arrow Books.

Gaunt, C. 2013. 'Government extends tax-free childcare to more families'. NurseryWorld. 4 June. Accessed 26 June 2014. www. nurseryworld.co.uk/nursery-world/news/1106667/government-extends-tax-free-childcare-families.

Giddens, A. 1998. *The Third Way: The Renewal of Social Democracy.* Cambridge: Polity.

Gilliland, J. 2012. 'Permanent worker, temporary resident: media representations of Canada's Live-In Caregiver Program'. Unpublished MA Dissertation, Department of Anthropology, University of Victoria.

Government of Canada. 2016. 'Hire a temporary foreign worker'. http://www.esdc.gc.ca/en/foreign_workers/index.page#a07

Government of Ontario. 2010. *Ontario Works Directives: Child Care Supports.* Ministry of Community and Social Services. Toronto: Ministry of Community and Social Services.

Gregson, N. and Lowe, M. 1994. *Servicing the Middle Classes: Class, Gender and Waged Domestic Labour in Contemporary Britain.* London: Routledge.

Harder, Lois. 2004. 'Child care, taxation and normative commitments: excavating the Child Care Expense Deduction debate'. *Studies in Political Economy* 73: 89-109.

Hayden, J. 1997. 'Caveat Australia? Child care under a neo-conservative agenda: a Canadian example. *Australian Journal of Early Childhood* 22 (3): 1-6.

Heckman, J. 2006. 'Skill formation and the economics of investing in disadvantaged children'. *Science* 312 (5782): 1900-02.

Hellgren, Z. 2015. 'Markets, regimes, and the role of atakeholders: explaining precariousness of migrant domestic/care workers in different institutional frameworks'. *Social Politics: International Studies in Gender, State & Society* 22 (2): 220-41. doi: 10.1093/sp/jxv010.

Hill, E. 2006. 'Howard's "choice": the ideology and politics of work and family policy 1996-2006'. *Australian Review of Public Affairs* 23: 1–8.

HM Government. 2009. *Next Steps for Early Learning and Childcare: Building on the 10-Year Strategy (Summary).* London: HM Government.

HM Revenue & Customs. 2013. *Paying for Childcare.* London: HM Revenue & Customs.

HM Revenue & Customs. 2014. *A Guide to Child Tax Credit and Working Tax Credit*. London: HM Revenue & Customs.

Hodge, J. 2006. '"Unskilled labour": Canada's Live-in Caregiver Program'. *Undercurrent* 3 (2): 60-6.

Holloway, S. and Tamplin, S. 2001. *Valuing Informal Childcare in the UK*. London: Office for National Statistics.

Howe, J. and Reilly, A. 2015. 'Meeting Australia's labor needs: the case for a new low-skill work visa'. *Fed. L. Rev.* 43: 259.

Human Resources and Skills Development Canada. 2013. 'Top occupational groups according to the number of temporary foreign worker positions on positive labour market opinions: Canada'. *Labour Market Opinion (LMO) Statistics Series. Annual Statistics 2012*. Ottawa: Government of Canada.

Indonesia Institute. 2014. *Submission to the Productivity Commission on the Childcare and Early Childhood Learning Inquiry*.

Jenson, J. 1997. 'Who cares? Gender and welfare regimes'. *Social Politics*, 4 (2): 182-87.

Jenson, J. 2008. 'Children, new social risks and policy change. A LEGO™ future?' *Comparative Social Research* 25: 357-81.

Jenson, J. 2009. 'Lost in translation: the social investment perspective and gender equality'. *Social Politics: International Studies in Gender, State & Society* 16 (4): 446-83.

Jenson, J. and Saint-Martin, D. 2003. 'New routes to social cohesion? citizenship and the social investment state'. *Canadian Journal of Sociology/Cahiers canadiens de sociologie* 28 (1): 77-99.

Jenson, J. and Sineau, M. 2001. *Who Cares?: Women's Work, Childcare, and Welfare State Redesign*. Toronto: University of Toronto Press.

Jha, T. 2014. 'Nanny rebates aren't about helping the rich'. *The Drum*. Accessed 13 December 2015. www.abc.net.au/news/2014-07-03/jha-its-not-rich-families-that-benefit-from-nanny-rebates/5569506

Jones, A. 1987. 'Tensions in community care policy: the case of family day care'. In *SWRC Reports and Proceedings No 70*, edited by P. Saunders and A. Jamrozik, 87-106. Sydney: Social Welfare Research Centre, University of New South Wales.

Karvelas, P. 2012. 'Regulation to allow subsidies for nannies a long way off, says Childcare Minister Kate Ellis'. *The Australian*, 9 August. www.theaustralian.com.au/national-affairs/regulation-to-allow-subsidies-for-nannies-a-long-way-off-says-childcare-minister-kate-ellis/story-fn59niix-1226446833517.

Kelly, P., Astorga-Garcia, M., Esguerra, and Community Alliance for Social Justice. 2009. 'Explaining the deprofessionalised Filipino: Why Filipino immigrants get low-paying jobs in Toronto'. In *CERIS Working Paper No. 75*, edited by M. Ali. Toronto: CERIS - Ontario Metropolis Centre.

Kelly, P., Park, S., de Leon, C. and Priest, J. 2011. 'Profile of live-in caregiver immigrants to Canada 1993-2009'. In *TIEDI Analytical Report*. Toronto: Toronto Immigrant Employment Data Initiative.

Kremer, M. 2002. 'The illustion of free choice: ideals of care and child care policy in the Flemish and Dutch welfare states'. In *Child Care Policy at the Crossroads: Gender and Welfare State Restructuring*, edited by S. Michel and R. Mahon. New York, NY: Routledge.

Kremer, M. 2006. 'The politics of ideals of care: Danish and Flemish child care policy compared'. *Social Politics: International Studies in Gender, State & Society* 13 (2): 261-85.

Kremer, M. 2007. *How Welfare States Care: Culture, Gender and Parenting in Europe*. Amsterdam: Amsterdam University Press.

Land, H. 2002. 'Spheres of care in the UK: separate and unequal'. *Critical Social Policy* 22 (1): 13-32.

Land, H. and Himmelweit, S. 2010. *Who Cares: Who Pays?* London: UNISON.

Le Bihan, B. and Martin, C. 2004. 'Atypical working hours: consequences for childcare arrangements'. *Social Policy & Administration* 38 (6): 565-90. doi: 10.1111/j.1467-9515.2004.00408.x.

Leach, P. 2009. *Child Care Today: Getting it Right for Everyone*. New York, NY: Alfred A. Knopf, Inc.

LeBaron, G. 2010. 'The political economy of the household: neoliberal restructuring, enclosures, and daily life'. *Review of International Political Economy* 17 (5): 889-912. doi: 10.1080/09692290903573914.

Lee, J. and Strachan, G. 1998. 'Who's minding the baby now? Child care under the Howard government'. *Labour and Industry* 9 (2): 81-101.

Leira, A. 2002. *Working Parents and the Welfare State: Family Change and Policy Reform in Scandinavia*. Cambridge: Cambridge University Press.

Leira, A. and Saraceno, C. 2002. 'Care: actors, relationships and contexts'. In *Contested Concepts in Gender and Social Politics*, edited by B. Hobson, J. Lewis and B. Siim, 55-83. Cheltenham: Edward Elgar.

Lewis, J. 1992. 'Gender and the development of welfare regimes'. *Journal of European Social Policy* 2 (3): 159-73.

Lewis, J. 1997. 'Gender and welfare regimes: further thoughts'. *Social Politics: International Studies in Gender, State and Society* 4 (2): 160-77. doi: 10.1093/sp/4.2.160.

Lewis, J. 2003. 'Developing early years childcare in England, 1997–2002: the choices for (working) mothers'. *Social Policy & Administration* 37 (3): 219–38.

Lewis, J. 2006. *Children, Changing Families and Welfare States.* Cheltenham: Edward Elgar.

Lewis, J. 2008. 'Childcare policies and the politics of choice'. *The Political Quarterly* 79 (4): 499–507.

Lewis, J. and Campbell, M. 2007. 'Work/family balance policies in the UK since 1997: a new departure?' *Journal of Social Policy* 36: 365–81.

Lewis, J. and Campbell, M. 2008. 'What's in a name? "Work and family" or "work and life" balance policies in the UK since 1997 and the implications for the pursuit of gender equality'. *Social Policy & Administration* 42 (5): 524–41. doi: 10.1111/j.1467-9515.2008.00615.x.

Lewis, J., Campbell, M. and Huerta, C. 2008. 'Patterns of paid and unpaid work in Western Europe: gender, commodification, preferences and the implications for policy'. *Journal of European Social Policy* 18 (1): 21–37.

Lister, R. 2004. 'The third way's social investment state'. In *Welfare State Change. Towards a Third Way*, edited by J. Lewis and R. Surender, 157–181. Oxford: Oxford University Press.

Lister, R. 2006. 'Children (but not women) first: New Labour, child welfare and gender'. *Critical Social Policy* 26 (2): 315–35.

Lister, R. 2008. 'Investing in children and childhood: a new welfare policy paradigm and its implications'. *Comparative Social Research* 25: 383–408.

Lister, R., Williams, F., Anttonen, A., Bussemaker, S., Leira, A., Siim, B., Tobio, C. and Gavanas, A. 2007. *Gendering Citizenship in Western Europe: New Challenges for Citizenship Research in a Cross-National Context.* Bristol: Policy Press.

Lloyd, E. 2008. 'The interface between childcare, family support and child poverty strategies under New Labour: tensions and contradictions'. *Social Policy and Society* 7 (4): 479–94. doi: doi:10.1017/S1474746408004442.

Lloyd, E. and Penn, H. 2012. *Childcare Markets: Can they Deliver an Equitable Service?* Bristol: Policy Press.

Lutz, H. ed. 2008. *Migration and Domestic Work: A European Perspective on a Global Theme, Studies in Migration and Diaspora.* Farnham: Ashgate Publishing Ltd.

Lutz, H. and Palenga-Möllenbeck, E. 2011. 'Care, gender and migration: towards a theory of transnational domestic work migration in Europe'. *Journal of Contemporary European Studies* 19 (3): 349–64.

Lutz, H., and Palenga-Möllenbeck, E. 2012. 'Care workers, care drain, and care chains: reflections on care, migration, and citizenship'. *Social Politics: International Studies in Gender, State & Society* 19 (1): 15-37. doi: 10.1093/sp/jxr026.

Mahon, R. 2004. 'Early child learning and care in Canada: who rules? Who should rule?' Paper presented at National Conference on Child Care in Canada, Winnipeg, 12-24 November.

Mahon, R., & Jenson, J. (2006). *ELCC Report 2006: Learning from each other: Early learning and child care experiences in Canadian cities.* Toronto: City of Toronto.

Mahon, R. 2007. 'Challenging national regimes from below: Toronto child-care politics'. *Politics and Gender* 3: 55-78.

Mahon, R. 2008. 'Varieties of liberalism: Canadian social policy from the "Golden Age" to the present'. *Social Policy & Administration* 42 (4): 342-61. doi: 10.1111/j.1467-9515.2008.00608.x.

Mahon, R. 2009. 'Canada's early childhood education and care policy: still a laggard?' *International Journal of Child Care and Education Policy* 3 (1): 27-42.

Mahon, R. 2010a. 'After neo-liberalism?: the OECD, the World Bank and the child'. *Global Social Policy* 10 (2): 172-92.

Mahon, R. 2010b. 'Learning, forgetting and rediscovering: producing the OECD's "new" family policy'. In *Mechanisms of OECD Governance*, edited by K. Martens and A.P. Jakobi, 198-216. Oxford: Oxford University Press.

Mahon, R. 2013. 'Childcare, new social risks, and the new politics of redistribution in Ontario'. In *Inequality and the Fading of Redistributive Politics*, edited by K. Banting and J. Myles, 359-380. Toronto: UBC Press.

Mahon, R., Anttonen, A., Bergqvist, C., Brennan, D. and Hobson, B. 2012. 'Convergent care regimes? Childcare arrangements in Australia, Canada, Finland and Sweden'. *Journal of European Social Policy* 22 (4): 419-31. doi: 10.1177/0958928712449776.

Martin, S. 1987. *Sharing the Responsibility: Report of the Special Committee on Child Care*. Edited by Canada Parliament. Ottawa: Queen's Printer.

Mas, S. 2013. 'Foreign nannies and caregivers fee to cost families $275'. 15 August. http://www.cbc.ca/news/politics/foreign-nannies-and-caregivers-fee-to-cost-families-275-1.1381800.

McCain, M.N. and Mustard, J.F. 1999. *Reversing the Real Brain Drain: Early Years Study Final Report*. Toronto: Canadian Institute for Advanced Research.

McIntosh, G. and Phillips, J. 2002. *Commonwealth Support for Childcare*. Canberra: Parliament of Australia.

McKeen, W. 2007. 'The National Children's Agenda: A neoliberal wolf in lamb's clothing'. *Studies in Political Economy* 80: 151-73.

McNicholas, L. 2014. 'A "nanny state" won't solve childcare problems'. *The Drum*. Australian Broadcasting Corporation. www.abc.net.au/ news/2014-07-03/mcnicholas-a-nanny-state-wont-solve-childcare-problems/5568734

Meagher, G. 1997. 'Recreating "domestic service": institutional cultures and the evolution of paid household work'. *Feminist Economics* 3 (2): 1-27. doi: 10.1080/135457097338681.

Meagher, G. 2000. 'A struggle for recognition: work life reform in the domestic services industry'. *Economic and Industrial Democracy* 21 (1): 9-37. doi: 10.1177/0143831x00211002.

Meyers, M.K. and Gornick, J.C. 2003. 'Public or private responsibility? Early childhood education and care, inequality, and the welfare state'. *Journal of Comparative Family Studies* 34 (3): 379-410.

Michel, S. and Mahon, R. 2002. *Child Care Policy at the Crossroads: Gender and Welfare State Restructuring*, New York: Routledge.

Michel, S. and Peng, I. 2012. 'All in the family? Migrants, nationhood, and care regimes in Asia and North America'. *Journal of European Social Policy* 22 (4): 406-18. doi: 10.1177/0958928712449774.

Militec, D. and Browne, R. 2013. 'Productivity Commission childcare hearings likely to pit nanny against centre'. *Sydney Morning Herald*, 18 November. www.smh.com.au/federal-politics/political-news/ productivity-commission-childcare-hearings-likely-to-pit-nanny-against-centre-20131118-2xrcl.html - ixzz2n8lUeZtL.

Morel, N. 2007. 'From subsidiarity to "free choice": child- and elder-care policy reforms in France, Belgium, Germany and the Netherlands'. *Social Policy & Administration* 41 (6): 618-37. doi: 10.1111/j.1467-9515.2007.00575.x.

Morel, N. 2012. 'The political economy of domestic work in France and Sweden in a European perspective'. *LIEPP Working Paper Series*. Paris: Socio-Fiscal Policies Research Group.

Morel, N. 2015. 'Servants for the knowledge-based economy? The political economy of domestic services in Europe'. *Social Politics: International Studies in Gender, State & Society* 22 (2): 170-92. doi: 10.1093/sp/jxv006.

Morel, N., Palier, B. and Palme, J. 2009. 'What future for social investment?', edited by the Institute for Future Studies. Stockholm: Institute for Future Studies.

Morel, N., Palier, B. and Palme. J. 2012. *Towards a Social Investment Welfare State?: Ideas, Policies and Challenges*. Bristol: Policy Press.

Morgan, K.J. 2005. 'The "production" of child care: how labor markets shape social policy and vice versa'. *Social Politics: International Studies in Gender, State & Society* 12 (2): 243-63.

Morton, K. 2012. 'New group to lobby government on registration of all childcarers'. NurseryWorld, 8 October. Accessed 03 February 2014. www.nurseryworld.co.uk/nursery-world/news/1106290/lobby-government-registration-childcarers.

Morton, K. 2013. 'Childcare costs - fears grow on the future of childcare vouchers'. NurseryWorld, 25 January. www.nurseryworld. co.uk/nursery-world/news/1097542/childcare-costs-fears-grow-future-childcare-vouchers

Morton, K. 2014. 'The Queen's Speech 2014: tax-free childcare and more support for free schools'. NurseryWorld, 4 June. Accessed 26 June 2014. http://www.nurseryworld.co.uk/nursery-world/news/1144622/queens-speech-2014-tax-free-childcare-support-free-schoolsx

Nannytax. 2014. 'Ofsted registration criteria'. Accessed 21 May. www.nannytax.co.uk/ofsted-registration-criteria.

Nannytax. 2015. *2014 Wages Survey: Annual Results Report.* Brighton: Nannytax.

National InHome Childcare Association. 2014. *Submission to the Productivity Commission Inquiry into Childhood and Early Childhood Learning.* http://www.pc.gov.au/inquiries/completed/childcare/submissions/initial/submission-counter/sub365-childcare.pdf

Newcombe, E. 2004. 'Temporary migration to the UK as an "au pair": cultural exchange or reproductive labour?' *Sussex Migration Working Paper no. 21.* Brighton: Sussex Centre for Migration Research.

Nordberg, C. 2012. 'Localising global care work: a discourse on migrant care workers in the Nordic welfare regime'. In *Transnationalism in the Global City*, edited by G. Boucher, A. Grindsted and T.L. Vicente, 63-78. Bilbao: Deusto University Press.

NurseryWorld. 2009. 'Analysis: a closer look at nanny workforce'. NurseryWorld, 24 November. Accessed 03 February 2014. http://www.nurseryworld.co.uk/nursery-world/analysis/1093825/analysis-closer-look-nanny-workforce

Nutbrown, C. 2012. *Foundations for Quality: The Independent Review of Early Education and Childcare Qualifications.* Runcorn: Department for Education.

O'Connor, J.S., Orloff, and Shaver, S. 1999. *States, Markets, Families: Gender, Liberalism, and Social Policy in Australia, Canada, Great Britain, and the United States.* Cambridge: Cambridge University Press.

O'Connor, J.S. and Robinson, G. 2008. 'Liberalism, citizenship and the welfare state'. In *Culture and Welfare State*, edited by W. van. Oorschot, M. Opielka and B. Pfau-Effinger, 29-49. Cheltenham: Edward Elgar.

OECD (Organisation for Economic Co-operation and Development). 2005. *Babies and Bosses - Reconciling Work and Family Life (Volume 4): Canada, Finland, Sweden and the United Kingdom*. Paris: OECD.

OECD. 2006. *Starting Strong II: Early Childhood Education and Care*. Paris: OECD.

OECD. 2012. *Encouraging Quality in Early Childhood Education and Care (ECEC)*. Paris: OECD.

OECD. 2013. *OECD Tax Database*. Paris: OECD.

OECD. 2015. *OECD Family Database*. Paris: OECD.

Ofsted. 2010. Common core skills and knowledge: A childcare fact sheet. Manchester: Ofsted. Accessed 3 July 2016. http://www.plymouth.gov.uk/documents-commoncore.pdf.

Ofsted. 2014a. *Childcare Register Requirements: Childminders and Home Childcarers, A Childcare Factsheet*. Manchester: Ofsted.

Ofsted. 2014b. 'The early years and childcare registers'. Ofsted. Accessed 14 May 2014. www.ofsted.gov.uk/early-years-and-childcare/our-early-years-childcare-work/early-years-and-childcare-registers.

Ofsted. 2015. 'Childcare providers and places: official statistics release'. In *Children, Education and Skills*, edited by S. Gibb. Manchester: Ofsted. ECD.

Orloff, A.S. 1993. 'Gender and the social rights of citizenship: the comparative analysis of gender relations and welfare states'. *American Sociological Review* 58 (3): 303-28.

Orloff, A.S. and Palier, B. 2009. 'The power of gender perspectives: feminist influence on policy paradigms, social science, and social politics'. *Social Politics: International Studies in Gender, State & Society* 16 (4): 405-12.

Owen, S. 1988. 'The "unobjectionable" service: a legislative history of childminding'. *Children & Society* 2 (4): 367-82. doi: 10.1111/j.1099-0860.1988.tb00559.x.

Owen, S. 2003. 'The development of childminding networks in Britain'. In *Family Day Care: International Perspectives on Policy, Practice and Quality*, edited by A. Mooney and J. Statham, 78. London: Jessica Kingsley Publishers.

Padamsee, T.J. 2009. 'Culture in connection: re-contextualizing ideational processes in the analysis of policy development'. *Social Politics: International Studies in Gender, State & Society* 16 (4): 413-45.

Parreñas, R.S. 2001. *Servants of Globalization: Women, Migration and Domestic Work*. Stanford: Stanford University Press.

Peng, I. 2011. 'Social investment policies in Canada, Australia, Japan, and South Korea'. *International Journal of Child Care and Education Policy* 5 (1): 45-53.

Penn, H. 2007. 'Childcare market management: how the United Kingdom government has reshaped its role in developing early childhood education and care'. *Contemporary Issues in Early Childhood* 8 (3): 192-207.

Penn, H. 2009. 'Public and private: the history of early education and care institutions in the United Kingdom'. In *Child Care and Preschool Development in Europe: Institutional Perspectives*, edited by K. Scheiwe and H. Willekens, 105-125. Basingstoke: Palgrave Macmillan.

Penn, H. 2011a. 'Policy rationles for early childhood services'. *International Journal of Child Care and Education Policy* 5 (1): 1-16.

Penn, H. 2011b. *Quality in Early Childhood Services: An International Perspective*. Milton Keynes: Open University Press.

Penn, H. 2012. 'Childcare markets: do they work?' *Occasional Paper No. 26*. Toronto: Childcare Resource and Research Unit.

Penn, H. and Lloyd, E. 2013. *The Costs of Childcare*. London: Childhood Wellbeing Research Centre.

Pfau-Effinger, B. 2005a. 'Culture and welfare state policies: reflections on a complex interrelation'. *Journal of Social Policy* 34 (1): 3-20.

Pfau-Effinger, B. 2005b. 'Development paths of care arrangements in the framework of family values and welfare values'. In *Care and Social Integration in European Societies*, edited by B. Pfau-Effinger and B. Geissler, 21-45. Bristol: Policy Press.

Pfau-Effinger, B. 2005c. 'Welfare state policies and the development of care arrangements'. *European Societies* 7 (2): 321-47. doi: 10.1080/14616690500083592.

Pfau-Effinger, B. 2006. 'Cultures of childhood and the relationship of care and employment in European welfare states'. In *Children, Changing Families and Welfare States*, edited by J. Lewis, 137-153. Cheltenham: Edward Elgar.

Phillips, S. and Mahon, R. 2002. 'Dual-earner families caught in a liberal welfare regime? The politics of child care policy in Canada'. In *Child Care Policy at the Crossroads: Gender and Welfare State Restructuring*, edited by S. Michel and R. Mahon, 191-219. London: Routledge.

Pratt, G. 1999. 'From registered nurse to registered nanny: discursive geographies of Filipina domestic workers in Vancouver, BC'. *Economic Geography* 75 (3): 215-36.

Pratt, G. 2003. 'Valuing childcare: troubles in suburbia'. *Antipode* 35 (3): 581-602.

Prentice, S. 2001. *Changing Child Care: Five Decades of Child Care Advocacy and Policy in Canada*. Halifax: Fernwood Publishing Co Ltd.

Prentice, S. 2009. 'High stakes: the "investable" child and the economic reframing of childcare'. *Signs* 34 (3): 687-710.

Press, F. and Woodrow, C. 2005. 'Commodification, corporatisation and children's spaces'. *Australian Journal of Education* 49 (3): 278-91.

Presser, H.B., Gornick, J.C. and Parashar, S. 2008. 'Gender and nonstandard work hours in 12 European countries'. *Monthly Labour Review*: 83-103.

Productivity Commission. 2014a. *Childcare and Early Childhood Learning - Draft Report*. Canberra: Productivity Commission.

Productivity Commission. 2014b. *Report on Government Services 2013, Early childhood Education and Care* (Chapter 3). Canberra: Productivity Commission.

Productivity Commission. 2015. *Childcare and Early Childhood Learning: Final Report*. Canberra: Commonwealth of Australia.

Professional Association for Childcare and Early Years. 2013. 'History of PACEY'. Accessed 27 June. www.pacey.org.uk/about/history_of_pacey.aspx.

Rabble.ca. 2010. 'No genuine national childcare until the Live-in Caregiver Program is scapped, Magkaisa Centre organizations assert', 10 February. www.rabble.ca/babble/news-rest-us/no-genuine-national-childcare-until-live-caregiver-program-scrapped-magkaisa-cen

Rammohan, A. and Whelan, S. 2007. 'The impact of childcare costs on the full-time/part-time employment decisions of Australian mothers'. *Australian Economic Papers* 46 (2): 152-69.

Randall, V. 1995. 'The irresponsible state? The politics of child daycare provision in Britain'. *British Journal of Political Science* 25: 327-48.

Randall, V. 1996. 'The politics of childcare policy'. *Parliamentary Affairs* 49 (1): 176-90.

Randall, V. 2002. 'Child care in Britain, or, how do you restructure nothing?' In *Child Care Policy at the Crossroads: Gender and Welfare State Restructuring*, edited by S. Michel and R. Mahon, 219-38. New York, NY: Routledge.

Rapoport, B. and Le Bourdais, C. 2008. 'Parental time and working schedules'. *Journal of Population Economics* 21 (4): 903-32.

Regulation Matters. 2013. Accessed 13 December. http://regulationmatters.co.uk/blog.

Regulation Matters. 2015. Accessed 1 December. http://www. regulationmatters.co.uk.

Richardson, B., Langford, R., Friendly, M. and Rauhala, A. 2013. 'From choice to change: an analysis of the "choice" discourse in Canada's 2006 federal election'. *Contemporary Issues in Early Childhood* 14 (2): 155-67.

Roeters, A. and Craig, L. 2014. 'Part-time work, women's work–life conflict, and job satisfaction: a cross-national comparison of Australia, the Netherlands, Germany, Sweden, and the United Kingdom'. *International Journal of Comparative Sociology* 55 (3): 185-203. doi: 10.1177/0020715214543541.

RPR Consulting. 2005. *Final Evaluation Report: In Home Care.* Canberra: Department of Family and Community Servcies.

Ruhs, M. and Anderson, B. eds. 2010. *Who Needs Migrant Workers?: Labour Shortages, Immigration, and Public Policy.* Oxford: Oxford University Press.

Rutter, J. and Evans, B. 2011. *Informal Childcare: Choice or Chance? A Literature Review.* London: Daycare Trust.

Rutter, J. and Evans, B. 2012a. *Improving Our Understanding of Informal Childcare in the UK: An Interim Report of Daycare Trust Research into Informal Childcare.* London: Daycare Trust.

Rutter, J. and Evans, B. 2012b. *Childcare for Parents with Atypical Work Patterns: The Need for Flexibility.* Informal Childcare Research Paper Three. London: Daycare Trust.

Salamon, L.M. and Elliott, V. eds. 2002. *The Tools of Government: A Guide to the New Governance.* New York, NY: Oxford University Press.

Schlesinger, B. 1971. 'Status of women in Canada: summary of commission recommendations'. *The Family Coordinator* 20 (3): 253-58.

Scottish Social Services Council. 2011. 'Qualifications for practitioners in day care of children services'. Accessed 21 May. www.sssc.uk.com/ All-about-Registration/qualification-criteria-managers-in-care-at-home-services.html.

Shaver, S. 2000. 'Inequalities, regimes, and Ttypologies'. *Social Politics: International Studies in Gender, State and Society* 7 (2): 215-19. doi: 10.1093/sp/7.2.215.

Shutes, I. and Chiatti, C. 2012. 'Migrant labour and the marketisation of care for older people: the employment of migrant care workers by families and service providers'. *Journal of European Social Policy* 22 (4): 392-405. doi: 10.1177/0958928712449773.

Simon, A., Owen, C., Hollingworth, K. and Rutter, J. 2015. *Provision and Use of Preschool Childcare in Britain*. Edited by Thomas Coram Research Unit Institute of Education. London: Univesity of Central London.

Simonazzi, A. 2009. 'Care regimes and national employment models'. *Cambridge Journal of Economics* 33 (2): 211-32.

Sinha, M. 2014. *Spotlight on Canadians: Results from the General Social Survey: Child Care in Canada*. Ottawa: Statistics Canada.

Sipilä, J., Repo, K. and Rissanen, T. 2010. *Cash-for-childcare: The Consequences for Caring Mothers*. Cheltenham: Edward Elgar.

Siraj, I. and Kingston, D. 2015. *An Independent Review of the Scottish Early Learning and Childcare (ELC) Workforce and Out of School Care (OSC) Workforce*. London: University College London.

Skinner, C. and Finch, N. 2006. 'Lone parents and informal childcare: a tax credit childcare subsidy?' *Social Policy & Administration* 40 (7): 807-23.

Smith, R., Poole, E., Perry, J., Wollny, I., Reeves, A., Coshall, C., d'Souza, J. and Bryson, C. 2010. *Childcare and Early Years Survey of Parents 2009*. Research Report RR-054. London: Department for Education.

Smyth, C. 2014. 'Boost your preschooler's brain power! An analysis of advice to parents from an Australian government-funded website'. *Women's Studies International Forum* 45: 10-18.

Social Issues Research Centre. 2009. *The Composition, Needs and Aspirations of the Nanny Workforce in England*. Oxford: Social Issues Research Centre.

Social Research Centre. 2014. *2013 National ECEC Workforce Census*. Melbourne: Department of Education.

Standing Committee on Family and Human Services. 2006. *Balancing Work and Family: Report on the Inquiry into Balancing Work and Family*. Canberra: Parliament of the Commonwealth of Australia.

Statham, J. and Mooney, A. 2003. *Around the Clock: Childcare Services at Atypical Times*. Bristol: Policy Press.

Statistics Canada. 2011. *National Household Survey, Catelogue no. 99-012-X2011033*. Ottawa: Statistics Canada.

Stiell, B. and England, K. 1997. 'Domestic distinctions: constructing difference among paid domestic workers in Toronto'. *Gender, Place & Culture* 4 (3): 339-60. doi: 10.1080/09663699725387.

Stiell, B. and England, K. 1999. 'Jamaican domestics, Filipina housekeepers and English nannies: representations of Toronto's foreign domestic workers'. In *Gender, Migration and Domestic Service*, edited by J.H. Momsen, 43-61. London: Routledge.

Strazdins, L., Korda, R.J., Lim, L.L.Y., Broom, D.H. and D'Souza, R.M. 2004. 'Around-the-clock: parent work schedules and children's well-being in a 24-hour economy'. *Social Science & Medicine* 59 (7): 1517-27.

Sumsion, J. 2006. 'From Whitlam to economic rationalism and beyond: a conceptual framework for political activism in children's services'. *Australian Journal of Early Childhood* 31 (1): 1-9.

Teghtsoonian, K. 1995. 'Work and/or motherhood: the ideological construction of women's options in Canadian child care policy debates'. *Canadian Journal of Women & Labour* 8: 411-39.

Thériault, L. 2006. 'National post and the nanny state: framing the child care debate in Canada'. *Canadian Review of Social Policy/Revue canadienne de politique sociale* (56): 140-8.

Thompson, S. and Ben-Galim, D. 2014. *Childmind the Gap: Reforming Childcare to Support Mothers into Work*. London: Institute for Public Policy Research.

Timpson, A.M. 2001. *Driven Apart: Women's Employment Equality and Child Care in Canadian Public Policy*. Vancouver: University of British Columbia Press.

Tronto, J.C. 2002. 'The "nanny" question in feminism'. *Hypatia* 17 (2): 34-51.

Tweed, J. 2003a. 'Nanny register is put off by minister'. NurseryWorld, 8 October. Accessed 3 July 2016. http://www.nurseryworld.co.uk/nursery-world/news/1082787/nanny-register-minister

Tweed, J. 2003b. 'New nanny register campaign'. NurseryWorld, 17 July. Accessed 3 July 2016. http://www.nurseryworld.co.uk/nursery-world/news/1099570/nanny-register-campaign

Tweed, J. 2004. 'Childcare tax credit extends to nannies'. NurseryWorld, 20 May. Accessed 3 July 2016. http://www.nurseryworld.co.uk/nursery-world/news/1098890/childcare-tax-credit-extends-nannies

Tyyskä, V. 1993. 'The women's movement and the welfare state: child care policy in Canada and Finland, 1960-1990'. Unpublished PhD, NN82775, University of Toronto.

Tyyskä, V. 1995. *The Politics of Caring and the Welfare State: The Impact of the Women's Movement on Child Care Policy in Canada and Finland, 1960–1990*, Helsinski: Suomalainen Tiedeakatemia.

Tyyskä, V. 2001. 'Advocacy ignored: child care policy in Ontario in the 1990s'. In *Changing Child Care: Five Decades of Child Care Advocacy and Policy in Canada*, edited by S. Prentice, 133-52. Halifax: Fernwood Publishing.

UK Government. 2014a. 'Au pairs: employment law'. Accessed 21 May. www.gov.uk/au-pairs-employment-law.

UK Government. 2014b. 'Help with childcare costs'. Accessed 21 May. www.gov.uk/help-with-childcare-costs/childcare-tax-credits.

Uren, K. 2013. 'Having a nanny is becoming a popular child care choice for families'. *The Advertiser*, 13 April. www.adelaidenow.com.au/ipad/having-a-nanny-is-becoming-a-popular-child-care-choice-for-families/story-fn3o6wog-1226618281224.

Van Oorschot, W., Opielka, M. and Pfau-Effinger, B. 2008. *Culture and Welfare State: Values and Social Policy in Comparative Perspective*. Cheltenham: Edward Elgar.

Vincent, C. and Ball, S.J. 2004. 'Middle class fractions, childcare and the "relational" and "normative" aspects of class practices. *The Sociological Review* 52 (4): 478-502.

Vincent, C. and Ball, S.J. 2006. *Childcare, Choice and Class Practice: Middle-class Parents and their Children*. London: Routledge.

Vincent, C., Braun, A. and Ball, S.J. 2008. 'Childcare, choice and social class: caring for young children in the UK'. *Critical Social Policy* 28 (1): 5-26.

Warner, M.E. and Gradus, R.H.J.M. 2009. *The Consequences of Implementing a Child Care Voucher: Evidence from Australia, the Netherlands and USA*. Amsterdam: Tinbergen Institute.

White, L. 2011. 'The internationalization of early childhood education and care issues: framing gender justice and child well being'. *Governance* 24 (2): 285-309.

White, L. and Friendly, M. 2012. 'Public funding, private delivery: states, markets, and early childhood education and care in Liberal welfare states – a comparison of Australia, the UK, Quebec, and New Zealand'. *Journal of Comparative Policy Analysis: Research and Practice* 14 (4): 292-310. doi: 10.1080/13876988.2012.699789.

Williams, F. 2004. *Rethinking Families*. London: Calouste Gulbenkian Foundation.

Williams, F. 2008. 'Migration and home-based child care in European welfare states'. Paper presented at ARACY seminar on Early Childhood Education and Childcare, Sydney.

Williams, F. 2010a. *Claiming and Framing in the Making of Care Policies: The Recognition and Redistribution of Care*. Geneva: United Nations Research Institute for Social Development.

Williams, F. 2010b. 'Migration and care: themes, concepts and challenges'. *Social Policy and Society* 9 (03): 385-96. doi:10.1017/S1474746410000102.

Williams, F. 2012a. 'Care relations and public policy: social justice claims and social investment frames'. *Families, Relationships and Societies* 1 (1): 103-19. doi: 10.1332/204674312x633199.

Williams, F. 2012b. 'Converging variations in migrant care work in Europe'. *Journal of European Social Policy* 22 (4): 363–76. doi: 10.1177/0958928712449771.

Williams, F. and Gavanas, A. 2008. 'The intersection of childcare regimes and migration regimes: a three-country study'. In *Migration and Domestic Work: A European Perspective on a Global Theme*, edited by H. Lutz, 13–28. Farnham: Ashgate.

Wincott, D. 2006. 'Paradoxes of New Labour social policy: toward universal child care in Europe's "most liberal" welfare regime?' *Social Politics: International Studies in Gender, State & Society* 13 (2): 286–312. doi: 10.1093/sp/jxj011.

Yeates, N. 2005. Global care chains: a critical introduction. *Global Migration Perspectives No. 44*. Geneva: Global Commission on International Migration.

Yeates, N. 2012. 'Global care chains: a state-of-the-art review and future directions in care transnationalization research'. *Global Networks* 12 (2): 135–54. doi: 10.1111/j.1471-0374.2012.00344.x.

Index

Please note: ECEC refers to 'early childhood education and care'